UPTON-BY-CHESTER

A PEOPLE'S HISTORY

Phil Pearn Kate Roberts Barbara Smith

extensively developed from the unpublished
Upton Village History Scrapbooks
compiled by the Upton Heath Women's Institute in 1951 & 1965

© Published by the Upton-by-Chester Local History Group
Upton-by-Chester UK

www.historyofuptonbychester.org.uk

ISBN 0-9548854-0-6

Design & layout by the editors

The book has been underwritten by an
'AWARDS FOR ALL' grant of £3000
and by loans from local organisations and members of the community

Proceeds from book sales will enable
further local community heritage projects by the
Upton-by-Chester Local History Group

Cover photo – Upton Mill c 1916 courtesy of Kath Griffiths
Back cover – sketch of the Village Pump c1950 by an unknown artist.
Opposite – Bryants Map 1831 – (ref M5.2)
reproduced courtesy of Cheshire and Chester Archives and Local Studies
Contents background – village signpost by Geoffrey Newcombe

Printed by W H Evans & Sons Ltd.
5 Knutsford Way Sealand Industrial Estate, Chester CH1 4NS
from typesetting in MS Word by the editors

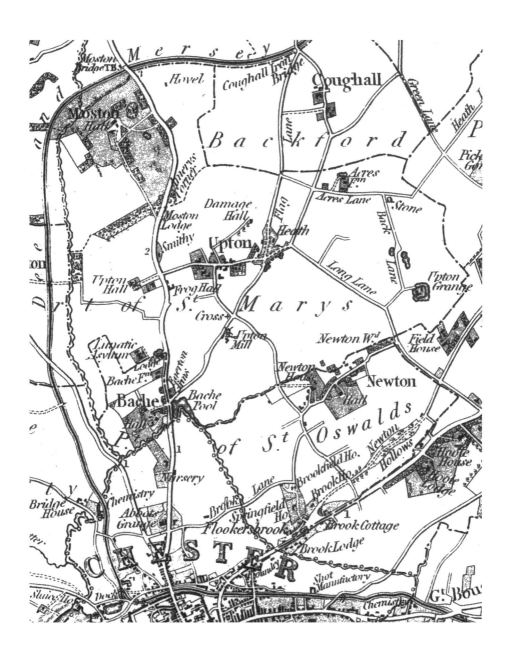

Book coverage – Upton, Bache, Moston,
& Newton (north of Plas Newton, Well & Shepherds Lanes)

Acknowledgements
for Support & Material

Cheshire and Chester Archives and Local Studies
Chester History & Heritage & Chester Photographic Survey
John Herson - Head of History, Liverpool John Moores University
John Peter Hess - Local Historian
Dr Jill Collens – Project Leader Historic Environment, Cheshire County Council
Gill Dunn – Chester Archaeological Service
Mike Emery – Site Director Poulton Research Project
Dan Robinson – Keeper of Archaeology Grosvenor Museum
Eric Illingworth – unpub 1990 report for 'Dip. of Local History' Liverpool Univ.
Geoffrey Newcombe - for photographic record of today's Upton area
Terry Clarke – for specific digital photographic processing

Many members of the local community have provided photographs, memorabilia and 'facts about their patch' – however, the following should be singled out for their considerable contribution across the content of many parts of this history.

Joyce Cook – tireless research in many areas and in proof reading
Peter Cooper, Eddie Edison, Joan Halbert, Jean Roberts, Des Robertson
For photographic archives - Barbara Cottrell, Kath Griffiths, Arthur Cooper

Researchers contributing on a specific topic are named within the relevent chapter.

This book has been underwritten by

Chester Civic Trust as part of its Millennium Festival	– 3 shares
The North of England Zoological Society	– 2 shares
The following members of the community	– 1 share each

Derek Barnett	Dorothy Joan Halbert	Kate Roberts
Jean Burtinshaw	David Hart	Alison Samuel
Barbara Capstick	David & Joyce Hooper	Colin & Barbara Smith
Irene & John Caswell	Councillor Pat Lott	Brenda Southward
Marjorie Elizabeth Case	Margaret Nash	Paul Stockton
Joyce Cook	Jane Nash	Elizabeth Submaranian
Barbara Cottrell	Bob & Pat Parker	Bob Thompson
Eddy Edison	Lynne Pearn	Bernard West
John Gough	Phil Pearn	David & Margaret Whaley
Max Green	Helen & Eric Povey	Paul & Chris Wilbraham
Eunice Grinter	Jean Roberts	

Foreword

I am delighted to have been asked to write this foreword having such fond memories of the Upton area where I still occasionally meet up with old friends. It's about time Upton had a local history book knowing how Eddy Edison loves to reminisce – glad you've made him an honorary life member.

I lived in Upton for a few years as a lad but they are the years you make some lasting friends and help form your thoughts for future years. We moved into Pine Gardens off Upton Drive. Ours was a new house but I believe many in Upton Drive had been built before the war. Upton had plenty of abandoned nursery areas in those days where we kids would play, but on one occasion my brother Ray and I were caught scrumping apples. It did mean coming up before our father in his official capacity as a JP.

The Headteacher of St Mary's Village School was a Mr. Chidlow but I was only there one term before going to Ellesmere Port Secondary Modern which meant catching the bus each morning from the Bache. I missed out on being taught by Joyce Cook your President but I did meet her in Chester a few years ago and enjoyed sharing some memories. Upton was a great place to live as a child, especially with the many visits to the Zoo – some official and often unofficial - under the hedge! I was married in Upton parish church which was also very much associated with my Cub Scout life in Upton.

Sadly my parents have missed out on reading this book with so much nostalgia but I'm very taken with the theme – *a people's history*. Whilst in Upton we travelled to Brighton because we were the runners-up in a national *'Britain's Most Typical Family'* competition. The presentation took place at The Dome in Brighton which I was eventually to return to for the Labour Party Conference – from Cub Scout to Deputy Prime Minister – so I think we qualify for inclusion in 'a people's history'.

Best wishes with the sales of the book and here's hoping you can use the resulting funds for some more good local heritage projects. – if you do a dig or need some diving expertise I'll see if I can help.

The Rt Hon John Prescott MP
Deputy Prime Minister
and First Secretary of State

Photo shows John aged 15 years as an Upton schoolboy in 1953

Dedications – submitted by some of the underwriters

Len Hughes, first Headmaster of Upton Manor School (1951 – 1977) who would have been delighted to hear about the Local History Group. Ex-pupils, throughout the world, remember his untiring efforts to stimulate their interest in Upton and local activities. **Joyce Cook**

Walter Cockram (1863 – 1961) whose unbounded interest in events and places has provided a legacy of photographs and information on life in Upton at the beginning of the 20th century. **Barbara Cottrell**

John Gough, sister Jill and their parents Stan and Jean, who have lived in Upton for over fifty years. **John Gough**

My parents without whom I wouldn't be here today. The War that brought me to Upton as an evacuee. My foster parents, Mr & Mrs H Hughes, to whom I am forever faithful for bringing me up as their son, making me who I am today.
Eddy Edison

For Joanna and Michael Whaley - born, bred and educated in Upton.
David & Margaret Whaley

To remember Frederick and Gladys Hooper who brought the family to Demage Lane in 1937. They chose wisely **David & Joyce Hooper**

To Kate and Andrew – too young to be in a History Book! **Eunice Grinter**

In memory of Bill Nash. **Margaret Nash**

With love to Cecilia, our dear son Bret, my brother Reg and late brother Ken. In affection for all my young companions in Upton during those happy, carefree, far off days. Dear to me are the memories still. **Derek Barnett**

I have had much pleasure in contributing to this book. It has brought back many happy memories of the first thirty years of my life and will be a source of interest to my wife Betty and my children Sally and Jonathan. **Bernard West**

In memory of Eric and Marjorie Christall who spent many happy years in Wealstone Lane from 1960 – 1990. With much love from their daughters.
Liz Case & Sylvia Dennett

To my mother Eunice Evans, sister Hazel and late father George Evans and my immediate family for being a loving caring family. Being born in Upton and still living here has brought me many treasured memories.
Former Parish Councillor 1994-2002 **Brenda Southward**

For Lydia Alice and Melissa Agnes with all my love, Mummy **Kate Roberts**

Norman and Ellen Mills came to live in Flag Lane in 1934. Gordon Mills lived in Upton until his marriage in 1964. Barbara Mills (now Capstick) has lived here all her life. **Barbara Capstick**

Preface

Today, most Upton inhabitants are incomers and so it is quite fitting that not one of the three, producing this book, is a 'true local'. Between us, we have only 67 years of local residential experience. Not trained historians; we have been on a fast learning curve, with the enthusiasm of the History Group members and the wider Upton community, keeping us on the task.

When our Local History Group was formed in 2002, the desire to publish a good quality history book was uppermost in our minds. We started gathering information on a website and gave ourselves three winters to meet our goal. The first winter got us well underway. The second, reached a state of maturity so that the Group could stage a successful exhibition and gain many more contacts. The third winter – more demanding than anticipated – has enabled us to 'fill the gaps' and compile all the 'scrapbook' information into a well presented book format. We have stuck to this timetable rather than publish when – if ever ! – the 'jig-saw' is complete.

Back in 'Festival of Britain' year – 1951 – the Women's Institutes around the country were encouraged to write up their local history. Upton Heath W.I. did an excellent job which has been preserved in the city archives and reproduced by the Upton Local History Group as a workbook to initiate our research.

Kate Roberts has written the three early chapters based on her previous project work; extensively advanced with research both in the Records Office and with early maps covering her dining room table. Her excitement has erupted everytime she has found some other piece of the jigsaw enabling a complete flow in our story. Her enthusiasm has ensured help from various professionals from within the college, the museum and local archaeologists.

I have picked up the story from Upton's first shift towards urban residential. As well as public records, this has meant talking to vast numbers of residents and delving into their house deeds and old snapshots to gain a good insight into our late 19th and 20th century history. As more information has been unearthed, interest in the community has snowballed and hardly a day has gone by without pursuing someone's memorabilia or querying some snippet of history. Quite often memories have been uncertain or conflicting and hence I have never taken a single source of memory as being historical evidence. The reader will find many occasions in the book with the words '*it is understood that...*' or '*a resident claims that...*'. Issues have been recorded as fact where there is substantial evidence although the reader must accept that our account is in good faith but subject to error.

The book has, rightly, been named 'A People's History' and this would not have been appropriate without Barbara Smith's six chapters (14–19). She has encouraged and chased local organisations, getting them to recall their histories and dig out their past memorabilia and photographs. Similarly she has pursued contributions from individuals either for personal reminiscences or to record the activities of those who have '*made an impact on our history*'. All these contributions have needed her editing into a well balanced picture of our community and the result of this thorough job is now available to the reader.

Throughout our research, our President Joyce Cook has been a constant source of help. Regularly at the Records Office, we have frequently turned to her for help pursuing numerous queries. Nothing we have requested has ever been too much trouble for her and her enthusiasm for the project has been delightful. Several members of our Local History Group have carried out research either relating to their own home or activity interest or, in fact, some have gained new interests as they have researched a topic allocated to them. The full committee has been busy, handling many of the 'behind the scenes' aspects needed for this publication.

Kate's early chapters come with a bibliography crediting the sources of her research and writing. For the recent history, Barbara and I have dealt with so many people and have been loaned so many photographs and memorabilia that it has not been practical to support our chapters in such a way. Hence we trust contributors will see this book as being a big 'thank you' for their efforts and generosity. We believe that all copyright issues have been addressed but clearly it has not been possible to identify let alone contact the originators of some old photographs.

Arriving at the content of a book is only one part of the story. From an early stage we have worked closely with our chosen printer – W H Evans – and their help has been invaluable enabling the three of us to carry out our own computer-based layout and typesetting. Over two, hard but enjoyable, years have gone into this book to ensure a quality of which Upton can be proud. We apologise for the inevitable mistakes and omissions and we look forward to wide community support in our future projects. Hoping all readers find the book both informative and entertaining.

Phil Pearn – Founding Chairman Upton-by-Chester Local History Group

Now that we have reached our goal of producing this book, there are three people who warrant a particularly big 'thank you' and without whom this publication would not have come to fruition on time. They are our three 'other halves' who have stood by us and supported us through the delights and frustrations of this project.

So thank you Lynne for all the listening, trying to improve my English and maintaining 'normal service' through the recent intense pre-publication period while I've worked with the other three ladies in my life.

Phil

Thank you Paul for being substitute Mum, your technical wizardry and for being unofficial sub-editor. *Kate*

And thank you Colin for your help with research, proof reading and ensuring that we had something to eat each evening. *Barbara*

Contents

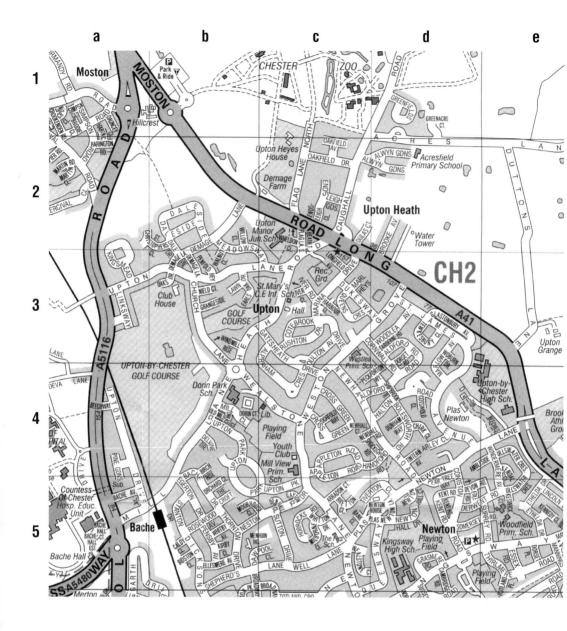

Street map of Upton-by-Chester & district produced in 2000
Reproduced by permission of Geographers' A-Z Map Co. Ltd.
Licence No: B3019.© Crown Copyright 2005.
All right reserved. Licence number 100017302

See gazetteer (back of book) for list of street names
within the coverage of the book.

CHAPTER 1

Introduction

The book aims to reveal the story of Upton's development, both in physical terms and through its community. The first chapters draw heavily on public archived material, analysed and presented for today's reader, telling the story from the earliest records through to the Tithe surveys of the mid-1800s. Subsequent chapters draw mainly on privately held material and memories. After following the growth from small rural village to city suburbia, the later chapters then focus on the people and their activities – both for employment and for leisure.

Location maps and illustrations

This introduction concludes with a set of eight full colour pages giving a brief, colourful, visual trip through our history. Throughout the other chapters, illustrations have been located alongside the relevant descriptive text. The double spread map on pages 98 / 99 and aerial photograph on pages 122 / 123 are useful references for chapters 5 to 10. To help the reader identify streets and some current day facilities, a modern map is featured opposite (x) and the gazetteer (end of the book) gives map grid references to aid their location.

The early years

We start by looking at some of the area's natural history and man's influence on the landscape. Then, from the first signs of man's presence, public archives have helped reveal the evolving story through Roman and Saxon times, Domesday, the diminishing Church control after the Reformation and then the disruptions of Civil War. Land ownership through the 'Lord of the Manor' is then covered and the evolving use of the land with enclosures and the formation of farms with various tenant farmers. Local 'antiquities' are examined and new theories revealed. Buildings dating back to Upton's agricultural past are discussed including coverage of what became of them. The 1839 Upton Tithe Survey presents a good snapshot of life at that time and chapter 5 is devoted to this period.

Shift to suburbia from the mid-1800s

The first incomers were wealthy businessmen seeking country estates. They became the 'local barons' and their resources strongly influenced the local community. By the turn of the century there was a trickle of the clerical and artisan classes – with both the Upton Heath area and Upton Park as significant communities, accounting for nearly half the population. Although the Asylum was established at the Bache, its impact on the Upton community was small. A thriving nursery business took up farm land in the south and from the 1930s, a major zoo has grown to cover a large part of our northern area, constraining housing development. The mid-1930s saw a significant increase in housing demand as Chester suburbs spread. Building was well underway when it was suspended by wartime activities. This war was 'close to home' with locally based military headquarters and hospitals. Post-war soon saw extensive housing development underway, building on fields after first mastering the streams and man-made pits and ponds. Due to Upton's location there were many proposals for canals, railways, trunk roads and even an airport that could have made Upton turn out very different from today. Upton is now reaching its residential capacity – held in by its greenbelt policy and kept green itself with its golf course, public greens and leafy verges.

The people and their activities and reminiscences

Moving on to community activities, we then get an insight into the businesses and employment through the last two centuries. All the major employers and many of the small business trades are covered. The story of the Village Hall has been given its own chapter and shows the major part it has played in the recreation of the area. This leads into a chronological look at the community-wide festivities such as those marking national celebrations. Looking at leisure activities, one of the earliest interests was growing and exhibiting flowers; this in time became the Horticultural Society. Another early recreation for the wealthy classes was Chester Golf Club which began its life in the Bache area, more than 30 years before Upton Golf Club became a reality. By the mid-1850s the growth of the village justified its own school and parish church.

Some members of the community have been singled out for coverage where they have made a wide impact. They have 'made their mark' in public service, such as civic or church, achieved something to make Upton proud or simply and humbly been part of the general well-being of the community. They are all remembered fondly by local residents. Under 'Reminiscences' we have selected some richly descriptive recollections and anyone who is of an age to remember schooldays of the first half of the 1900s will be magically transported back in time. Finally, 'Tale Ends' is an amalgamation of amusing stories told by residents – whether you believe them all - is in your hands.

Abbreviations used throughout the book

'WI Book' – The 1951 Upton Village History Scrapbook compiled by the W.I.
'CRO' – The Cheshire and Chester Archives and Local Studies.

Upton's Plague Stone – or is it? See page 54
Photo – Kate Roberts

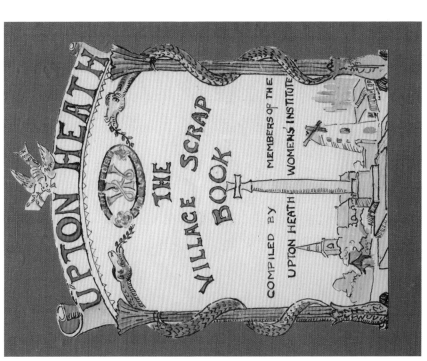

The 1951 W.I. Village History Scrapbook
Image reproduced courtesy of the Cheshire and Chester Archives and Local Studies

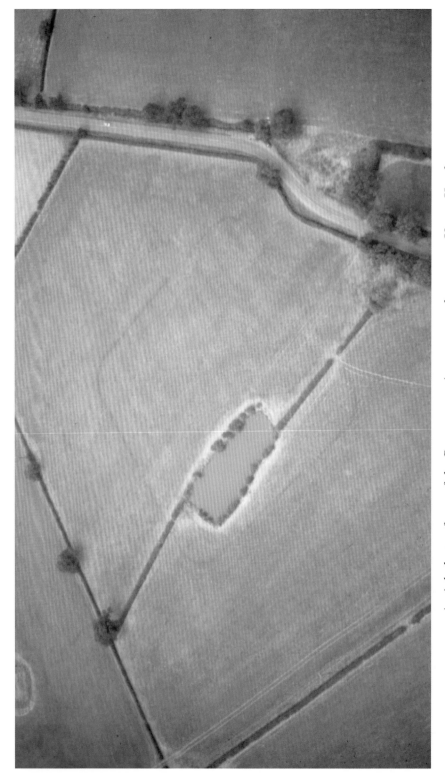

Aerial photo of one of the Roman practice camp enclosures on Upton Heath
Copyright Cheshire County Council

UPTON HALL

COPIED FROM A WATER COLOUR DRAWING BY D.FROST— 25-9-20.

Reproduced from 'The W.I. Book' courtesy of the Cheshire Federation of Women's Institutes

5

"The Oaks," Upton by Chester

C. Norwood.

The Oaks, formerly Upton Bank, the first of Upton's Gentleman's Country Estates. Now part of Upton Golf Club

Reproduced from 'The W.I. Book' courtesy of the Cheshire Federation of Women's Institutes

Mr Godwin passing 'Nixon's Land' – now the Bache supermarket entrance
Date and photographer unknown

The 1977 Silver Jubilee Carnival Procession
Photos – David and Ailsa Clegg

An Upton entrance – Demage Lane   Photo – David Hooper

An Upton entrance – Bache Roundabout   Photo – Kate Roberts

Stanton Drive, 1953 Coronation   Photo – Francix Fox

Pine Gardens, 1977 Silver Jubilee   Photo – Jill Smith

Some members of Upton-by-Chester Local History Group, March 2004, at the Village Hall

Photo – Geoffrey Newcombe, History Group Official Photographer

CHAPTER 2
Natural History

Upton-by-Chester is found to the north of Chester city centre, just over one mile from The Cross. The two-mile post is on the Liverpool Road opposite the site of the old smithy, almost marking the northern most limit of Upton itself. The Township of Upton covers an area of 1154 acres, its near neighbour, Bache, whose own history is often hard to separate from Upton's, covers an area of 95 acres. Upton is sheltered by the Clwydian Mountains and they can be glimpsed from many sites in the locality. As Upton is higher than the city, this too can be viewed, with its illuminated Cathedral by night.

Upton has become part of the suburbs of Chester, as there is now no differentiation between the villages that once surrounded the city. Although Upton has had a very close association with Chester, right from the earliest of times, it has retained it's own identity. This has been revealed through its history, people and natural history.

Geology of Upton

The underlying bedrock at Upton is Triassic sandstone, also known as the Chester Pebble Beds because the sandstone contains pebbles. This is the oldest rock in the local sequence and is overlaid with drift deposits of boulder clay. The soil that has developed is typical of the type widespread throughout Cheshire. It is finely textured and ideal for grassland that has been a major contributor to the development of the dairying industry in Cheshire since 15th century. It is prone to surface wetness, but in the more favourable places it is good enough for market or nursery gardening. Glacial sands and marl have been deposited by the retreating ice sheet where the boulder clay was missing, or in the many pits. When a sand deposit was found it was worked and used for road and property building from the 18th to 20th centuries.

Bache brook and cliffs

11

Topography

The western part of Upton formerly consisted of heathland at an approximate level 40m above Ordnance Datum; this is about as high as Upton gets. To the north, a deep valley running between the former estuary of the River Gowy and the River Dee interrupts this plateau. This is called the Deva Spillway and the hill that was formed is known locally as Butter Hill. It originated as a drainage channel for the River Mersey which was blocked by ice approximately 11,000 BC, water cut across to the River Dee estuary at a point between Chester and Blacon. At the lower end, the Upton/Bache border lies at 15m OD; the brook that runs through has worn the stone into cliffs 4 – 5m high.

Marl Pits

Marl pits have been a feature of Upton for hundreds of years. Marl is a naturally occurring resource that was easily utilised by farmers as a fertilizer.

At the end of the last ice age the retreating ice sheet left behind various deposits. One of these was marl, a soft concentration of secondary calcium carbonate. It was found at a depth of 1-2m in the underlying till (clay) layer and as it was dug out a pit was left behind. It had been known, probably since Roman times, that spreading this clay over sandy soils enriches it and improved its water-holding ability. This practice was known as marling. By digging the marl into the field it interacted with the soil, changed it physically and released its nutrients.

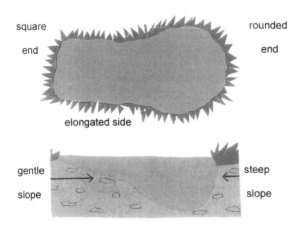

Marl was applied in summer and was effective for about 12 years, the value of adding manure to fertilise was well known but as much of the winter stock was slaughtered each autumn, it was therefore not so readily available. Marl was in general use between the 16th and 18th centuries. Marling was carried out by a group of 5 or 6 men under a leader known as the 'Lord of the Pit' and usually took about a fortnight to complete. The practice eventually died out even though it was freely available as it took a great deal of labour for excavation, haulage and spreading. The availability of quarried lime became the replacement for marl. A marl pit is different from a sand or clay pit and is easily distinguished by its shape. It has a square edge, with gentle slope at one end and a steep rounded slope at the other. This shape was the result of the heavily laden carts being hauled up the sloping end; the deep end was where the marl was taken.

Eventually the pit would fill with water, so another would be dug, sometimes very close by. Later, pits were dug in the middle of the field to make the spreading of marl easier. The colour picture of the Roman practice camp enclosure shows a disused marl pit in its centre, see Ch1. As the seepage of water out of a marl pit is very slow, surface water is enough to keep it full and as a result, the marl pits have survived to the present day. This process was repeated over and over again leaving Upton to be dotted with marl pits.

Upton Heath

An Egerton family estate map of 1735 shows, the proposed enclosure of the heath which had been until this time an open, flat area of the township with no natural drainage. There had been several Acts of Parliament to enclose such areas but there is no evidence to support this for Upton, and the enclosure was probably done privately by the Egerton estate. The enclosure award dates from 1767. It can be noted from the map that all the field boundaries inside the enclosure are straight lines whereas the fields outside show a more natural shape. What is now Long Lane is also drawn straight and would have been an access road put in at the same time.

One curious addition to the map is the inclusion of what was then called Upton Green but known today as Upton Heath. There are several references to a property from at least the Elizabethan period, called Hogg House, in the vicinity. The map shows further growth in this area which continued to develop.

Manor of Upton, Chester St Mary, 1735

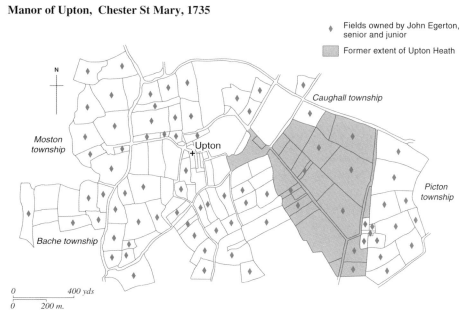

◆ Fields owned by John Egerton, senior and junior

▨ Former extent of Upton Heath

Reproduced from A.D.M.Phillips and C.B.Phillips, (eds), A New Historical Atlas of Cheshire, Chester, 2002, p 55, with kind permission of the editors and author.

Farming in Upton

Agriculture has been the backbone of Upton for hundreds of years. There have been at least eight farms and numerous small holdings and, going back further, everyone who lived in Upton would have grown their own produce on some scale. We have one farm left in operation and it is also one of our oldest.

Upton Grange (Lot 2).

Upton Grange c.1900

The Dutton family has farmed at Upton Grange since John D Dutton took on the tenancy in 1906 from the Shrewsbury estate. The farm then was 166 acres with a rent of about £250 per year. The Shrewsbury estate sold the property and others held in the neighbourhood in 1916. John Dutton took the opportunity to buy and carried on with a mixture of arable and livestock farming. Cattle, sheep and pigs were reared alongside oats, barley and root crops, cheese was made and horses were bred, bought and sold. In those days farming was still very labour intensive and many people made their living on the farm. When John Dutton died in 1950 his youngest son, Tom, took over. By then more machinery was in use i.e. tractors and milking machines, and by 1978 a partnership was formed – father and two sons – who acquired more land and concentrated on dairy and beef farming. The two brothers, Tim and Piers Dutton, now run Upton Grange; their herd of 110 dairy cows is certified organic and all the field work is carried out by contractors. We will have to wait and see if their sons continue working the farm through this century.

The Duttons method of mixed farming is one that goes back a long way due to the types of soil found in Upton. The heavier clay soils hold water and are difficult to cultivate and more adapted to grass that can support animals. The lighter sandy areas are free draining and easier to plough and more suited

to growing crops; the extensive nursery lands are testament to this.

An early 19th century map of the Upton Hall estate tells us which crops were being grown; they included potatoes, barley and pasture.

There are two references to ridge and furrow cultivation. These were recorded in the early 1960s and have now been lost to housing developments. The first instance was in the playing field of Upton Heath Primary School where 12 strips were to be seen. Secondly behind the houses of Endsleigh Gardens there were three strips identified. Part of the Wealstone Lane playing field may also show the remains of ridge and furrow field marks.

One lost relic of a farming community is the penfold for impounding stray animals. Upton's stood somewhere near the bottom of Demage Lane by the Upton Lane junction and is marked on the first edition OS map of 1871-72 as 'pinfold'. The WI Book suggests that it could have been demolished at the time the Vicarage was built in 1889. By the time of the 1899 OS Map it is missing. This shows the decline in farming within the village though its name is now remembered in the road Penfold Hey that is close to the site.

Field names on our old maps also show us other types of crops grown, for example, peas, beans, wheat, rye as well as clover. The rural landscape was also recorded in 1721 at the Cheshire Sessions; the document describes the manor of Upton as containing cottages, orchards, gardens, meadows, pasture and heath. This paints a pretty picture of a rural landscape that was once Upton.

Trees

Upton is blessed with many trees and there are several, which are well over 200 years old. Trees, in particular oaks, were used to mark field boundaries when

Heath Road

Upton was a farming community, and there are a number of these trees that have survived. The large oak at the top of Demage Lane is an example. (See colour picture chapter 1). The owners of the larger houses built during the 19th century used a variety of tree specimens to enhance their gardens. Although we have lost several of the houses, we are fortunate that many of these trees have been incorporated into the modern re-developments. A considerable number of trees in Upton have Tree Preservation Orders served on them and this will protect them for many years to come. One part of Upton that has many protected trees is the area that covered the former residence Upton Lawn. Not only are there trees remaining from around the old house, but on the opposite side of the golf course running along Heath Road are a great many large trees which once

15

Tree planting at Upton Heath School, 1991

formed the edge of the property. There is a famous local story concerning Upton Lawn. In 1919 Earl Douglas Haig visited Chester to be made Honorary Freeman of the City. He lunched with the Mayor, Sir John Frost, and Mayoress, at their residence, Upton Lawn. Whilst there he planted an oak tree raised from an acorn which was brought from the WWI battlefields of Verdun, France. It was known locally as 'Earl's Oak'.

More recently there have been several tree-planting occasions. In 1991 school playing fields were being sold off for development, at Upton Heath School. It was decided to plant a mixture of trees on the corner of their playing field to prevent it being sold. On Saturday, 2 November 1991 350 trees were planted by residents, guests and children, Gyles Brandreth MP, and Councillors John Butler and Gerald Grant each planted an oak tree.

At Moston a landfill site was turned into a wildlife retreat by volunteers and the Cheshire Wildlife Trust in 2003. Many trees and plants were included.

In November 2004 the Parish Council, with the help of children from Upton Heath and Dorin Park Schools, planted several trees at the Chemistry Pits field to encourage a wildlife area.

References

A New Historical Atlas Of Cheshire, Philips and Philips 2002

Geological Survey Chester And Winsford, British Geological Survey Sheet Memoir 107.55, Earp and Taylor

The Dutton family at Upton Grange, contribution from Piers Dutton

Upton Hall Estate Map CCRO DEO 206/7

Cheshire Sheaf III Series (1957-1961)

Cheshire Sessions 1721 CCRO Egerton Family Bundle

1735 Upton Heath Enclosure Map CCRO DEO 1/7

ULHG History Sheet 6, Des Robertson

Pits and Ponds Past and Present, Joan Springett

Upton's Trees, contribution from Dorothy Clift

Upton County High School Trial Excavation Report 1994, Matthews, Emery, Edwards, Harrison

CHAPTER 3
Early History

Man's occupation of Upton dates back to the earliest of times. Prehistoric sites are extremely difficult to locate, and it is only a chance find that usually reveals its possible location. The other surprising area is the Saxon period, where the outline of Upton's original settlement has begun to show itself. This chapter also contains a glimpse of the awful times when the plague visited, with a detailed description of how the bodies were to be buried. It also became apparent as the research developed that there was a continuous time line of ownership for Upton. This too is presented but it must be noted that there have been many other people over the centuries who have also owned large parts of Upton. Too many to mention every one in this book.

The Prehistoric Period

Upton's history begins far back in prehistory. Evidence of man has been found in the Mesolithic Period some 11,000 to 4,350 BC. A local man, William Shore Jr, found several pieces of flint on the edges of Bache Pool about the time it was drained and filled in 1892. He published a work in 1911 entitled Prehistoric Man Cheshire, in which he recorded the flints and other finds and sites he found with other people. The Bache Pool site came under closer scrutiny more recently when an archaeological investigation was undertaken prior to the supermarket site expansion in the late 1990s. Another flint flake was found of the

Photographs with the kind permission of the Grosvenor Museum

17

same type. These flakes were used for cutting, chopping or as weapons by securing several pieces into a wooden handle. It was hoped to find the possible location of a settlement site, as a find of this kind is very unusual for Cheshire, though sadly none was found.

So why was man drawn to this particular spot? The name Bache means 'valley stream', which aptly describes the area's main feature. Such a freshwater source would have been a natural asset. The lightly wooded valley with sandy soils and the pool's animals and plants could have given the opportunity for settlement or cultivation on a permanent or temporary/seasonal basis.

The Roman Period

Only trace activity had been found in Upton until recently, stray coins and pottery shards but nothing structural. The area Upton covers forms a sort of no-mans-land immediately outside the Fortress City between two Roman roads. One runs on a NW alignment from Chester, although its exact course is not certain. It is thought that the Parkgate Road is the most probable. The other also comes close, as traces of it were found at Liverpool Road/Parkgate Road junction leading to Brook Lane and on to Hoole Bank.

As the Bache/Upton area was so close to the fortress it is unlikely to have had any widespread settlement except for the land used for agricultural purposes as it fell within the Prata Legionis, i.e. The Fields of the Legions. This was a specified area of land probably between the Rivers Dee and Gowy, including the Wirral, which would have supplied the fortress with produce, crops, leather, wood – anything in fact that was needed.

Upton Heath

In the summer of 1986 the Environmental Planning Service Department at Backford Hall was doing aerial recognisance in the area. They spotted features in the fields around Upton Grange Farm on Upton Heath. By 1989 a total of 5 enclosures were found lying between Acres Lane and Long Lane. The sites are roughly rectilinear with rounded corners and of a similar size, the shape of a playing card that is typically Roman. (See colour picture Ch 1)

There have been several investigations as to what exactly they are but it now seems clear that they fall into the category of practice camps. Roman soldiers used them when out on campaign or for practice and were only meant to be temporary, even for overnight.

In 1997 there was an evaluation of one of the enclosures which found a ditch and a row of postholes, which was interpreted as the remains of a wooden palisade. Radiocarbon dating from the bottom of the ditch gave a Roman date.

The Saxon Period

When the Roman occupation of Britain finally came to an end at the beginning of the 6th century, the county fell into a quieter period with the Saxon's gradual arrival. This period is often referred to as the Dark Ages but a lasting legacy of this era are the place names in our area.

Upton means the 'Higher-up farm' or enclosure and is of Saxon origin. Many of the surrounding villages also have names with Saxon origins – for example –

Picton	}	Pica's enclosure/farm
Chorlton	}	Churl's enclosure/farm
Newton	}	The new enclosure/farm
Moston	}	The moor-fold enclosure/farm

British (Celtic) names are still present in Cheshire mainly in the hills, rivers and streams, but as this area was a frontier zone between Saxons and Britons there are many TON settlements. The Saxons liked a rural setting but the economic importance of Chester would have drawn them to the vicinity. Chester was a market centre with sea trading links with the Irish Sea routes. It is at this intriguing time that Upton gets its first direct written mention and its first connection to the Cathedral that was St Weburgh's Abbey at the time.

Edgar, King of the Mercian's, granted St Werburgh's Abbey land for its foundation and Upton was part of the gift. Here is an excerpt from the document which is now lost but was copied at several times at later dates.

*Almighty father, only hope of the world. Creator of the heavens. Founder of the earth. Who traverses the day by illuminating it with the burning rays of the brilliant Titan. And He dresses the night in the splendour of radiant Diana. He has given all goods to us, bestowing on us more than we merit. Just as in turn he was such an example through the gospel to others, so he has taught us through a corpus of other writings to give back in return. On account of which, I, Edgar, of the Kingdom of the Mercians, by the protecting grace of Christ, exulted to the rooftops, for the expiation of my soul and of my predecessors....... I give and freely grant to almighty God, to the (monks) in honour of the ever most holy virgin Werburg ..... thus they are Hodeshlid Ceofanlea Huntingdun **Huptun** Easton Barue. I, Edgar, King of the Mercians have ordered this to be written with the agreement of the rest of the tribes. With the sign of the holy cross I have affirmed and corroborated it.*

The language used is a good illustration of the transitional times of the period. Christianity was the new religion that promised so much but there were those who still could not leave their old gods completely and this document shows that perhaps by mentioning everyone, you kept a foot in each camp and caused least offence. It is beautifully written, colourful and shows the importance of family past, present and future. The document is dated AD 958.

Henry Bradshaw was a monk from St Werburgh's Abbey who, just before his death in 1513, aged 48, wrote a book on the life of St Werburgh. The saint had an unusual connection with Upton.

Werburgh was the daughter of Wulfere, King of the Mercian Saxons, and was descended from four Saxon Kings. She gave up her life of royalty and riches to enter into holy orders at Ely Abbey as a Virgin. When she died her body was buried at Hanbury in Shropshire where she had founded a nunnery. There she lay for 200 years until the Viking invasion of 875 reached Mercia. The Danes got close to Hanbury so her shrine was moved to the secure city of Chester. It was here that the miracles started. Henry Bradshaw tells us tales of the Saint saving Chester from the Welsh, the Danes and the Scots. She cured the sick and brought an unlawfully hanged man back to life. She saved the city from fire when her shrine was carried in procession in 1180 and of course was responsible for the miracle of Upton Heath.

Bradshaw's story of

Howe at the manor-place of Vpton saint Werburge restrayned wylde horses from distruction of cornes put in by theyr ennemyes.   Cap xiii

The Danes were threatening Chester so the people moved their valuable cattle and crops out of the city to the safety of Upton Heath, which was land owned by the Abbey. As the wild horsemen attacked, the Saint intervened striking them down with palsy, leprosy and blindness. Not only did this miracle save the day but also made sure they did not try again. St Werburgh's shrine can still be found inside Chester Cathedral today.

By 1066 St Werburgh's Abbey was the second richest landowner in the county after Earl Edwin, and this included the manor of Upton.

This concludes the literary sources for the time, so what other evidence is there for Saxon Upton? By the careful study of old maps information reveals itself that can be looked for in the present day surroundings. Three maps have been sourced; the 1735 Enclosure map of Upton Heath, the 1801 Estate map for the Egertons, and the 1839 Tithe map, and these have been used in combination. The earlier map shows the layout of what was probably the original settlement.

St Weburgh's shrine.
With kind permission of the Chapter of
Chester Cathedral

One field in particular, in the very centre of the map, is surrounded on all four sides by lanes. Next to it are strip fields that indicate croft and toft farming facing on to what is now Upton Lane. We know that this stretch of Upton Lane was called Smoke Street until the first half of the 20th century. It has been previously remarked that the term street stands out when all other roads are called lanes. This is another piece of evidence as it indicates a very old name and derives from – STRETE – Old English for road.

By the time of the 1801 map, changes have been made, Smoke Street/Sandpit Lane has been straightened, losing the T junction at one corner of the enclosure, and a lane has also fallen out of use and become a field boundary. Although some older features have gone, it does show an increasing concentration of dwellings around the junctions of Church Lane and Upton Lane.

On the 1839 Tithe map the lost lane can still be seen as a field boundary and the field is called Footway field confirming the previous significance. The shape of the lost T-junction is visible as the boundary of Upton Lawn House and even though this property has also gone, the same shape is retained today in Lawn Drive.

Other field names of interest are on the 1735 map. Port, Tapa and Wing Fields are grouped together along Liverpool Road behind the Egerton Arms – Upton Drive area. Tapa is a personal name (NB Pica in Picton), words beginning with 'wing' in the Old English dictionary relate to vines but Port is the important name. Port means a town with market rights or entrance / portal. The position of this field on the edge of the city limits and on a main route does suggest that it could well of been the site of trading of some kind. This area is on the very doorstep of the City and could well have been the original starting point for settlement.

We can therefore find an enclosure, farming evidence, a well, road network, all forming a main settlement and 3 large fields of a possible secondary centre. There are important elements missing; the boundary of the area and a place of worship or church. The 1735 map has another large road marked which is another casualty on the 1801 map. Acres Lane continued straight into the zoo, crossing Flag Lane, and onwards arcing across open country to join Liverpool Road.

This could well form the northern limits of the settlement area – part of it still does today being the Upton/Moston boundary. There is no place name or map evidence for a church site in Upton and it seems most likely that there never was one. The nearest known church from this period is St Werburgh's Abbey in the city centre, and it was here that people from the outlying communities would worship. But, there is one last piece of evidence we are left to consider - Upton Cross. When the name was checked, four words of Latin and a date of 1398 were found and this led to an alternative story for Upton's plague stone. (See Ch 4)

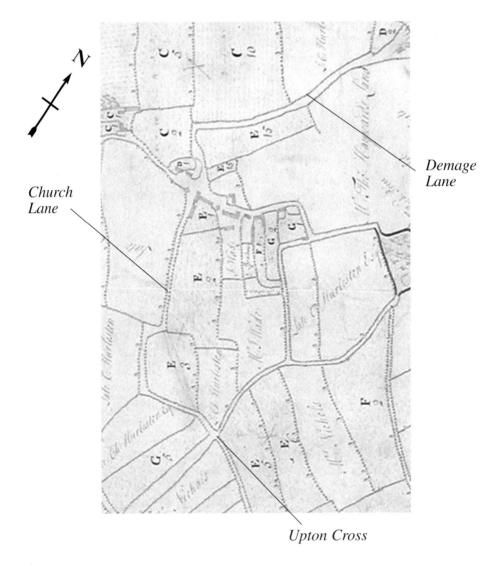

N

Church Lane

Demage Lane

Upton Cross

Part of the 1735 Upton Heath Enclosure map from the Egerton estate. This shows the focal point of the initial development of Upton, including its road lay-out and field patterns.

The Medieval Period

The end of the English era was marked by the Norman invasion of 1066, though the North of England was slow to acknowledge William as King. The Norman armies moved north, first to Northumbria and subsequently down through Cheshire to help change people's minds. They devastated everything in their way, burned houses and crops, killed or chased people away and laid many parts of Cheshire to waste. This was the winter of 1069-70.

King Edgar's Charter of 958 was made just before he became King of England and suggests that Upton was a Mercian royal vill. This is confirmed by its status in 1066 as a possession of Edwin, Earl of Mercia. This high status continued after the conquest when Upton became the possession of Hugh I, Earl of Chester.

Upton's entry into the Great Domesday Book of 1086 is as follows –

In Wirral Hundred
Upton. Earl Edwin held it.4½ hides paying tax. Land for 12 ploughs.
In lordship 1; 2 ploughmen;
12 villagers and 2 riders with 5 ploughs.
Of this land, Hamo holds 2 parts of 1 hide of this manor;
Herbert ½ hide; Mundret 1 hide. In lordship 4 ploughs; 8 ploughmen.
2 villagers and 2 smallholders with 1 plough. Meadow, 1 acre.
Value of the whole manor before 1066, 60s; now the Earl's lordship
45s, his men's 40s.

Parts of the manor were let to three others: Hamo de Macsi held two parts of one hide (about 80 acres of arable), Herbert held half a hide (about 60 acres) and Mundret. The Domesday survey for the area does have several omissions particularly in our immediate area north of Chester City. As we can see from the

Domesday entry for Upton its value was 60s in the reign of Edward. This was quite a high value locally compared to Wervin 30s, Croughton 10s, Chorlton 2s or Picton 40s. It does suggest, and so does Ormerod, *'that Upton was at this time head of several dependant estates'*. The three sublet portions of the vill were probably the later manors of Moston, Bache and Caughall. The manors of Bache and Moston continued to have lands at Upton as did the Abbot of St Werburgh's. The Abbey had lost its holdings in the township before 1066. Not until Earl Hugh I granted the tithes of Upton to the Abbey, when it was re-founded as a Benedictine House in 1293, was the connection remade. He did not, however, give land, just its income and neither did his successor Earl Richard. The third Earl, Ranulph le Maschin, did donate the manor of Upton to the Abbey as a *'post obit'* gift and this is where it stayed until the Dissolution of 20th January 1540. Upton was included in the Wirral Hundred for the Domesday survey, but it was probably moved to the Broxton Hundred about the time the third Earl was dividing his lands as gifts for the Abbey and rewards to his barons.

Bache Mill

The Township of Bache originally consisted of a single estate, Bache Hall was a moated manorial site of medieval date. There was a water mill associated with the Hall; the earliest reference to it was when it was granted to St Werburgh's Abbey by Earl Richard in 1119. Bache Mill pool was located where the current supermarket entrance and petrol station stands and was almost to Garth Drive. The mill building was on the other side of the road.

Watermills of this time were associated with well-established areas of arable farming and were costly installations, but very profitable. Earl Richard had also given the monks the land between the Abbey and Bache Mill, ie. Northgate Street. The soke rights that this gave the Monks meant that their tenants living on Northgate Street had to take their corn to be ground only at the monks mill at Bache. These rights were rigorously kept; milling at home was forbidden. The mill was therefore a financial asset to the owner and to the miller, especially if he leased the mill. A fascinating dispute is recorded between the Bache Mill and the Dee Mills. This took place in 1567 concerning these very rights.

1801 Estate map showing location of Bache water mill

Thomas Bavand worked the Bache Mill and had been Sheriff of Chester in the same year that Ralph Goodman had been Mayor, 1547. Goodman leased the Dee Mills. Bavand died leaving his Widow, Margaret, dependent on the mill for a living. She carried on the business and kept the old connections, including the businesses of some citizens who did not live in Northgate Street. The Goodmans did nothing whilst Thomas Bavand was alive but did take actions against his widow.

The Goodmans' court case was also against four other local millers who were also taking lawful business away from them. The four gave in immediately with two of them giving evidence against Mrs Bavand but she stood firm declaring she acted within the law. Evidence was called on to prove her wrong and a court order was issued to prevent her, or her servants, from carrying on the practice.

Three years later in September 1570 a second Bill of Indictment was issued as she was in daily breach of the first. Another order was issued in March 1571, Margaret was taken to Chester Castle to be punished and kept until she could enter into bonds with sufficient sureties not to break the order again. She also had to pay the Goodmans 35 shillings in cost. The last piece of this story is that her son, Richard, takes over Bache Mill.

The mill stayed in operation and ownership of the Dean and Chapter of Chester Cathedral until it was sold off in March 1816. The Indenture shows that the Mill had already stopped milling grain and was used by John Dodd who was a skinner. It does provide the only physical description of the mill, which consisted of the mill building, shippon, sheds, pool, ponds, watercourses, floodgates, streams, fishing and Bache Pool. The exact end of the mill is not known, but it had stopped milling corn before 1816 and the millpond had mostly been allowed to silt up before it was filled in.

For over 700 years local people brought their corn to Bache Mill yet nothing physical remains of so many centuries of continuous industrial activity. Although in September 1973 workmen uncovered what was first thought to be a wooden dugout canoe but on removal to the Grosvenor Museum for cleaning and examination it was identified as a chute made from a single piece of oak measuring 3m long, 50cm wide and 35cm deep. The core had been dug out to create a trough with an opening cut at one end. It had peg holes and some pegs still in position. This is probably the last remaining piece of the lost mill.

Oak chute being removed from its find site.
Photographs used with kind permission of Chester City Council.

The Plague

The plague visited many times during the 16th and 17th centuries but in 1603 we have a detailed account of one such visitation. In the Mayor's Book for October of that year a decision was made to allow the burial of several Upton residents who had succumbed to the plague, including Widow Davy of Hogg House, in the churchyard of the Cathedral. The people of Upton could claim this right as part of Upton lay in the Parish of St Oswald i.e. the parish church of the Cathedral. Certain strict conditions had to be followed. They could take the usual route to the graveyard but when they reached Richard Bavand's house next door they could take some of the wall down to make it easier to carry the bodies. The dead were to be brought in at 6 o'clock in the evening by people carrying white rods to denote their business. After the bodies were buried they had to leave, still carrying the white rods in their hands, and were not allowed to converse with any inhabitants of the city or enter into any house.

The city was taking every step it could to contain the plague and prevent it spreading further. It must have been hard for the living to keep up with the plague and perhaps it was too dangerous to take the dead across the city to be buried at St Mary's on the Hill. It would make sense not to carry them through the city but take them to the nearer graveyard.

Beside the doorway of Holy Ascension Church can be found Upton's plague stone with an inscription put there in 1938 after some restoration. It had been found when the War Memorial foundations were begun in 1920. Between then and 1938 the stone seems to have moved location several times depending on various stories. It even spent some time back in its original position but upright, being used as a stile with villagers utilising the hollow as a step up.

In the church porch hangs an inscription offering an explanation of the stone, which details how people could use the stone as a place to pay or barter for food. This may have been necessary if people wanted to trade with one another but keep the risk of catching the plague to a minimum. The stone bowl was put there to represent where the coins would have been placed into the disinfectant. (See Ch4)

The Civil War – The Siege of Chester

The English Civil War was a time of great unheaval and divide in the country and our area was greatly affected. The Siege of the City of Chester meant that the close proximity of Bache and Upton brought war to the doorstep.

By the summer of 1642 Chester had begun to prepare itself for the imminent war. The City Assembly set about repairing the walls and gates and formed a City Regiment. Chester came into Royalist control when most of the leading and powerful men who controlled the city's trade were for that cause more than there being any organised opposition for the Parliamentarian side.

It was Sir William Brereton who commanded the Parliamentary forces in Cheshire. He had business interests in Chester where he owned a town house. He had been unsuccessful in some of his business enterprises because of opposition from the local authorities, including the Gamul family. This meant that he had more than a passing interest in seeing Chester brought into Parliamentarian hands.

The defences of the city were expanded in 1643 to include some of the northern and eastern suburbs. This included an extended mud/earth wall and trench, fortified with strategically placed bastions or mounts. This was to enclose extra space to be used by incoming Irish troops. The wall ran north from the NW corner of the City Walls and on to the first mount called Morgans, then NW to the Stone Bridge that carried the Neston Road over Flookers Brook, where another mount was built.

It then turned NE across two roads out of the city. Northgate Street was covered by a mount and this was also covered by another one the other side of Bache Lane (Liverpool Road) – called Dr Whalley's mount, and on to Flookers Brook mount. These mounts covered not just the roads but also the turnpikes and gates that cut through the wall. Flookersbrook Hall was initially protected. The wall went on to Boughton and down to the river. A deep lane was cut through the rock linking Stone Bridge Lane (Parkgate Road) and Bache Lane (Liverpool Road). This allowed the rapid movement of artillery; the road is still called Rock Lane.

The siege was biting hard by November 1643 when Colonel John Morrow was ordered to burn the Handbridge suburb, and this was done to prevent the rebels sheltering or attacking from so close to the city. The following day, Bache and Flookers Brook Halls were also burnt for the same reasons. This was a drastic action to take but the city was desparate to protect itself and its Royalist status. Upton Hall faired better being just out of the immediate vicinity of the city. Early in 1644 when the Parliamentarian Colonel Brereton was trying to tighten his stranglehold on Chester, he established several new garrisons, and one of these was Upton Hall. A detachment of troops from Christleton Hall moved in.

The inhabitants of Upton and the surrounding area would have felt the full force of the war. The sound of cannon fire and the sight of soldiers would have been an almost daily event. The scarcity of food had its own effect on the locality; not only were families to be fed but the soldiers garrison at Upton Hall would have taken anything available, leading to great deprivation. This eventually brought the siege to a head.

There were frequent skirmishes between both sides and each side built extensive earthworks in the area and across to Newton and Hoole. It seems that there would also have been such earthworks around Upton Hall, but they were mostly demolished when fighting finished and the remnants dispersed as the suburbs grew in later years.

From this time we have two cannon balls, both allegedly local, one found in the 1950s in the vicinity of Flag Lane, and now in the keeping of our Local History Group.

Small cannon ball
diameter 9cm

ULHG Cannon Ball

The siege ended in 1646 when the Royalist Commander, Lord Byron, surrendered the exhausted City to Brereton. The city was starving, impoverished and wrecked. The suburbs of Broughton, Handbridge and the Northgate area had been levelled, and Bache Hall was one of six large houses that were lost. It was the property of Edward Whitby at the time, he was a Recorder for the city and part of the City Assembly. The house was rebuilt as we can still see today.

A final legacy of the war was a re-visit of the plague, the citizens were weakened and in poor health and were very easy victims of the disease. Over 2000 died in and around Chester between June 1647 and April 1648. They either died or fled to the surrounding countryside leaving the city. The city, like Bache Hall, did rebuild itself and its economy.

The Ownership of Upton

Before 1882 when Upton became a Parish in its own right, it held the status of Township being mostly in St Mary's-on-the-Hill with a small piece in St. Oswald's Parish. Before this, Upton was a manor, which initially meant that it was a definite area of land under the outright ownership of one. The revenue from a manor, land within it, or indeed the whole manor was often used as gift or reward by the owner. Ancestors commonly re-granted these gifts in memory of their predecessor but manors could be bought, sold or inherited, and these situations have all happened to Upton.

It is possible to trace most of the chain that leads up to Upton becoming a Parish and its last Lord of the Manor, Sir Philip Grey-Egerton.

The first known owner was the Mercian King Edgar, and this reflects the Anglo-Saxon origins of Upton. There is no evidence to suggest that there was any kind of settlement here before this time. Edgar gave the manor to St Werburgh's Abbey, Chester, in 958, but between then and the Domesday record the land falls back to the Mercian Earl Edwin. The Norman Earl of Chester, Hugh I, takes over and grants the tithes to St Werburgh's in 1093, but Earl Ranulph I gives Upton Manor to the Abbey 1121-1129. These Norman earls were probably giving back what they had taken by force when they first came to power.

It seems that the Abbot's rule may have been a hard one as in 1381 news of riots in London reached Cheshire. The King's letters denouncing the rebellion of the Peasants' Rising were read at Chester. Cheshire had remained peaceful but some bondsmen of the Abbot held secret meetings in the woods in Wirral. A proclamation was issued forbidding the meetings; it also forbade the collection of money to help the disputes. Despite this, several men from Upton met with others at Lea-by-Backford and rose in arms, damaging goods and property belonging to the Abbot. This rising was typical in England at the time as social discontent was widespread, but the men of Chester were not treated any worse than others.

The Abbey, by way of confirmation, stays in possession of the Manor until the Dissolution of the Monasteries in 1541 when King Henry VIII confiscates all land owned by the St Werburgh's into crown hands. The Abbey was restored as a Cathedral with Dean and Chapter, but then fell on hard times after the reformation.

By 1552 the Dean of Chester and two canons had been imprisoned in Fleet, London, at the hand of Sir Richard Cotton, their crime – taking and selling the lead off the Cathedral roof. This seems an unduly harsh punishment but Sir Richard had very strong personal motives for manoeuvring the Dean – he wanted land and lots of it. Under intimidation the Dean signed over most of the Cathedral's land in return for a fixed annual payment, Sir Richard's blow was doubly hard as he also managed to get the lands for almost £100 less than their true value of over £700.

The lands were later sold on to many Cheshire gentlemen by George Cotton, Sir Richard's son, as he had died in 1556. These fee farmers had a fight on their hands to keep the land for which they were paying, as a peculiar situation had developed by the time Queen Elizabeth had come to the throne. With the huge amount of paperwork generated at the Dissolution and Reformation, errors were made with the wording on some documents. The flaws proved crucial, effectively rendering grants null and void and the Crown still in possession of the previous Abbey lands. Upton fell into the category of these 'concealed' lands. Queen Elizabeth commissioned Peter Grey to investigate Chester Cathedral's situation in September 1577. It did not take him long to find quite a long list of lands in error, including Upton, Moston and Wervin, a total value of £200 pa in all. Grey was in league with two others and sold on the leases as his reward to them, (Hitchcock, and Bostock who soon died). The fee farmers found that those leases were in danger and most came to terms with Hitchcock. The final outcome of the whole business was a court judgment of 1580, where the Dean and Chapter lost their freehold right to the lands to the fee farmers but were given the rents including a rise to a true value.

A document in the Egerton family deposit in the Record Office shows George Cotton selling Upton to George Calveley in 1580. It includes the signatures of George Cotton, Sir Hugh Cholmondeley, Sir George Calveley, Thomas Leigh and others who were the witnesses to the sale and the main Cheshire gentlemen who bought the land taken by Sir Richard Cotton from the Dean and Chapter. They were obviously a tight-knit group. This ends this turbulent time in our history but from now onwards the landowners were also residents.

Two families in particular became the major players. The Browns, who lived in Hoole, and the Brocks who became the Lords of the Manor and lived at Upton Hall. There are other Latin manuscripts left behind by the Brock family to be translated, and these will reveal yet more of their story. For many generations the Brocks held Upton – until 1734 – when the last William Brock died. His two sons had died before him and so it was to the eldest daughter, Elizabeth, and her husband, John Egerton of Oulton, that Upton Manor came. The Egertons, or various branches of the family, held Upton until 1828 when it became invested in the Grey-Egertons of Oulton. The last Lord of the Manor was Sir Philip Henry Brian Grey-Egerton, 12th Baronet who, from 1891 until his death on 4th July 1937 saw the last of many hundreds of years of ownership of Upton as an estate. His sons had died in the First World War leaving no male heir but his daughter did take over the last few pieces of land that had not been sold to private developers.

References

Prehistoric Man In Cheshire, W Shone 1911

Unpublished Site Evaluation Report For Safeway Ltd, M M Emery 1997

West Cheshire From The Air, S Rhys Williams 1997

Roman Roads In Britain, Margary 1973

The Place Names Of Cheshire Part IV, Dodgson 1972

Pre Conquest Cheshire 383-1066, J D Bulock 1972

Cartularium Saxonicum folio 1041, W G de Gray Birch (ed) 1885-93

The Life Of St Werburge Of Chester, Henry Bradshaw 1513,
Re edited C Hortmann 1889, Early English Text Society 2002

1735 Upton Heath Enclosure Map CCRO DEO 1/7

1801 Egerton Estate Map CCRO DEO 1/18

1839 Tithe Map and Apportionment CCRO EDT 401/1&2

Domesday Book Cheshire: including Lancashire Cumbria and North Wales,
P Morgan 1978

History of Cheshire – Broxton Hundred – Upton, G Ormerod

Caligraphy contribution from Hazel Petch

The Chartulary and Register of the Abbey of St Werburghs, J Tait

St Oswalds Church in the Parish of Backford, J P Hess

The Monks of Chester, RVH Burne 1962

History Of Cornmilling IV – Some Feudal Mills, Bennett and Elton 1904

Indenture from Dean and Chapter of Chester Cathedral 1816 for Bache Mill
CCRO EDD 10/2/1 and 10/2/2

Cheshire Archaeological Bulletin 2 1974

Mayor's Book 28 Folio 152 CCRO

The Great Siege of Chester, J Barrett 2003

The Great Leaguer of Chester, S Pickstock 1994

Excavations at Chester. The Civil War Siegeworks 1642-6, S Ward

Victoria County Histories of Cheshire volumes I, II, III

Chester Cathedral, RVH Burne

The Peasants Rising and the Lollards, E Powell and G M Travelyan

Grant of Upton Manor 1580 CCRO DEO 206/1

Sites and Monuments Record 2035 Cross at Upton

Public Monument and Sculpture Association, War Memorial and Plague Stone
at Upton

Latin translation and interpretation Brian Lewis

CHAPTER 4

Historic Upton

This chapter explains the sites and properties in Upton that were known to exist before the Tithe Map of 1840 was drawn up. Many of those properties have been lost over time but we are fortunate to still have several with us today. We are left with cottages, former farmhouses, a public house, one hall, boundary stones and the ancient stone at the side of the church. Not forgetting many of the roads we use today.

Upton Hall

The pretty watercolour picture of Upton Hall from 1920 shows two houses in one; a farmhouse and a decaying hall. (See chapter 2). The hall appears to be of Elizabethan period with stone mullioned windows and had cellars. The house was between what is now the end of the hospital complex and the Dale Camp; the Chester to Birkenhead railway was put across the Hall's drive in 1840. The house had fine views across to the Welsh hills but its location does feel isolated from the rest of Upton being separated by the railway and main road. Maybe this is what the original owners intended.

The origin of the property is not known, nor is it possible to tell if there was another house on the site previously. If we assume that this house was the property of the Lord of the Manor of Upton it could well be that the Brock family, who establish themselves at the head of Upton Manor, were the most likely builders. Ormerod starts the family with John Brock, gentleman, who left his second wife a widow in 1594. The family were landowners not only in Upton but Newton, Moston, around the Christleton area and as far afield as Moreton, Wirral. There are many instances of them renting out their land to farmers.

The Brocks played a prominent position not just in Upton but in Chester, and served as Aldermen, Councillors, Sheriff, as well as Churchwardens of St Mary-on-the-Hill Church. They intermarried with other local gentry including the Greggs of Bradley, the Hurlstones of Picton, and the Hockenhulls of Shotwick. When the male line ran out in 1734 it was the last time that the Lord of the Manor lived in Upton Hall. It was then rented out by the Egerton family and became more of a large farm than a gentleman's residence.

From the mid 1800s to 1923 the Hall was tenanted and farmed by the Ithell family, Thomas Ithell moved from a farm by the sand pit in Upton Lane to the Hall until he died in 1876 at almost 100 years old.

In 1897 a surveyor from Mollington, John Davies, came in July of that year to make a valuation on the property for the Egerton family. He has left a good description of the Hall at almost the end of its long life when it was already in decay. Davies described two approaches from the main road, fields in a good state of cultivation, especially wheat, but the *'accommodation was old and considerably out of repair'*. He valued the whole property and land as comprising over 46 acres at £11/7s/4ᵈ. The Ithells kept the tenancy within the family until Richard Ithell finally left for his own house in Upton. The last tenant was Arthur Hinde and he farmed until 1933 when the Hall was finally demolished. Although the Hall is no longer, the field it stood in is still farmed to this day.

In the summer of 2004 a History Group member unearthed an old gun on the Hall field whilst walking her dog. It was taken to the Grosvenor Museum for identification and turned out to be a gentleman's pocket pistol with a percussion cap firing mechanism. This dated it to between 1840-1850 but the gun itself could have been much older as it appears that the firing mechanism is an addition, probably an upgrade.

Robert Brock

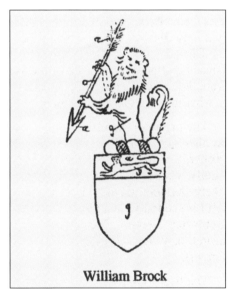
William Brock

Brock family coats of arms

Bache Hall

The house that now carries the name of Bache Hall was built in the early 18ᵗʰ century. It is of plain brick, two storeys, has 5 bays and is Grade III listed. The house is situated on a gentle rise; below is a rocky valley with Bache Brook running through. It was rebuilt after the old house was demolished during the Civil War siege of Chester. This older property is listed as having a medieval moat, but there is no trace of it now as modern housing covers the site but on the 1844 tithe map of Bache, field No.3 is called Moat Field and could possibly be the site of the original house.

The first references to various families who have held the manor start in the 13th century with several people having Bache as a surname, it is probable that they did represent the ownership. By the 14th century it was held by the Donecaster family and in the next century the Chauntrells take over. There are references to documents with various members of the family listed right through until William sells the manor to Robert Whitby in approximately 1606. It is during the Whitby's custodianship that the old house is lost and a new one built. From the Whitby's the estate passed, partly by purchase and partly by marriage, to the Cromptons. About 1720 the manor passes via an heiress of the Cromptons to the Morgans of Golden Grove in Flintshire until they sold it to Samuel James Broadhurst of Chester. The property descended to various members of his family who, as part of the Will terms, had to change their name from Jenks to Brodhurst (sometimes listed as Broadhurst). In 1874 Samuel Broadhurst Hill sold the estate to the Hudson family, and finally a Major MacGillycuddy who was the last private owner. He sold it to the neighbouring Mental Hospital in 1922 and the Hall has just undergone restoration and expansion by Chester College as a School of Midwifery.

In 1973 Liverpool Road was widened to a dual carriageway ending at Bache Hall; a lodge house and Bache Cottage were demolished. In the 1990s a new road, Countess Way, was put in, running along the lawns parallel to Bache Brook underneath the Hall. It joins Parkgate Road and Liverpool Road.

Bache Lodge house, Liverpool Road

Moston Hall and The Dale

Moston Hall was built in the early part of the 19th century and was the seat of the Massey family. Built of red brick it was partly restored and added to in 1870. When the estate was sold off to the Swetenham family an unsold portion descended to Miss Massey who, in the 1880s, built The Dale. Mr Reginald Potts later bought it as a present to his wife and they moved there from The Oaks. In 1938 The Dale was purchased by the War Department from Mrs F Potts and became the Depot of the Cheshire Regiment.

Heath House

There are references to this property going back to the early 17th century, and its location is revealed in the St Oswald's Vestry Orders of 1656. It describes the parish boundaries and says that the house stood on the Upton-Picton boundary

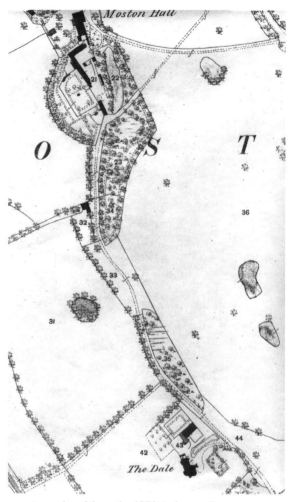

Reproduced from the 1873 Ordnance Survey map

'*at the north end a lane led to Picton on the east a meere stone parted Upton and Picton Heath*'. This leads us to what is now Upton Grange Farm. The large house that is just set back from the lane is a much later building, but behind in the farm courtyard stands a large cottage of a very much earlier date. This is in all probability Heath House, if not the site of it. Early records of St Oswald's and St Mary's churches have accounts of the Robinson family of Heath House in their books.

Recently local archaeology students gained permission to fieldwalk on the field next to the scheduled moat field. This was a simple exercise of dividing the field in 10m surveyed squares and retrieving objects found on the newly ploughed and rolled soil surface. A diverse collection of pottery was found from Roman to Willow pattern, lots of broken clay pipes and very thick pieces of glass from wine bottles. This shows activity across many centuries, but particularly by the agricultural worker who was smoking and taking refreshment from the 17th century onwards.

The Acres – Acres Lane

This is another of our very old sites. The Cheshire Sheaf records the sale of land here at the end of the 16th century. Firstly in 1587-8 R Browne sold land in Upton and Wervin to Henry Birkenhead (of Backford Hall). Called The Acres, it consisted of 16 acres in all lying between Upton Common, Wervin Common and the high road that led to Caughall. Secondly, in 1595-6 R Browne again sold land, this time to Will Aldersey. Called Great Acres, it had a value of £80 and was again in the vicinity of the first sale.

The exact age of the farm is not known, and it does not appear on a map until the 1831map of Bryant by which time it is a large farm house and outbuilding arrangement. At the time of the Tithe survey eight years later it was owned by Samuel Brittain, who owned various other pieces of land in Upton, including the Mill and farm next to it, but did not live at the Acres.

It continued to function as a farm right through to the early part of the 20th century when the Dean family (of Upton Mill) lived and worked here for several decades. It is not known exactly when the Deans left and the farm became semi derelict until the early 1980's, when the outbuildings were converted into residential properties called Green Acres Court. The main house became a country hotel for a while, then in the late 1980s it was significantly refurbished and extended to become the Orchard Manor Nursing Home. 'The WI Book' notes how much the display of daffodils in the old orchard was admired at the time.

Upton Farm – Upton Lane

The origins of this building are not known for certain but research leads us to a possible date sometime between the post-Civil War era and the early 18th century. The farm started life as a two-room small holding with a central entrance door facing west and an inglenook fireplace at each end. There may well have been a wooden ladder giving access to the loft space. Another room was added at right angles, on the north side, almost doubling the property and is shown on the 1735 map. It has been previously written that wattle and daub walls are in the building. Extensive restoration in more recent years has failed to locate any, but reed and plasterwork has been found in a wall and as a ceiling. It is believed that the house was extended into a farm in 1842, as there is a set of initials and the year scratched into the rough plaster upstairs in the stable block. The roof was also raised by some 6-8 courses and the farm then took its distinctive quadrangle form remembered by many today.

It has been recorded that a 'Spence' was located in the kitchen. This was described as an area partitioned off – the lower part filled in and the upper part railed. A separate area might be needed for the making or storage of products made on the farm. One hidden feature of the house is the cellars that an ex-employee of a previous owner report as being barrel-vaulted, but they were

filled with sand at the insistence of the owner's wife. There is a substantial amount of sand under the present kitchen floor but no way of verifying the report. The farm had its own water pump, which also supplied the cottages in the vicinity.

Upton Farm had grown from a smallholding into a farm, which was working until the middle of the last century. In the 1920s and 30s it operated as a pig farm run by the Brickland family. When it changed hands it still kept to the business of animal keeping, slaughtering and selling the products from the farm.

After WW2, the property and some adjoining land, was owned by Mr Shinn who was a speculative builder. He built and sold plots around Upton Lane and he also sold off part of the farm; the demolition of most of the quadrangle buildings allowed the development of Penfold Hey. His son, Arthur Shinn, later took over the property before he sold it in 1990 to the current owners, Mr and Mrs Stockton, who have taken great care to restore some of the period features of the house. When Upton Lane was widened the end of the building was demolished and the garden wall built.

Rose Cottage - Upton Lane

This house has had many changes of name. It has been known as Rose Bank, Rose Bank Cottage, and Rose Villa and is on the site of the Man in the Moon public house as marked on the 1735 map. The front of the building shows a date of 1745. The house is earlier than this but its exact date is not known. In the decades that followed the Civil War there was much regeneration and building, Rose Cottage probably fits into this era. The windows on the front of the house are very distinctive, in a gothic style, which was popular in the 18th century. At some time the roof has been raised; this quite often happened and there are other examples in Upton. The house has several outbuildings including a former wash house in the back yard and a coach house at the end of the property on Demage Lane. The coach house was once a separate family house in the 1930's and was also a cobbler's business. The garden seems to be missing one side, and this is because there was once a lane next to the house. A later cottage was built in the gap.

Tenants even from its early history have usually lived in the house. From Richard Pierce in 1735 to Samuel Brittain, a land owner and Chester solicitor who owned the house in 1839, but the Whitelock family were the tenants, through to the 20th century when David Watkins owned but rented to several tenants all with military connections. One was a Cheshire Regiment Colonel, Sir Napier Crookenden, who was born in the house in 1915. The present owners, Dr and Mrs Bowra , have lived in Rose Cottage since 1977.

Hogg House and The Manor House

There have been several references to a house that is no longer standing, but has some significance as well as great age. 'The WI Book' first notes Hogg House as belonging to St Werburgh's Abbey and quotes an as yet unfounded reference to a grant of 1579. It was included with other land in a grant to the Glaisser family of Lea-by-Backford and was in the holding of Robert Davye, who paid rent at the West Gate of the Abbey on Michaelmas and Lady Day. Robert Davye's widow was to die of the plague in 1603; although several died and were buried at the same time it is only Widow Davye's name that gets mentioned. This shows that the Davyes and their house were of some minor importance. Though none of this information helps to locate the property 'The WI Book' gives another description of a very old house that was demolished at the turn of the 20th century. It was thatched with clay floor downstairs and was reputed to have been the only cottage on the Heath and one of the oldest cottages in Upton. The location of this house is known now as the site of Woodbank and Heath House cottages on Heath Road.

Our earliest map which includes residents' names is the 1735 map and on this, John Ithell is listed as tenanting this same piece of land; there are three houses on the site. The Ithell family connection with the site is a long one and at some unknown time they must have purchased the site, as by early 20th century Richard Ithell retired from farming at Upton Hall and moved into his own house very close by.

This house was known as the Manor House but was formally called the Beeches; again it was reported to be an old house with rush ceilings and stone foundations. This picture of the house shows it in its modernised form in the mid-20th century. The house was demolished and the bungalows of Wheldon Close now stand on the site.

The key to unravelling the site is the Ithell family, whose repeated connection over several centuries is highly significant. We have a lot of evidence for various branches of the family living all over Upton but the Heath site must have become their home as they were usually tenants. It has already been suggested that Hogg House was a property of some significance, as were the Ithell family, and it is just possible that they acquired the site and built the Manor House when they needed a bigger or newer property. Hogg House remained but lost its significance until it was demolished in 1905 when the land was sold by Richard Ithell to build the pair of cottages called Heath Cottages. Further evidence, which could substantiate the claim that there was an old cottage on the site, has been found. Cellars were unexpectedly discovered when alterations were made to Heath House Cottage.

The Ithell Family

The Ithell family have had a constant presence in Upton like no other family. They farmed for the Brock and Egerton families and can be found in local records going back to at least 1631, when William Ithell buried his wife, Elizabeth. Throughout the 18th and 19th centuries various members of the family occur in the Parish Records for St Mary's-on-the-Hill, the Township Minute Books, maps and in the Egerton family papers. For example, in the 1730s we can locate three branches of the family living in Upton at the same time.

Thomas Ithell was a labourer living at Bache Pool with his wife Mary and their two children, Martha and Thomas.

John Ithell was a Yeoman living at Upton Heath with his wife Margaret and their son, John.

William Ithell was a Churchwarden at St Mary's-on-the-Hill.

As you can see the family used the names Thomas and John frequently, and this makes unravelling the families quite difficult. They have also managed to live in many of the known properties in Upton, e.g. The Golden Ball Inn (The Egerton Arms), the Manor House (Upton Heath), Demage Farm and Upton Hall. In 1820 Thomas Ithell moved from a farm in Sandpit Lane to take the tenancy of Upton Hall from the Egertons. Between the various family members they farmed a considerable amount of Upton whilst owning very little, yet achieving the status of Yeoman farmers. This Thomas Ithell died in 1876 aged 99 years and 9 months. Eventually his nephew Richard was the last to take over the Hall farm in 1890 until he gave up possession in 1923 when he retired to his own house. Mr Richard Ithell held the Hall from Sir Philip Grey-Egerton and was the oldest tenant on the estate at the time of the Silver Wedding celebrations of Sir Philip and Lady Grey-Egerton in 1936. These were held at Oulton Park and representatives from Upton gave a gift of a silver cake basket presented by Mr Ithell. In the speeches that followed Sir Phillip noted the strong family tradition on the estate exemplified by the Ithell family's four hundred year association.

Mr Richard Ithell died in 1947 having served on the Parish Council, the Highway Board and the District Council.

The Brewers Arms, Frog Hall and Bridge Farm Cottage

The area that now comprises the Frog Public House and its near vicinity has a very integrated history. No buildings appear until after the 1735 map but the land here was not part of the Egerton estate. The 1801 map has Jane Jones cottage and one other building marked. The northern block we understand to be a compact set of dwellings, the southern block the farm cottage. A lease from 1835 has John Gill paying Mr Jones a peppercorn rent for 1 year, for the house that became the Brewers Arms. The 1839 Tithe map and Apportionment now shows three properties on the site; the public house, a cottage and garden and 5 dwellings and gardens owned by John Axe (the owner of the Victoria Hotel). Lloyd Branford is listed as owning the other two properties but further information has a Joseph Hughes as owner of the cottage and Richard Jones as occupier.

The name Frog Hall is introduced on the 1871 OS map and the 1881 census records 30 adults plus children residing in Frog Hall – presumably the set of cottages and the farm cottage together. The 2nd edition OS map at the end of that century shows the farm cottage increasing in size. The cottages and Brewers Arms are demolished in the 1930s and the present building 'The Frog' is built set further back from the very front of the road where the old inn was position. The Frog Hall cottages were probably demolished in the 1940's. By 1960 the farm cottage – now called Bridge Farm Cottage - has fallen into such a state of decay, that Chester Urban District Council issued a demolition order, with the premises to be vacated within 12 months. Eventually a planning application was granted in 1962, which stopped the demolition of the cottage, and led to its sale and renovation. Mr and Mrs Shipley have lived at Bridge Farm Cottage since 1978.

The name that unites all the properties that have stood in this area is 'Frog,' and there has been a great deal of conjecture as to its meaning. Here are two explanations – simply that there was a large number of frogs as the area was low and therefore damp – or – Frog Hall like Rats Castle, Bats Hall or Owl Castle, is supposed to have applied to ruined buildings. There is no definitive information available and it will probably never be explained.

Upton Cross House – Heath Road

The house has been a private residence for more than 140 years, but before then it was an inn called the Victoria Hotel. It stands at the meeting of the roads leading to Upton Heath, the Bache and Newton, occupying a prominent location in the village.

The property is large with obvious additions made to the original house, but its exact age is unknown. 'The WI Book' has a date of 1790 for cockfighting at the premises and the house probably dates from around this period. There are many references to the hotel and gardens in the commercial directories from 1850 to 1864, with Mr John Axe as the owner. One Victorian guide book for the Chester area records *'The Victorian Tea Gardens, the property of Mr John Axe, are extensively and tastefully laid out with shrubs, flowers and evergreens and form a place of great attraction in the summer season to the numerous visitors who have the pleasure of paying a visit to them'*.

When 'The WI Book' was first written it recorded several alternative names for the Inn as well as telling of the use of the skittle alley in the back yard which was popular with local people. This obviously shows that the old inn was still in living memory even then, and must have been a popular place within the community.

The house became the property of the Potts family who let it to various tenants from the 1860s until 1904. In the 1950s and 60s the Rev. Canon Harvey and his family lived at Upton Cross House. Canon Harvey was the Headmaster of the King's School, Chester, and was responsible for moving the school out of its old site to its present location on Wrexham Road. Canon Harvey often assisted Canon Wheldon-Williams at services at the Parish Church and his wife was President of the Upton WI. It was Canon Harvey who gave the Cockpit to the people of Upton.

On an outside wall overlooking the rear yard once hung a large bell. It is not known why the bell was needed, but the present owners of Upton Cross House brought the bell to the ULHG exhibition of 2004 where it was rung with great effect.

The Cockpit – Upton Cross-roads

To the side of Upton Cross House is what is known locally as the Cockpit. This was once the front garden of the Victoria Hotel and was used as a tea garden. The sport of cockfighting was somewhat shady which is why the only references to it have been as reminiscences and there are none officially recorded anywhere. The Victoria Hotel was a very popular venue and the story goes that local gentry from the surrounding locality spent their evenings here after the Chester race meetings.

In 1978 The Clerk of Upton Parish Council invited the Grosvenor Museum to investigate which sadly did not reveal any new information. One clue to the origin of the 'pit' comes from the field name on which the house and cockpit stand; this was called Sandhole Croft. It may have been an 18th century sandpit that was subsequently used as a cockpit. The cockpit is open to the public.

Cockpit garden 1951

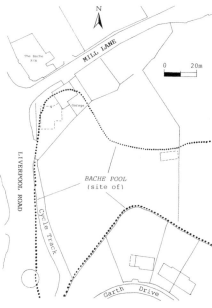

The former extent of Bache Pool

Bache Pool

The pool was enlarged in medieval times by damming the brook. This was needed to keep Bache Watermills wheels turning even in times of low water. It also had several other functions. The monks of the Abbey were forbidden to eat meat for most of the time but could have fish and would probably have had fishponds at their mill. The pool was a large landmark in the area and was used in the defining of the limits of the Chester City boundary. It also took the place of the village green as a meeting place for locals. We note in May 1744 that the meetings for the Township of Upton were to be held at the house of Thomas Ithell at Bache Pool. Again in May 1751 a meeting to settle the accounts of the Overseer of the Highways at Bache Pool.

The Egerton Arms – Liverpool Road

One cannot say for certain that John Ithell's house at Bache Pool from 1751 and the Golden Ball from 1735 are the same place. All that can be noted is that this corner of Upton has held significance for a very long time, and in particular has been the place where the community met to arrange its affairs. It has not been possible to find out when first an inn was built on the site, but the 1735 map has John Hughes living at the Golden Ball with house, garden and wheat field behind.

An inn sited here would be ideal as it was not only on the Turnpike road but was also the very last stop before you entered the City of Chester and paid city prices. The building may even be on the site of much older buildings.

The inn was the focal point for the Township meetings and we also have another name from around the 1860s, the Bache Hotel. When the inn became the Egerton Arms we do not know, but it was customary to name the inn, where people collected to pay the Lord of the Manor their dues, after him. Sir Philip Egerton is the owner of the Egerton arms in the Tithe Apportionment and the family does so until 1911 when Sir Philip Grey-Egerton sells the public house with its yard and gardens to the Northgate Brewery. The pub has had several name changes in the 20th century but it now retains it old name.

1741 Township Minute Book

This hand written bound book contains the Minutes referring to *'The charge of the poor for the Township of Upton'*; the initial signatories were John Wade, John Johnson and William Shone. Throughout these Minutes William Shone signs on behalf of John Egerton, Lord of the Manor, and principal land owner, whenever he is absent – although by 1760 John Egerton is often in attendance. The ratepayers met, typically 5 or 6 of them, and names were nominated as eligible to be an 'Overseer of the Poor'. Each year a single Overseer of the Poor was designated and they had the duty to both collect the rate and meet the needs. The Minutes therefore not only record those assigned these duties but also the accounts of how the rate was spent. Named ratepayers and their duties seemed to cycle annually with most ratepayers doing the role at some point. The 'Overseer of the Highway', later known as the 'Way Warden', seemed only to be assigned to certain ratepayers and for a number of years at a time. Even after 1760 when John Egerton attended these meetings he was never assigned a duty. During much of this period Richard Roberts was the Constable. It is assumed that the Constable was appointed from amongst the Township.

Here is an example of the type of items paid out to local people in need as discussed at the Township meetings.

From the account of 1751/2

Ann Downs coffin 9/-

Burial of Ann Down 6/2

Some items to Old Nell £1/9/7

Some items to Old Nell 52wks £1/6/-

Ralph Wilkinson for John Downs rent 15/9

Linen drapers bill £1/2/3

Mr Price for 52wks £3/18/-

John Price and Ann Stouts child £6/10/-

Widow Jones for 52wks @ 12^d £2/12/-

Mrs Price's bread 15/6

Shoes for the poor 16/-

Shurtt cloth 8/-

Coals £2/7/6

Upton Mill – Off Mill Lane

The mill is purported to have been built in 1775; the building and equipping of a tower windmill would have been an expensive investment for someone. Not many people were capable of such an outlay and the Egertons may well be the likely candidates. Prior to the windmill being built, grain was milled at the Bache water mill, but this was at the end of its working life and it is conceivable that the Egertons saw fit to make their own arrangements for their estate. The mill first appears on the 1801 Egerton estate map but there is unfortunately no detail as to who the owner or tenant was at that time.

The windmill itself was a brick tower 5 storeys high and was topped with a wooden cap which held the sails, it could turn to face whichever direction the wind took, and this was achieved by the small set of fantail sails at the back. It seems that the sails were made of cloth until 1901 when they were replaced with wooden louvered type made by a Newark firm of millwrights. It is this image that has appeared on so many pictures of the mill; it even featured on a postcard in 1918. On the Tithe map of 1839 we see that Samuel Brittain is the owner of the mill house, buildings, the farm house next door (which fronts Mill Lane today) the orchard and several fields, one with a lane connecting to Mill Lane. The Miller was William Carter, who eventually bought the mill and sold part of the grounds to create the Mill Lane entrance to Upton Park in 1857. In the 1871 Census William Carter, now aged 60 is recorded as being the miller, baker and farmer; his daughter had married Edward Dean. The name Dean figures largely in the history of the mill, the Dean family baker business is covered in Chapter 11. Upton Mill lost its sails sometime in the 1920s and was used as a bakery until a new one was built on the site in 1929. The expanded bakery business is shown on the OS map for the 1930s, so much so that it was proposed to demolish the mill by 1954 but this was opposed by residents. In 1956 the bakery business transferred to larger premises at Saltney, and the site and buildings fell into a state of disrepair. There were various uses for the mill until the firm of T Houlbrook and Sons, wholesalers and vegetable merchants, took over the site in the early 1960s. Their use provoked considerable local concern. A newspaper article from October 1969 shows that the situation had reached government level as the County Council Planning Dept had reported the case to the Ministry of Housing and Local Government. The Houlbrooks moved out and the site was cleared with bits sold off for housing development. The bakery chimney came down, allegedly by Blaster Bates. By 1979 the mill itself was up for sale, and was purchased and converted by Mr M Field.

Cottages

We are fortunate to have several cottages that were built before the 1839 Tithe still standing. One group can be found at the lower end of Upton Lane, next to Rose Cottage; there are 5 of them. There were more cottages in this area, a little further up each side of what was then called Smoke Street. The cottages were known as the Smoke Street Cottages and were demolished in the 1940s. It is not surprising to find such a concentration of older properties in this one spot, as it was around here the initial settlement formed and developed.

Another 'hot spot' can be found at Upton Heath, of the many cottages there, the pair on the Long Lane/Heath Road corner have particularly distinctive windows. Again the Gothic style could be an indication of its age. We do have some information about these houses, one in particular. They seemed to be owned by

Samuel Brittain in 1839 and from 1876 the Darlington family ownership with tenants. Previously owned by joiner Bob Jones and his sisters, the cottages were in poor condition with no lighting in 1932. The houses are currently owned by Mr S and Mr G Ryder, who have renovated them retaining the character of the building.

There are a further two cottages next door but one, whose age is unknown but again appear on the Tithe map. With these cottages and the ones that existed opposite, they formed another early nucleus of development at this end of the village.

One other cottage can be found on church Lane, between the Churchyard and the Cock Pit. Oak Cottage is of unknown date and is another example of a property where the roof has been raised; it was allegedly once thatched. The cottage was also reputed to have been used as a toll cottage from which tolls were levied on loads of sand coming from the sandpit on Upton Lane. It was also once the abode of the village cobbler, but now retains a great deal of the character shown in the illustration.

The Water Pump – Heath Road

Until 1880, when the Chester Waterworks Company brought water to Upton, residents used their nearest well. The last remaining communal pump has become a local landmark, and is believed to be more than 200 years old. During the early part of WW2 it was decided to make the pump ready for use, it was still found to be in working order and the water usable. Post-WW2, railings were put around the pump and the well itself, at the side, covered over.

Boundary Stones

The present day boundaries of Upton are almost exactly as they were on our earliest known map, the 1735 enclosure map. There have never been any outstanding natural features that have been used to delineate the boundary; therefore boundary stones were used as markers. Only one stone is marked on the current OS map; earlier OS maps have an increasing number of stones marked, the further one goes back in time. If the location of all the stones is noted from all maps, including the 1801 Egerton Estate map, a total of twelve positions are found.

We have been able to find three boundary stones, two of which are in their original positions. All three have a similar inscription on them, SMP and a date of 1731. These obviously were used to mark the division of Upton, i.e. the line between St Mary's and St Oswald's parishes. The date helps to confirm this as we must not forget that Upton as a parish in its own right did not exist until 1882, from its consecration in 1854 to 1882 it was a Chapel of Ease to St Mary-on-the-Hill, Chester.

The boundary stone on Long Lane by the sports ground footbridge was not marked on an OS map until the 1936 edition; just one field away the position of a stone is marked at least back to 1801 and this could well be its original position.

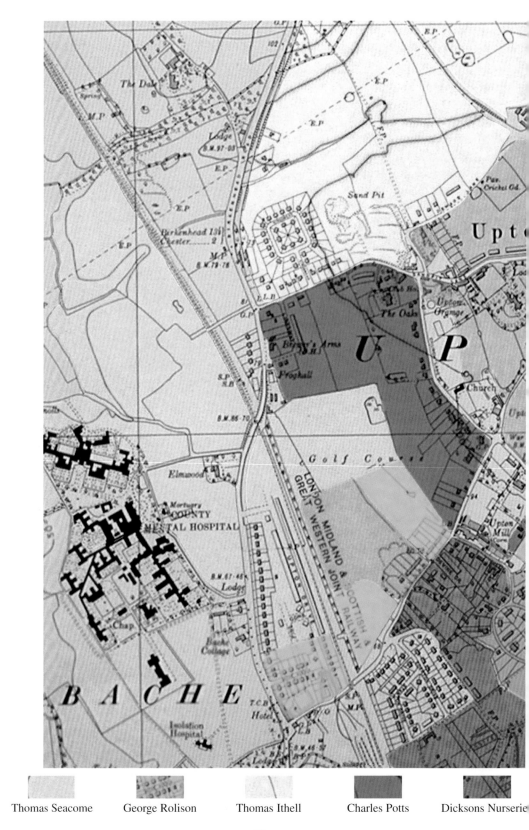

Thomas Seacome   George Rolison   Thomas Ithell   Charles Potts   Dicksons Nurseries

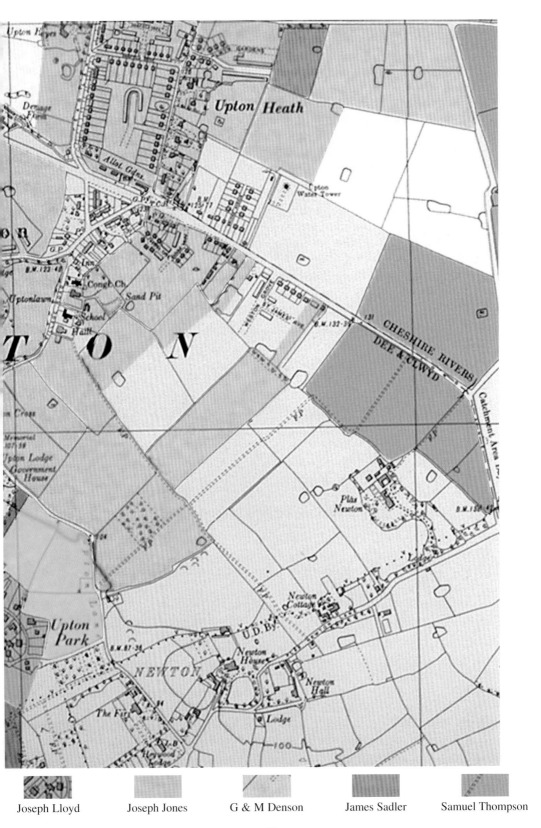

Joseph Lloyd   Joseph Jones   G & M Denson   James Sadler   Samuel Thompson

Roads and Footpaths

The roads and lanes of Upton have their own story to tell of the development and growth of the area. Some of the oldest trackways are still with us today; some have disappeared, but are remembered in other ways. The old maps for the Heath enclosure, Egerton estate, and Tithe Apportionment give us a snapshot of the lay-out at those dates. The Ordinance Survey maps and local people's living memory give an opportunity to compare information. We can therefore see the approximate order in which the road links developed.

There are two categories of roads we will look at; firstly local roads that connected various parts of Upton together e.g. Mill Lane, Upton Lane. Secondly, the roads that connects with other villages, e.g. Liverpool Road, Caughall Road, and Wealstone Lane. Several have been listed below to give more detail.

Mill Lane c.1912

Mill Lane is one of our oldest roads as it connected the ancient cornmill at Bache with the Upton inhabitants. Later, as Upton Windmill was also located on this road, it may well have been know as Mill Lane for a very long time.

Church Lane has changed its name and its layout in the last 270 years. It obviously has not always been called Church Lane but 'The WI Book' records locals remembering it as Port Lane prior to the church being built. This can be confirmed on the Tithe map as it lists the spare piece of land created when the road was straightened as Port Croft. This is another very old local road as it connected the central settlement with Upton Cross.

Upton Lane is another of our old local roads and it too has had several other names. The lower part joining with Liverpool Road was called Sandpit Lane in relation to the large sandpit that was excavated in the 19th century, alternatively Frog Lane, as it led to the Frog Hall. The stretch from Upton Farm upwards towards the Heath was called Smoke Street; the smoke element was from the fires of the cottages on that stretch but the Street element denotes its Saxon origins (strete OE) and may have more simply been called the Street originally. The road was straightened and connected to Heath Lane sometime between 1735 and 1801 and renamed Upton Lane in the 1930s.

Demage Lane connected the central community with the outlying Demage Farm. The field at the end of the lane was called Demage Croft on the 1735 map, though no building is recorded.

Heath Road too has had other names; it was called Main Road at the top and is marked on the 1936 OS Map as Village Road.

Wealstone Lane was previously called Upton Lane from pre 1872 to 1911 as it is so marked on the OS Maps that cover that time period. This must have been very confusing for all concerned as the name transfers to the other side of Upton. As the road connects Upton and Newton it is quite probable that it was also called Newton Lane depending on which direction you were coming from. It has had its present name since pre WW 2 and could well fit into the changes around the War Memorial at that time.

Acres Lane is another road that connected other communities. It was a very significant road, much longer than at present as it joined Picton, skirting the edge of Upton before crossing to join the Birkenhead toll road. Acres Lane stops when it meets Caughall Lane but would have carried on crossing Flag Lane and arcing across open fields. It has been noted in the past that this road could have been part of the Salters Way. (See chapter 2)

Flag Lane leads out of Upton, northwards, across Butter Hill and on to Chorlton. This very old trackway has many local stories attached to it to explain its name. They include lepers, monks, Flag Iris and route markers. The name Flag could also be an indication of its age as Old English dictionary lists 'Fleag' as meaning to fly, possibly confirming it as an exit route from the village.

Long Lane aptly describes this road. It connected those who lived on Upton Heath with Heath Farm (i.e. Upton Grange Farm) and on to Hoole. From the Cheshire Sheaf in 1750 it was announced that 'All the Freeholders in the township of Upton are desired to meet on the 12th September 1750 by 10 in the morning at Thomas Ithils at the Beach Pool to settle each one's share of land on Upton Common and to fix on proper roads to be made over the same'. The straightness of Long Lane may indicate that although it may have been a track or footpath for a long time it was not upgraded to a road until after this date. A direct route as opposed to an Old English winding lane.

Liverpool Road begins as Upper Northgate Street, which goes straight out of the City. The Wirral-bound Roman Road that left the fortress via the North Gate veered to the left along Parkgate Road, making Liverpool Road a more local road of a later unknown date. It was called Bache Lane in the medieval/Middle

Ages as it led to the Bache and the end of the City Liberties, i.e. Boundary limits. From here it becomes the Chester to Birkenhead Road, eventually being turned into a toll road.

The position of some of our more modern roads has not always been the whim of the developer. For example, Weston Grove, Gatesheath Drive and several others follow the line of the old field boundary that the houses have been built on. We can also see from the old maps that there are even a few lanes which have been lost long ago and others which have fairly recently become obsolete.

One very old footpath, which was once a popular and pleasant walk for locals, disappeared with the housing development of the late 20th century. It began on Heath Road at the side of the Village Hall and ran across the fields to meet Plas Newton Lane at Newton Cottage. This track is marked on many maps going back to the 1735 one and from this its position suggests that it could be a much older track still. It was known locally as the Stile (or Style).

Of the other footpaths that have come and gone with time, there are two remaining; one is a short cut between Upton Lane and Demage Lane and is known as the Twitchell. The other runs from the back of Daleside across open land, over a footbridge crossing a drainage stream and out onto Liverpool Road at Moston.

Upton Cross

Where the roads Church Lane, Mill Lane, Heath Road and Wealstone Lane converge it has always been a feature of Upton. Around the crossroads there has been the Victoria Hotel (Upton Cross House), the Cock Pit, Upton Lodge and the War Memorial, but these come relatively later on historically. In the main the area has remained quite open. It is not the only crossroads in Upton as Upton Lane crosses Demage Lane and Church Lane, but it is the only one to be called 'cross'. The name is therefore significant and becomes the first place to start investigating.

In Dodgeson's book Place Names of Cheshire Part IV it lists The Cross in the entry for Upton, 'a house named from a cross shown 1831 Bry at the crossroads'. This is explained by looking at Bryants map of 1831 (see page iii) and there is the site of an ancient cross marked. The book entry also includes a Latin reference from 1398 as 'landas terre iuxta crucem'. We can therefore see the possibility that the name comes not from the crossing of these old roads but from some kind of ancient monument.

Official records also need to be consulted and these turn out to be the Sites and Monument Record (SMR), the Public Monument and Sculpture Association National Recording Project (PMSA) and eventually the Upton Township books for the early 20th century. The SMR also has the same reference to a 14th century cross but when checked no further information was found, though the Environmental Planning Dept, Backford Hall were able to clarify the Latin reference. It comes from a document once in the keeping of the British Museum now transferred to the British Library. It must be noted that there are two other Upton's in Cheshire and great care must be taken before any confidence can be put in a document unless it can be seen in its original context. The two entries on the PMSA are for the Plague Stone and the War Memorial. The plague stone reference does not include any extra information it just records the inscription inside the church; the War Memorial does have one very interesting sentence. *'When the foundations for the war memorial were being dug, the workmen discovered the old plague stone from the 1660's'.* Again caution is required but it does marry up with the inscription in the church that the stone's location originates at the crossroads. The date of 1920-22 is the date given as the period when the memorial was designed and built and presumably when the stone was found. The Upton Township Book 2, which recorded the minutes of their meetings, is the next reference point, and this has occasional entries concerning an ancient stone, over a period of 8 years.

The story starts in 1931 when Mr Potts offers a stone to the Upton War Memorial Committee. February 1932 Professor Newstead examines the stone and in his opinion says that it is probably the base of a cross. The stone is to be placed at the rear of the War Memorial and in the accounts, a Mr Clegg is paid for removing the stone from Mr Pott's house. April 1932 sees the stone set back into the hedge where it now stays until 1938. By 1937 it seems the committee had decided the stone needed to be moved from that site and an inscription was to accompany it. A Mr Collins from the Blue Coat School and Upton resident was to add the stone cup. (This is the first reference to a stone cup). From January 1938 the stone was recorded as the Ancient Plague Stone where previously it was recorded as the Ancient Stone. In correspondence with Prof. Newstead he recommends Mr W F Irvine of Corwen on the inscription and explanatory note. A revised caption is submitted and approved, but does not record by whom and the stone was cleaned and taken to Upton Church where the bowl was fixed to constrain its removal.

This fascinating and revealing story from the Township Minute Book means we need to have another look at our Plague Stone, as it seems to be hiding another story altogether. It was in fact felt that professional help was required to further the research for this book and Chester Archaeology, the Chester City archaeological unit, were called in. After very careful examination of first the stone and then the paper evidence the archaeologist was able to confirm that the stone was not a plague stone but was the base of a cross as originally thought. That is, the remains of an ancient monument – probably all stone that was made up of a base, shaft and cross on the top. There is nothing in the minutes recorded to suggest why they thought that the stone was a plague stone, except perhaps that this was an unusual idea for an unusual stone. It has not yet been possible to date the base, as it has no distinguishing features to suggest a style. Crosses of this type were not uncommon features in the local landscape. There were for example sites at Vicars Cross, Christleton and of course the cross in the city centre. The Puritans pulled down most and this could be why only the base of ours remains. Crosses were erected from the Saxon period right through the medieval period and would have been repaired or replaced when needed. It seems we have therefore something much older and more special than a plague stone and it is very fitting that the remains of the early Christians focal point of worship is now in the safety of our Parish Church. More work is needed to complete the story and this will be an ongoing project for Upton Local History Group, but steps have already been taken to correct and update the official status of the stone and so give Upton's oldest relic more protection.

Upton's ancient cross base

References

The Brock Family of Upton, contribution from Max Green

1897 Valuation of Upton Hall J Davies, CCRO Egerton Family Deposit

Bache Tithe Map and Apportionment CCRO EDT 30/1& 2

The Cheshire Sheaf 1941 (8007) The Broadhurst Family and the Bache Estate, 1941 (8009) Brodhurst or Broardhurst Family 1917 (3273) The Morgan and Crompton Families

Sites And Monuments Record 1921 The Cockpit

Upton Township Book 2 CCRO RP/12/2

Boundary stone image, Mrs Lott
Boundary stone image Eric Illingworth
Simon Ward from Chester Archaeology, Chester City Council

CHAPTER 5
Tithe Surveys around 1840

The years around 1840 are well recorded thanks to the 'Tithe Surveys & Apportionments' which noted ownership, occupation, value and usage of each parcel of ground. This period also serves as a good 'watershed' from the historic rural setting towards the residential suburbia we know today. The chapter analyses the Upton Tithe survey with reference to those of Bache and the northern parts of Newton. Census records and Bagshaw's 1850 Directory cast further light on picturing this period. The remaining source is the Upton Township Minute book.

The 1839 Upton Tithe Survey Map

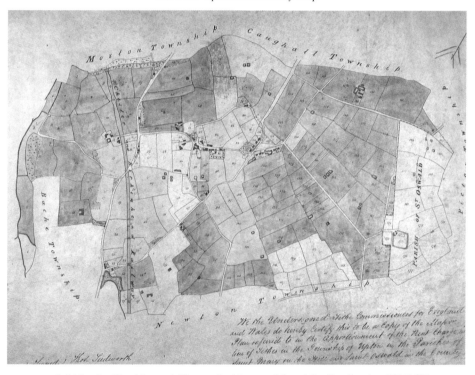

as held by the Cheshire and Chester Archives and Local Studies Service (EDT407)

From an 1801 Upton population of 173, by 1821 the figure had reached 206. Of the 30 families, 28 were chiefly employed in agriculture and only 2 in trade. By 1831, the population had increased to 289 but this was largely attributed to the new asylum. Of the 43 families, in 39 dwellings, only 33 were engaged chiefly in agriculture. The 1839 Tithe Survey records 62 dwellings – up 50% in a decade. The 1841 census records 274 for Upton, 18 for Bache Township and 163 in the asylum. There was new labouring work with the railway and access to and from Upton was improving.

Upton Township in 1839 included some of what we know today as The Bache. It bordered onto the Townships of Bache, Moston, Caughall, Picton and Newton. Upton contained 1106 acres of which over half was owned by Baronet Sir Philip Egerton whose family line Brock/Egerton had been 'Lord of the Manor' since Elizabethan times. Other major landowners were Land Agent Samuel Brittain, Lloyd & Henry Bamford (they owned land bordering Newton and may have held Newton's Manor) and Charles Potts of a long-established Chester family. The Earl of Kilmorey still held most of Upton and the 1839 Tithe Apportionment recorded his dues from each land plot.

There were two main clusters of dwellings

- **Upton Heath** – cottages around the triangle we know today as adjoining Flag Lane South
- **Upton Village** – mainly farm houses/yards but some cottages – the area we know today as Church Ln / Upton Ln / Demage Ln junction near the Golf Clubhouse.

and two smaller clusters

- Bache – around the Egerton Arms
- Upton Hall / Frog Hall / smithy – the area we know today as the Liverpool Road / Upton Lane junction.

and a few individual or pairs of dwellings.

Most farmers were tenant farmers leasing fields which were not always adjacent and changed hands according to demand. Hence 'farms' couldn't be defined as specific single entities. People recorded on the census as 'farmers' occupied land from only two acres up to a few hundred acres. Clearly farmers often occupy fields outside of their own township and so a full understanding of Upton's farm land requires investigation of all the surrounding township tithes. This has not been done and so no reference is given to land outside Upton farmed by Upton farmers.

At this time, Upton had no school or church or shops. Dwellings however sold the products of their occupier's trade. The asylum had been recently built (the 1829 building) on a site of a few acres – known as the asylum gardens with a lodge and tree lined drive – all in the ownership of the County Magistrates. There was only one 'gentleman's estate', that of Charles Potts who owned the building where the Golf Clubhouse now stands. There are some references to this having been the old 'Upper Upton Hall' but any suggestion of this being another historic manorial hall are unsubstantiated as yet. The Chester & Birkenhead railway had only recently acquired ownership of the route cutting north to south through the western part of the township. This split many fields in two and ran very close to the manorial hall of Upton Hall.

Working the land

This section should be read in conjunction with the double spread coloured map on pages 50 / 51. To help the reader associate the map with the known layout of today's Upton, a 1936 map has been used as the background with coloured overlays relating to the use of the land at the time of the 1839 Tithe Survey – that is a century earlier. Only the main Upton farmers and nurserymen have been given coloured overlays. The fields without a coloured overlay were occupied either by farms from outside Upton or by local smallholders.

The text and the map are intended to be indicative only. For a more definitive picture the reader should refer to the 1839 Upton Tithe Survey & Apportionments (EDT 401/1&2), held by the Cheshire and Chester Archives and Local Studies.

Tenant farmer - Thomas Seacome occupied Upton Hall – with most of the fields to the west of the railway line but also much of the Bache pool area and part of the golf course. Arable use seemed to dominate rather than pasture.

Tenant farmer - Thomas Ithell (a father and son both Thomas – aged 59 and 23 in 1839) occupied the farmhouse & yard in Upton Village (north of Upton Lane by the sandpit) with some surrounding fields to the north. They also had fields west of Grange farm and west/north of the Demage cottages. The 1851 census records the Ithells as farming 267 acres – at a quarter of Upton's land area - theirs was the largest 'farm' although they only owned some 4 acres in 1839.

George Rolison – born 1801 - (he signed Rolison but many records show Rolinson) occupied the Egerton Arms public house and a few acres to the north of Mill Lane from Liverpool Rd to the Mill Lane rise. He also had hay fields (now Wealstone Lane playing fields) and part of the golf course. He is recorded in the 1851 census as a farmer of 40 acres but in Bagshaw's directory as the victualler of the Egerton arms.

Tenant farmers – George & Martha Denson occupied the house where the Grange was later built (opposite the house now named Upton Farm). The survey records this property as having a walled garden. The Tithe survey records the occupation in the name of Martha. She is recorded as occupying much of central Upton bordered by Church Ln /Heath Rd/ A41/Demage Ln. as well as Marl Heyes and much of the land between Flag Ln Nth. and just beyond Caughall Rd. By the 1851 census and Bagshaw's 1850 directory the Densons are no longer mentioned even though they would have only been in their early 60s. William Beecroft is named in the 1851 census – aged 34 years – and farming 140 acres. It appears that he took over this main 'central Upton' farm since the 1874 Directory lists him as farming Upton Green – which from the Ordnance survey we know was the former name of The Grange. When the buildings on this south side of Upton Lane ceased being a farm house and farm buildings is not known but it appears that the buildings on the north side expanded and, to this day, they have retained the name of 'Upton Farm'.

Tenant farmer - Samuel Thomason occupied the moated farm Upton Grange and surrounding fields. Besides his tenancy, he also owned the field, that was later, the site of Upton High school & its playing fields. In the 1851 census he is recorded as aged 50 and unmarried; farming 165 acres. Today, this is Upton's only working farm with a spread of fields very little changed from 160 years ago.

Tenant farmer - Joseph Jones occupied a house on the corner of Church Ln (later the site of the Lodge serving The Grange – now Nield Court) His fields were fairly scattered - around the Westlea school area, around Caughall Rd and going towards Duttons Ln. He also farmed the SW of the golf course, the Church Hall/Vicarage site and the Alpraham Cres / Cross Green area.

Tenant farmer Joseph Lloyd occupied the farmhouse by Upton Mill and occupied the Mill orchard and nearby fields. These some fifteen years later became the new residential development of Upton Park.

James Sadler – occupied the Acres farmhouse/yard and adjacent fields.

William Carter was the tenant miller & farmer of Upton Mill occupying only two fields – off Wealstone Lane near Newton and the other NE of Long Lane.

Nurserymen Francis & James Dickson owned and occupied Upton Villa (later known as Upton House & Stanton House) within large grounds. They also owned and used fields on the southern boundary with Newton and Bache. Presumably, these were nursery ground, with one field contained a building that may have been the working centre of the nursery business. They also rented a field between the Mill and Upton Cross. See page 152 for more on Dicksons Nursery.

Charles Potts (Solicitor & Chester Borough County Clerk - of a long-established Chester family) owned the orchard homestead along with fields – all now part of the golfcourse. He also owned an isolated field between the mill and Wealstone Lane. (see page 92)

Edward Evans owned and occupied some fields that latter became Plas Newton.

The following occupied other fields in Upton but resided outside the township.
- Henry Hesketh - on the Newton boundary
- William Fox - Cornwall Rd area
- John Dinwoodie - in the far NW of Upton may have farmed in Moston – even from Moston Hall.
- Richard Massey had two fields to the south of the Moston boundary. One between the railway and the main road, and the other, the plantation.
- James Price had a small field just north of Newton.
- Charles Billington had two fields just north of Newton
- Robert Rolison had a meadow on the western boundary – possibly with more land further west beyond Upton.
- Isaac David Jacques occupied a field on the border with Picton – possibly with other fields in Picton.

The Upton Heath dwellings

Upton Heath – the Wheatsheaf area – had 6 cottages owned by Samuel Rushton and used by George Blake, John Smith, Miss Smith, Thomas Tasker (Agricultural labourer married aged 59 in 1851), George Taylor, Charles Williamson (Railway porter married aged 36 in 1851). On the Upton Ln / Heath Rd corner – a dwelling owned by Lloyd Bamford and occupied by Samuel Blake.

Upton Heath – the north side of Heath Rd heading up towards the pump - lived Mary Darlington. Next door - owned by Lloyd Bamford lived Mary Farrington (Charwoman married aged 57 in 1851) who also occupied a thin strip of land alongside Brook Av. Next door - owned by Lloyd Bamford lived William Parsonage who also had a garden in the triangle opposite the later site of the Wheatsheaf; and a field owned by the Cathedral now partly the site of the A41 between the traffic lights and Flag Ln. Next were three dwellings – owned by Sir Philip Egerton. One was occupied by John Jones who also occupied the field – the site of the current Baptist church. Another, John Reeves occupied a garden - part of the wedge between Flag Ln Sth and Heath Rd. The third, was occupied by James Speed. Another five dwellings were owned by Samuel Brittain and occupied by Isaac Blackman, Richard Challoner, John Pulford, George Reeves, James Roberts.

The Upton Village dwellings

Rose Cottage – owned by Samuel Brittain was occupied by Miss Whitelock. The two dwellings next door were owned by Egerton and occupied by Mary and John Hughes, who also occupied a small field by the Demage cottages. Mary Brooks and the Misses Hibbert occupied two cottages alongside the Upton Ln farm (later The Grange). Two cottages alongside Martha Denson's farmhouse were occupied by John Sauntley and John Tasker. The house later known as Upton Farm with a small croft (field) at the back was occupied by William Cardwell

The Bache dwellings (as part of Upton Township)

Two dwellings were occupied by Mary Dutton & Samuel Massey with a garden adjacent to the Bache pool.

Other dwellings

Upton Cross was owned by John Axe who occupied Sand Hole croft and the house and cottage and garden. John Dane tenanted either the house or the cottage. Frog Hall, also owned by John Axe, was recorded as five dwellings occupied by Matthew Fayle, Samuel Hignett, Joseph Johnson, Samuel Lloyd and Thomas Reeves. The public house (believed to be the Brewers Arms – part of Frog Hall) owned by Lloyd Bramford was occupied by Robert Jones and the cottage also owned by Lloyd Bramford was occupied by Jane Jones. The smithy on the Liverpool Rd and field opposite, owned by Sir P Egerton, was occupied by William Darlington (blacksmith) and family. Demage Cottages - site of the future Demage Farm - were both owned by George Blake (of Upton Heath?) and occupied by Thomas Bennett (an agricultural labourer) and by Mary Jones. Surrounding fields were occupied by other farmers. Two dwellings just south of the plantation boundary with Moston were occupied by Game Keeper Moses Lanceley & George Wynne.

From the Upton Township Minutes

The following are recorded as Councillors for 1839 (although the Minutes do not use the the term 'Councillor').

- Sam Thomason (farmer at the moated Grange Farm)
- Francis Dickson (Nurseryman)
- Thomas Ithell (farming over 25% of the township)
- George Denson (village centre farmer)
- George Rolison(Egerton Arms & a land owning farmer)
- Thomas Seacombe (farmer at Upton Hall)
- Charles Potts (Chester gentleman of Upper Upton Hall estate)

By the 1850s, Ithell resided at Upton Hall - but this may have been Thomas's son Thomas. Thomason & Rolison were still Overseers but new names had appeared as follows -

- William Beecroft - farmer of 140 acres – employing 3
- William Evans - farming 80 acres from the village centre – employing 1
- William Carter - of Upton Mill
- William Hughes
- John Edward Norton
- Thomas Wilcoxan of Acres
- John Axe - property owner incl. Victoria Hotel (Upton Cross)

The Township Council was run by the farmers and two incomer business men – Francis Dickson and solicitor Charles Potts.

CHAPTER 6
Developments 1840 - 1899

This period saw the shift away from a truly rural agricultural economy towards a residential area. First to move in were the wealthy families seeking country estates that could now be readily created and accessed. As they moved in using the new railway and improved road network these gentlemen became 'local squires' often playing a major role in the community through their provision of employment, sponsorship, community venues and no doubt a belief that they were bringing useful expertise to the evolving community. Today most of these country houses have been demolished and built over. Some remain, belonging to organisations, with only Upton Lodge retained as a private residence.

The population for Upton, Bache & Moston grew nearly three fold from around 270 to just over 750 without including the Asylum whose numbers outstripped these. With this growth came the need for community facilities – the churches and school as well as public houses, shops and the improving utilities.

The wealthy who chose Upton were prepared to travel to Liverpool or Manchester for business but also some Chester shop keepers and other businessmen were looking to move further outside Chester than the Hoole and Newton areas. While there was extensive housing development closer to Chester, including the Hoole and Newton areas, Upton's mass housing development did not start until the 1930s.

This chapter looks first at these gentlemen's country estates although some such as Bache Hall and The Dale have already been covered in Chapter 4. Three of these were developed in what was then the centre of Upton village.

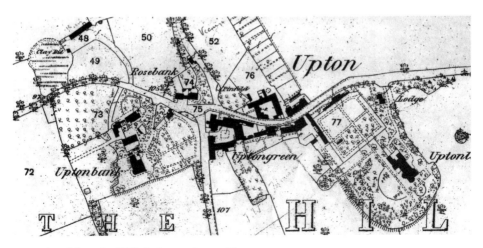

Reproduced from the 1873 Ordnance Survey Map

The Oaks (formerly Upton Bank) - known today as the Upton Golf Clubhouse.

This residence was already established by the 1839 Tithe survey but is covered in this chapter as the first of Upton's 'Gentleman's Country Estates'. Charles Potts had a solicitors practice in Chester and was the Clerk of the Chester Borough County Council. He is listed with his wife in the 1841 Upton census but not for 1851. By 1881 Charles Townsend – County Treasurer – is recorded as the resident and then by 1902 Reginald Potts was in residence before moving to The Dale. It is suggested that this was only one of the Potts residences and that a farm bailiff ran the estate during their absence. The extent of dwellings for estate workers within the estate can only be assumed from studying the map.

The Oaks, Upton by Chester

'In late Regency style, it stands on a slight rise and commanded a pleasant vista of lawns and trees with pastureland beyond'. (see also colour photograph – page 6)

William Richardson Moss acquired 'Upton Bank' in 1903 and carried out extensive alterations to the house including changing its name to The Oaks. Prior to his retirement he had been a successful cotton mill owner in Bolton. William Richardson Moss was a keen patron of the arts and having accumulated wealth through the cotton industry loved to spend it on art treasures of any kind. He had a tremendous collection of china, embroidery, pictures and books. He died 24th Aug 1915 and is buried in Upton churchyard with his second wife Helen Eveline (1851-1909). Although the property no longer houses any of these contents - the downpipes dated 1903 remain and the painted glass lights in the banquet room window have been retained within Upton although the window itself is now a new double glazed unit. This painted window bears the initials of William and his second wife Helen.

Mr Andrews Crompton J.P. was the next owner occupier acquiring The Oaks in 1916/7. He had married William Richardson Moss's elder daughter Teresa. The Andrews Cromptons became involved in the community. Mr Andrews Crompton was the first Vice Chairman of the Upton Village Hall and Mrs. Andrews Crompton became the first president of the Women's Institute. They lived at The Oaks for 15 years prior to the sale in 1931 to G J (Fred) Owen (see page 93).

Upton Lawn

According to Ormerod this large and spacious brick residence was built in the 1850s by T Helps, whose initials are entwined on the front of the lodge. By 1859 there was a curved walled garden, the line of which was still clear in later maps.

The property was sold first to the Logan family who were generous benefactors to the church, and then on to John Meadows Frost, who was Mayor of Chester during the WW1 period and knighted shortly afterwards.

The house is seen here in a photograph c1950 after it had been converted into flats. After that it gradually degraded until it was demolished c1970. The grounds were enhanced by the many lovely trees with rhododendrons in flower in spring. Many of the periphery trees still remain to this day along the wide verge of Heath road. Sir John and Lady Frost frequently opened their grounds for community events and were renowned for their generosity – see later chapters. This photograph of the 1933 Rose Queen festivities shows some of the grounds.

Parish records show the existence of a lending library in 1884. *'By the kindness of T. Walton Thomson, Esq. a handsome gift of new books has been given for the use of Upton parishioners. These books are for the present placed in the Reading Room at Upton Lawn and are now ready for use. The library will be open every Monday evening from 7-8 o'clock. Subscriptions one penny per month (payable in advance). The*

Library is not confined to members of the Reading Room but open to all Residents in the Parish'

The most notable visitor was Earl Haigh in the immediate post-WW1 period. He planted an acorn from Verdun which grew to a large oak around which the Earls Oak development was built in the 1970s. The tree standing in a private garden was later felled. Also now demolished are the several estate workers' cottages – see the map at the start of this chapter. All that remains is the refurbished lodge and the many fine trees. See chapter 9 for the coach house and post-war development of this estate.

The Grange

The modern housing developments, Grangeside and Nield Court, both take their names from the gentleman's country estate that stood there for over a century. Apparently the middle part of Upton Grange was built first around 1830 and then two wings were added later at different times. Named 'Upton Green' in 1872 it

was extensively developed by 1898 and renamed 'The Grange'. Not to be confused with Dutton's farm 'Upton Grange', this was a fashionable name for the site of a former farmhouse. It is shown here looking west down Upton Lane in what is understood to be an early 1960s photograph.

'The W I Book' notes that *'There is a secret room, a very small one, between the dining room and study, whose door is opened by treading on a knob in the dining room floor. The dining room and study are panelled in three different kinds of wood; this panelling was made by the Upton villagers. The tower was only built to hide a water tank. The lodge, behind which are stables and garages, has been converted into two cottages'.*

The original owner has not been identified but may have been the wealthy Brittain family who owned land in Upton. In the early 1900s it was the home of Colliery Manager Thomas Morris and then Sir Helenus Robertson. For several years between the wars it was the home of High Court Judge Sir Basil Nield who succeeded Sir Charles Cayzer as Chester's Member of Parliament. During WW2 it was at least partly used as the headquarters of the National Fire Service for this area. From February 1947 it became the Forestry Commission HQ for the North-West of England until June 1965. From then on demolition was on the cards. The Lodge entrance off Church Lane and its associated cottages – all now demolished - housed staff for the big house including the gardener and driver. During the WW2 years these were gardeners – Jim Stacey & Mr Hughes – with chauffeur Mr Harris.

Upton Lodge

Croft field - of nearly 4 acres - had passed from Lord of the Manor ownership prior to 1735 when it was part of the Nicholls farm covering much of central Upton. By 1801 it was farmed by a member of the Hesketh family and by 1839 was one of the few fields actually owned by the long established Upton farmers - the Ithells.

In the 1840s Croft field was sold for the house and grounds of Upton Lodge. The house is believed to have been built around 1848 (the 1848 date displayed on the cottage and former stables) - although the 3-storey house may have just preceded the cottage and outbuildings. One of the first occupants may have been Mr Tilston - a cheese maker (factor). It is also believed that in 1874, retired nurseryman James Dickson was living there shortly before he died. The 1881 census records it being the home of Captain Henry Hall (aged 35yrs) of the 22nd Cheshire Regiment - living there with his family. On 7th November 1885 the house with its out-offices, stabling, coach house and grounds were auctioned as three lots - Lot 1 being the house and gardens with two fields, Lot 2 and Lot 3 being potential building land. However it appears that all three lots went to a single purchaser - the estate staying intact. The next known owner was Mr B I Kemp but it is not known whether he was the 1885 auction buyer. Mr T A Beckett then bought the house and grounds from Mr Kemp sometime in the early 1900s. He later raised some finances by selling some land adjacent to the Mill to the Mill owners and then sold the house and remaining ground in 1927 to the War Department.

The illustration is taken from a 1994 full colour painting by George Thompson - reproduced here by courtesy of Dr. John Charles-Jones.

The 1963 aerial photograph on page 122 shows the kitchen garden to the side prior to it becoming a small public park.

Dorin Court (later Government House)

Chronologically this should be covered in the next chapter since it was built c1902 but is included here as the last of the gentleman's country residences to be built.

Clothier Mr S J W Clerk bought land to the south of Upton Cross from Egerton on which to build a house which was known either as Ravenscourt or Dorin Court. It was built in the ornamental style of the late nineteenth century. Later it became Government House because from the 1930s until c1970 it was owned by the army (see Chapter 8) before demolition to make way for the Cheshire County Council Care (CLS) residential home Dorin Court (now known as Weal Stone).

Mrs Lilian Edmunds (nee Halford) – (seen here with other staff) was a kitchen maid from 1937 – 39 and recalls the staff of General and Lady Jackson

being invited to live on the premises for a month every summer and a month at Christmas while the Jacksons were away in Dorset. They were encouraged to enjoy the tennis courts, the summer house and the whiskey and cigars while looking after the property.

The Oakfield estate

The original smaller Oakfield, as shown on this 1872 Ordnance survey, is understood to have been built in the 1850s. Complete with its lodge (long since demolished) it would appear to have been the home of a gentleman farmer with fountains and fishponds. It was later acquired by Benjamin Chaffers Roberts - a wealthy Liverpool Tea Merchant – who built the current familiar Oakfield building and the new lodge across the drive.

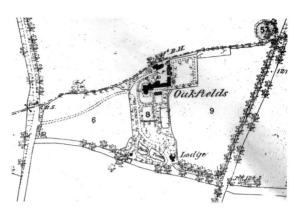

Reproduced from the 1873 Ordnance Survey Map

This was complete before the next Ordnance survey of 1898 and the later plan, also shown here, relates to sale particulars c1913. It was bought by Mr. Beresford Jones and then let during WW1 to Belgian refugees and to Lady Arthur Grosvenor for her hospital (see page 108). Post-war, Oakfield changed hands twice before it was bought, with its much reduced land, by George Mottershead in 1930 for his zoo (see page 149).

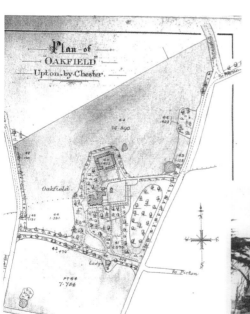

Oakfield pictured c1950

Roberts acquired considerable land around the Oakfield estate. Some properties were built specifically to service the estate while it is likely that some dwellings were initially built for his estate workers.

Properties within or surrounding the Oakfield estate

Within this section some of the properties were clearly part of Roberts' Oakfield estate whereas others may have been attracted to develop nearby.

The corner field in Upton Heath known as 'the Horse Pasture' had been acquired by Hesketh from the Egertons in the 18th century. By the 1872 OS survey a property and outhouse had been built on Long Lane - presumably Heath Cottage – shown to the east of the encircled area. By 1881 this was the home of spinster schoolteacher Emma Frith and her lodgers. The corner field was then owned by Robert Spear Hudson (a manufacturing chemist) of Bache Hall and he sold to Ben Roberts of Oakfield in 1885. A row of four cottages (shown here encircled) were then built in 1891 possibly for Ben Roberts estate workers. When Roberts put the estate up for sale in 1913 the southerly end of the former 'Horse Pasture' along with the cottages was sold to Mrs Martha Dean of Upton Mill. It was acquired with sitting tenants (H Dutton, T Garner, W Williams, P C Bratt, G Brown and J Baird). This may have been when the 'Heath Cottage' dwelling had its name changed to Nos: 1 & 2 Mill View. Possibly the Deans (see page 156) wanted all 6 dwellings to house the growing force of mill workers. With the later demise of the mill the cottages were gradually sold into private householder ownership.

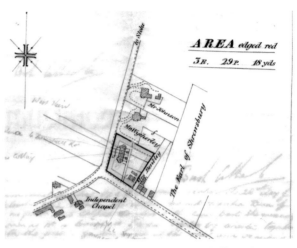

Plan from deeds covering Long Lane/Caughall Road junction

Ben Roberts also acquired the north end of the fields up as far as the pond that still remains today. By the 1898 Ordnance survey, 3 large detached houses - Rosedene, Heathfields and The Grove (built 1878) had been built possibly for estate managers. These properties and further developments in this area are covered in later chapters.

Shown here - the property that was used as the laundry for Oakfield still stands near the corner of Flag Lane North.

Upton Heyes & Demage Farm

Demage (or Damage) cottages existed at the time of the Tithe (see Chapter 5) but expanded later to become known as Demage Farm. This was reached by a lane (Demage Lane) that ended at the cottages/farm. In the 1890s stock broker's agent Harold Broadbent bought land from Egerton including fields called Hay Field and Near and Further Hay Field. When he built Upton Heyes off Flag Lane is not known – still not shown on the 1898 Ordnance survey. The next owner was Thomas Arthur Rigby – a flour miller of Waterloo Dock Mill, Liverpool. It is understood that he may have built up Demage Farm. The Upton Council minutes record the dispute of the ownership of Demage Lane during Rigby's ownership when he sealed off the lane only to have this torn down by annoyed locals before the issue was amicably resolved. Rigby is understood to have built the two Heyes Cottages in 1900.

Reproduced from the 1911 Ordnance Survey Map

In 1923 Mr. Beresford-Jones bought Upton Heyes and the family lived there until 1947, when it was taken over by the Cheshire County Council for use as Judge's Lodgings. A famous visitor there in November 1950 was Lord Goddard, Chief Justice. The 1965 WI History update records the judges arriving during April, May, July and November - the traffic on the A41 being halted by the police to allow the safe crossing of their official cars. In the 1950s / early 1960s Mr & Mrs Thornton were the wardens and the grounds are remembered for their unusual trees - Tulip & Handkerchief - as well as the grass tennis courts. This Upton Heyes photograph features Lady Grosvenor during her 'gypsy' era in attendance to present the prizes to the Upton Scouts in 1912.

The Firs

The origin of The Firs is not known but first appears on the 1872 Ordnance survey; its style suggests another gentleman's country residence. It sat alongside Heywood Lodge in the corner of Well Lane and what is now Wealstone Lane. After use by the military it was demolished c1980 and the housing estate around Horrocks Road built. A sample of the sandstone boundary wall and many tall trees are all that remain.

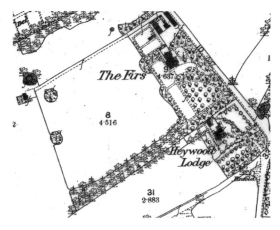

Reproduced from the 1873 Ordnance Survey Map

Heywood Lodge

The 1841 Newton Tithe survey shows a large field at the Wealstone Lane / Well Lane junction known as Heywoods Field. By 1854 Heywood Lodge was the home of the Rev. R D Thomas - and it is assumed that the house was built for him shortly before that date. In 1851 Rev. Thomas had become the minister of Christ Church Newton and died in the 1890s. By 1896 Thomas Ledsham Wilkinson - a Chester fishmonger and game dealer - was in residence and it is assumed that he built the snooker room - later used as the school dining room. It was later owned by Mr Maitland and then by

the early 1900s, by Charles Anderson Earle - a Liverpool cotton broker. His uncle, also named Charles, was a well known landscape watercolourist and many of his paintings still hang on the walls.

The photograph supplied by their descendant - Sally Symes - shows C A Earle (on the left) with other members of the family all in the garden of Heywood Lodge. Joseph Cooper was the coachman - later chauffeur - to the

Earles for some 30 yrs pre-WW2. Wartime use of the building and grounds is covered on page 106. By 1952 it had become a co-educational secretarial college called 'Normain College'(proprietors - Norman & Main) - providing a dual role of a secretarial college and a private school for children who had failed the newly introduced 11-plus. Later under new management the school started suffering dwindling numbers and closed in 1961. At this time, there was already a flourishing school accommodated in the army huts of The Firs. They purchased Normain College in 1962 and relocated the school into Heywood Lodge – see page 256.

Newton House (north of Plas Newton Lane)

Newton House was probably built c1830. It is located near the earlier Georgian-style Newton Hall. It is shown on the 1840 Newton Tithe Map – in the ownership of Henry Hesketh who possessed considerable land in Upton. This photograph of Newton House was taken in the early 1950s after the house had been bought by Cheshire County Council for use as a Care Home for the Elderly.

The last private owners were the Darcys – a brother & sister. The Darcy name occurs in the early Upton Township minutes. Cheshire County Council bought the full estate - subsequently selling land for housing development (incl Tiverton Close and the Boys Home - Appleton House - which was later demolished for the Bellway development - Arradon Ct & Breton Cl). In the early 1990s, Newton House, now owned by Chester City Council, was demolished and the new Care Home built.

The only remaining original building is the set of four tied cottages pictured here from a recent photograph. The stables at the far end of the cottages have since been demolished and garages built.

Plas Newton (north of Plas Newton Lane)

Plas Newton is not recorded on the 1839 Upton Tithe survey but a driveway is shown on the 1841 Newton Tithe survey. This suggests that Plas Newton – '*a fine country house*' - was built in the early 1840s. The first churchwarden of Upton church (before it became the parish church) was Col. E Evans-Lloyd who reputedly lived at Plas Newton in 1843. The 1873 map, shown here, records Plas Newton and its Lodge much as it remained. Its most famous owner was Alfred Tyrer - a senior partner of a Liverpool-based solicitors; he was believed also to have been the son of a Liverpool shipping owner. Reputed to have played polo for England and written a book on the subject, he was clearly a gentleman of considerable wealth, stabling many polo ponies. Alfred and his wife Ida Elizabeth played an active part in Upton village and church life. Garden parties were held on the lawns. Evacuees were billeted in the house during WW2. Alfred is reputed to have been among those who travelled on the first train to Hoylake in 1869 and he died at Plas Newton in 1946 at the age of 98. He is buried in Upton Parish church along with his wife who died in 1942.

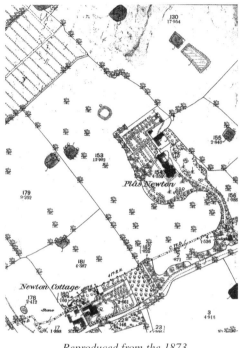

Reproduced from the 1873 Ordnance Survey Map

Their Head Gardener was William Morgan who moved into the Lodge c1925. His son Bill who was born in Long Lane Upton in 1923 recounts his reminiscences (see Chapter 18). After Tyrer's death the house was cleared of its treasures through a major auction that drew buyers from far and wide. One of the later owners was Mr. Tyler - choirmaster/organist at the parish church. The Plas Newton estate has been gradually reduced until today only the name remains.

Newton Cottage is recorded on both the Upton 1839 and the Newton 1841 Tithe surveys although as a smaller set of properties than in the 1872 OS above. During WW1 Miss Clark-Lloyd of Newton Cottage was host to the family of the Emperor of Abyssinia and governess to his daughter. They were remembered attending Upton Church with brightly coloured umbrellas on wet days.

The Lloyd-Jones family farmed the Plas Newton estate for many years finally selling up farmland in the 1950s. Campbell Lloyd-Jones left the area in the 1960s moving to Bala where he started a golf course The farmhouse (see photograph page 117) and outbuildings were demolished/refurbished and the current modern Newton Mews built in 1989.

Other individual notable properties

Stanton House (previously known as Upton House & Upton Villa) was the home of part of the Dickson's dynasty (see page 152). All that remains today is the Lodge on the corner of Mill Lane and Bache Drive. The 1881 census records 'The Melford' inhabited by Mrs Longworth – wife of a retired clergyman. Two other dwellings are another Upton Villa inhabited by watch repairer Joseph Price and Cromwell Bank by boot manufacturer Frederick Jones. It is assumed that these are all part of the 1870s building to the north of the school.

In the Bache area, to the south of Bache Pool, stood the Bron-y-Garth estate only remembered today as the site of Garth Drive built in the 1950s. The Lodge to Bache Hall (see page 34) was lost as part of the Liverpool Road widening and development of the hospital. Similarly the hospital expansion saw the eventual demise of Bache House to the south of the hospital main entrance.

Within the northern part of Newton, Rose Cottage (see page 130) seems to have been built c1850 accessed down Well Lane and surrounded by Dicksons Nursery. Early in the 1900s Woodbine (later renamed Broomhurst) was built nearby off Well Lane but subsequently demolished and now the site of Dawpool Rd. Another cottage was surrounded by nursery – now known as WealStone cottage on Wealstone Ln. This first appears on the 1872 Ordnance survey and is understood to have been a school house at some point. Moss Bank (between the Firs school and Newton House) first shows on the 1872 Ordnance survey, develops on later maps and is still on the 1957 but now is remembered as the modern housing development, Bank Close.

Governance of Upton during the period 1840-1899

For Upton, Moston and the Bache, the population grew through the 1840s and 1850s from approx. 270 to 370 and then doubled to 750 by the end of the century (excluding the growing asylum numbers). Council was held at the Egerton Arms. Following an Act of Parliament in 1834 - the Township appointed a Guardian (of the Poor) who was that town's representative for the 'grouped' administration of 'the poor'. In 1871, Upton became part of a new grouping known as the Chester Union. Compared to the earlier role of 'Overseer of the Poor' there was now a reduced responsibility of settling the value of the 'rate' and ensuring its collection. The pages from the Upton Minutes mainly record the quarterly accounts along with any meetings - all relating to setting a rate (local tax) and administering local public costs. The key costs were the payment to the 'Union' and to the County. Meetings were still held at the Egerton Arms with a typical attendance by six ratepayers - all local males of some 'local standing' either farmers or significant property/land holders.

After a period, any new attending ratepayers were nominated as eligible to be 'Guardians'. Chairing the meetings and preparing the accounts seemed to circulate around the membership - each 'doing their bit' for a year or so (see page 62 for the names of ratepayers in 1839). Meetings set the rate e.g. '6^d in the £' based on the rateable value of land/property and occasionally discussed the need to reset certain rateable values. As well as electing in new 'Overseers' to collect the rate they elected other roles within their number such as 'Surveyor of Highways' and 'Guardian of the Township' - whose duty was to represent the interests of Upton's poor at the Chester 'grouped workhouse'. Meetings sometimes discussed the state of certain roads (on one occasion Charles Potts even offering to pay £5 if used on the road providing access to his estate).

A typical quarterly account, based on an income of around £60, recorded –

13/9^d - constable R Turpin (25% salary - he served other townships)
£7/0/^{d} - County rate;   10/0^d - magistrates fees;   £40 - to the 'Poor Union'
highways; general expenses; auditors fees etc (one case noted of paying a surgeon)

In 1840 Police Officer Robert Turpin served Upton and other parishes but after the County Police Act of 1856 there was a permanent police officer for Upton. When the first constabulary was actually set up in Upton has not been identified but we know from the 1881 census that Constable Francis Hindley lived in the Heath with his family (see below).

Towards the end of the century, the number of ratepayers (at least attending the meetings) had now doubled. It now included professional and business incomers as well as the vicar. Minutes included special meetings such as a meeting in the 1890s at the school for *'Property owners of Upton Heath'* to address concerns about a sewerage scheme for the area.

Upton Heath developments

By the 1839 Tithe survey, Upton Heath had become the main residential area of more modest cottages This was further expanded during the mid to late 1800s. The row of terraces – often referred to as Heath Row – were probably built around 1850. The photograph dates from c1920 and shows the cobbled pavement and gutter. The row acquired the nickname of *'Sheep's Head Row'* -

so named by the reputation that heads would appear at the stable doors whenever incidents happened in the road.

Heath Row is Upton's only terrace directly onto the road, with no set of front gardens, and is probably due to the large pond or pit to their rear.

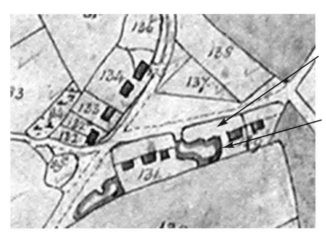

Upton Heath – taken from the 1839 Tithe survey

This small section of the 1839 Tithe survey shows why these later buildings took place where they did. The large pool – the Chemistry Pit – is still clearly marked and avoided by buildings in both the 1872 and 1898 Ordnance surveys. The area behind Heath Row acquired the name of *'Chemistry Pits'* and excavations during recent building work has revealed past use as a rubbish dump. No convincing explanation for the use of the term 'Chemistry' has yet been identified.

The Heath's first shop (and possibly at some point a tearoom), is generally now remembered as Brookfields It was built in the late 1800s (see page 164, which includes a 1960s photograph). The 1881 census records a Heath grocer – Edward Swindley. Various references are made to Swindley's Row including early 1900s Upton Council minutes recording sanitation concerns over their privies. The location of this 'Swindley's Row' has not been identified but is likely to be either Heath Row or nos: 48 -64 Heath Road.

Cottages between the Wheatsheaf and the former 'Brookfields' shop existed at the time of the 1839 Tithe survey but were extended significantly in the late 1800s. Around 1897 two gable ended cottages were added to nos:54/56 - one at each end - and this presumably explains the name '1-4 Gable Cottages' as shown on early maps for nos:52-58 Heath Road. Shortly afterwards c1900 the building was extended west giving nos:48/50. No:48 had the name of Jubilee Cottage and became the police house while no:50 may have became the Post Office / grocers run by Swindley. Shown on the 1936 OS, this building was demolished later to extend the Wheatsheaf car park (the site of the other pond shown above)

The drive way to the east of no:58 led to a modest coal yard during the first half of the 20th century – run by Tom Harrison of no:58. Garages and remodelled gardens are there now. No:62 is shown on early maps as '1-3 Farm Cottages'. No:60 was only added in 1986/7

Across Heath Road from Upton Heath Motors, another property was built during this period. It was the only building on *'the Heath triangle'* until the 1900s but this has recently been replaced with a modern bungalow.

The first school arrives (see also page 239)

Upton had its first church school and school house before its first church. The first St. Mary's School was built in 1843, by the Rector of St. Mary's-on-the-Hill, on part of the Footway field donated by Egerton. This first school stood in front of the present school, much nearer to the road. Alongside the school ran a path to the brickyard at the rear, while opposite stretched fields. It was a Mixed School with an Infants' department and according to Ormerod accommodated 80 children. In 1859 the average attendance was 55.

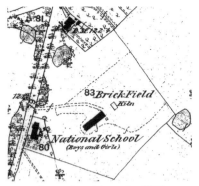

*Reproduced from the 1873
Ordnance Survey Map*

Church services were held on Sundays until the church was built eleven years later. From 1877 it was a meeting place for the ratepayers of the township.

The old school was demolished in 1884 and on 24th July 1884, the corner stone of the new buildings was laid by Miss Mary Humberston. The school and house were built and presented to the parish, by the Humberstons of Mollington Banastre, to open on 16th April 1885. The new red brick school, described as *'very handsome and commodious'*, had a single large schoolroom with a platform at one end. On the 27th May 1885, an 'Industrial & Art Exhibition' was held in participation with surrounding villages. Later, an infants' classroom was erected at the expense of Miss Mary Humberston, and in 1896, it was further enlarged. In that year, too, water was laid on at the school. The photograph shows the class of 1907.

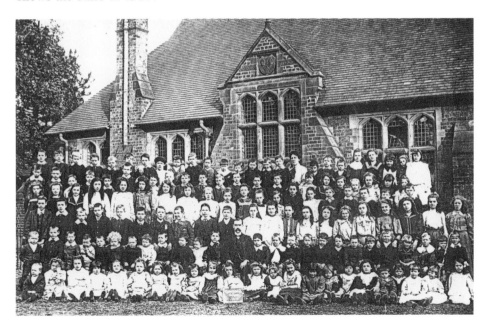

The Parish Church (see also Chapter 15)

The Church of the Holy Ascension was built in 1854 and came into being as a chapel of ease to St Mary-on-the-Hill, Chester. The rector of St Mary's at that time was Rev. William Henry Massie, who saw the need for places of worship in the more remote parts of the parish. Rev. Massie employed the eminent local architect James Harrison and the building began on land given by Sir Philip Grey Egerton. Richard, Marquis of Westminster was Patron of St. Mary-on-the-Hill and gave £1000 towards the building fund and a similar amount for the endowment. There were, of course, other contributions in cash and kind. Local people carted materials and the Rector rode out frequently to keep his eye on quality and progress. The foundation stone was laid by the Marquis on 10th March 1853, and only fourteen months later the church was consecrated by John Graham, Lord Bishop of Chester. On that day only £13 of the total cost remained outstanding.

About thirty years after the establishment of the Chapel of Ease, the population of the village had grown so much that it was decided to take steps to make Upton a parish in its own right. In February 1874 the Patron had been created Duke of Westminster and when he had settled the necessary compensation to St. Mary's, the new parish of Holy Ascension Upton was established on 8th December 1882. The photograph shown here dates from c1950.

Seven years after the appointment of Rev. Sparling as the first vicar it was decided that the new parish should have a vicarage. By the efforts of Colonel Evans-Lloyd a fund was started, generously supported locally and the balance made up by the Duke. The decision to build was made in March 1889, the foundation stone laid by Mrs Emily Logan on

August 15th of the same year and the vicarage finished and occupied eleven months later. This was achieved without any financial help from the Ecclesiastical Commissioners. The photograph shows the centenary celebrations held by the church congregation

The first Chapel (see also Chapter 15)

In 1858 six young men from Queen Street Congregational Church began to hold open-air religious meetings in the wheelwright's yard where the Wheatsheaf Inn was later built. The interest in these gatherings increased, and the group of wor-

shippers, which included the owner himself, began to use the wheelwright's shop for their meeting place.

As the congregations increased the County Union resolved to build a chapel at Upton. In 1860 the first Congregational Church building was completed and opened and a Sunday school was formed.

As the years went by, this first building became too small and inconven-

ient for the growing population. Plans were made and funds raised, and in June 1900 the foundation stone was laid for the new Congregational Church situated near the site of the original meeting-place. The sketch here dates from c1950 from 'the WI Book'. The old chapel became the Upton Heath Post Office for many years and also a newsagents – still known by its long established name of 'Jacksons' – see page 165.

Wheatsheaf public house

Thomas Knight acquired this plot of land in 1845 and a few years later built a wheelwright's shop. About 1850 he built a bake-house near this shop but in the directories and census still described himself as a wheelwright. Between 1857 and 1861 he altered and converted the bakehouse into a dwelling house, which sometime between 1864 and 1867 became a public house. In the 1874 Trade Directory he was both a wheelwright and a beer seller. The Birkenhead Brewery Company acquired the house from Thomas Knight on 17th February 1877. It is shown here towards the end of the 19th century.

In 1934 an outside covered stairway was erected on the far side to give easier access to a large room used by the British Legion.

Upton Park

Queens Park – on the south side of the River Dee from Chester city – had been a fairly successful early-1850s development, offering superior residences just outside the overcrowded city. In the mid-1850s three Chester entrepreneurs – land agent William Shone with Willian Pitt and Thomas Wood – engaged the same surveyor, John Hitchen, to design a 'Park' for Upton on similar fashionable lines. The following is redrawn from the existing original plan and shows the grand scheme that was never realised. The plots failed to sell as hoped and Upton Park developed over many decades as an enclave surrounded by countryside.

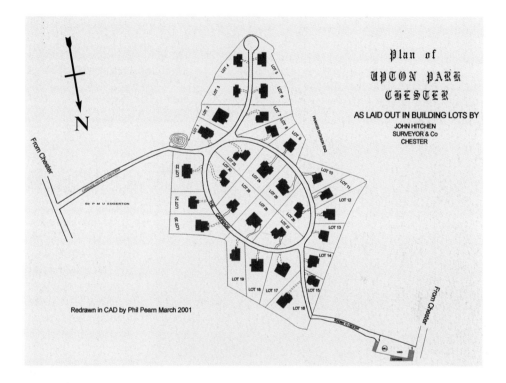

By 1857 the three estate developers had acquired all the land utilising the track off Mill Lane past Upton Mill and they created a circular carriageway and entrance drive out to the main lane linking Upton to Newton. By the 1861 census only four households existed with Pitt and Wood being two of these. By the 1890s however, all the inner circle plots and many of the outer had been developed although acquisition by Dicksons nursery had removed the intention of the cul-de-sac.

The Park grew as plots were individually bought and developed, providing housing referred to as 'artisans' villas'. The residents were a mix of owners and tenants – some the new clerical and professional classes and others *'living on annuities'*.

Some properties had stables and quarters for several servants while others were compact pairs of semi-detached cottages. By the 1880s, there were over 100 residents including servants – representing about one in six of Upton. This was a significant proportion of Upton's increase for the last few decades.

The tree-lined Avenue entrance has remained a feature of the Park and the high holly hedges and many trees have contributed to the City Council's decision in the late 1990s to make Upton Park a conservation area. All the photographs shown here were taken around 1912.

The Avenue poplars have been replaced and the diseased elms were felled in 1979.

The restrictive covenant covering much of the current Upton Park has been closely protected over recent decades. While some in-filling has continued until recent times, the density rules of the 1870 revised covenant have been retained.

The book 'Upton Park Chester – a community for 150 years' by Phil Pearn, published in 2001, provides an in-depth history of the development and its community up to the present day.

Life in Upton in the late 1800s

An analysis of the late 1800s census records with the 1872 and 1898 Ordnance surveys allows a picture to be painted of life in the village as the century drew to a close. Unfortunately the archived Upton Township Minutes do not cover the period 1894 – 1912. The first Minute book following the 1894 Local Government Act has not been lodged with the Cheshire Records Office and its whereabouts is unknown.

There were four Upton farmers working approximately 50% of the Upton & Bache area although they could have farmed further land outside the parish. It appears they were all mainly tenant farmers but may have owned some land.

> John Wainwright at the Acres (125 acres)
>
> William Heath at Grange Farm (168 acres)
>
> John Dickinson at Upton Farm (101 acres)
>
> Thomas Ithell at Upton Hall (168 acres)

Much of the land in the south of the parish was either nursery land with the Dicksons or farmed out of Newton. So although there were several Gentleman's Country Estates, most only took a small proportion of the total land area for their private use. Roberts' Oakfield estate was easily the largest but he probably let some agricultural land to Upton farmers.

On the whole the small cottages and terraced property was occupied by labourers and their families or by those in domestic service but not living on their master's or mistress's premises. The larger houses either housed the 'nouveau rich' or those living comfortably 'from their own financial means'.

The parish church now had its established vicar – Rev. Wilfred Sparling - settled into the new Vicarage and active in village life. The new school provided education for the area and apparently for canal boat children who spent the day there while their parents by-passed Upton. The 'local barons' from the grand houses provided employment and a degree of the social fabric. Their influence along with the main farmers on the Council, was reducing as more of the professional classes were moving into the area.

By 1890, mains water was available throughout the area. When gas arrived has not been identified but some gas street lighting is known to have been established fairly early in the next century.

CHAPTER 7
Developments 1900 - 1939

Despite Egerton's 1899 plans for large housing estates on most of the land remaining in his ownership, only modest ribbon development occurred until the mid-1930s. The new century started with a local population of some 750 plus an asylum population approaching twice that number. By the outbreak of WW2 the local population had risen to over 3000 with the much improved shops and services and with wider main roads. These roads generally had houses along at least one side. The first decade saw housing developments mainly around Upton Heath. The second decade saw a few detached houses on individual plots but by the late 1930s several green field housing estates were either complete or well underway. Modernisation of the infrastructure was the key issue of Parish Council concern. The Council now had incomers offering specific expertise blending with the views of the big private estate 'barons' whose control of village life was fading.

Egerton's 1899 plan for clean new city suburbs

By 1899, Lord of the Manor, Egerton, had reduced his land ownership in Upton to around 50%. His detailed plans for 'greenfield' housing estates are archived with the Cheshire Records Office (DEO 206/5). The marked up 1936 OS Map (page 87) shows the extent of these proposals. The original plan not only shows the proposed areas for development but all the proposed new service roads with each house plot marked out. In common with other major landowners in the Chester area this was not to be high density development. A number of estates with say 100 detached or semi-pairs were proposed. Restrictive covenants to establish a high standard of housing were the norm at this time for the landed gentry. Note that even by 1939 only Kingsmead and the Upton Drive area had been developed on land he designated in 1899.

Not only was Egerton thinking this way but the declining Dicksons Nursery, which began selling land in Newton and Hoole, was also attempting to sell some of its Upton land as shown in this failed Auction Sale proposal. The area was developed later in the 1930s incorporating Delvine Drive. Properties were built in 1904 on the plots shown as 'SOLD'.

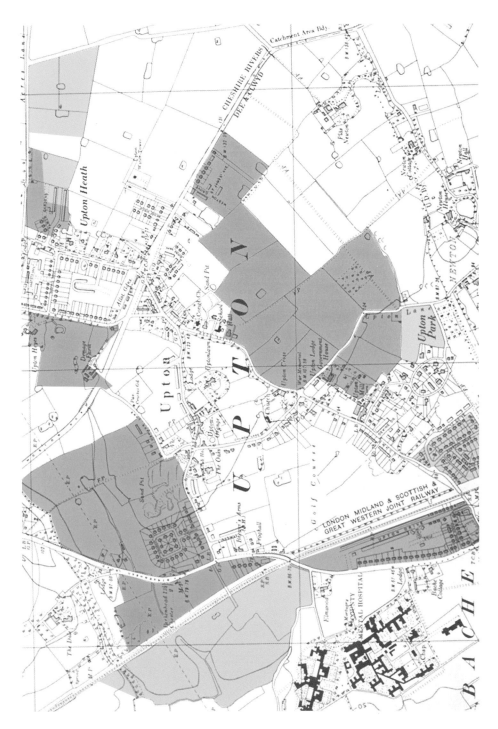

Reproduced from the 1936 Ordnance Survey Map – manually marked up to show the 1899 housing development proposals (deep shading) and the relatively small amount of other Egerton land (pale shading)

Upton Heath development in the early 20ᵗʰ century

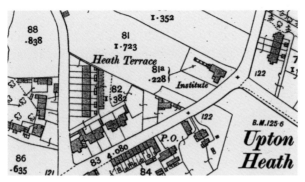

The Upton Heath 'triangle' –
Reproduced from the 1911 Ordnance Survey Map

Upton Heath was the main focus of new building in the opening years of the 20ᵗʰ century. Builder George Austin bought the triangular plot in 1903. The deed describes land and cottages - but from the 1899 OS map we see that the only property was that in the eastern corner of the plot. Austin raised a mortgage and first built The Gables on the southern corner. It is understood that he made this his home. In 1905, he then built 2 pairs of semis on Heath Road (formerly Main Road) and the set of terraces (Heath Terrace) on Flag Lane. It appears that Austin retained the land behind the terraces as his builder's yard. Much later, the end semi and yard were sold to Mr Davies who used the yard for his engineering business. This c1913 photograph shows the area now well established.

The gable end cottages (in the right of the photograph) had only been added in 1897 and the pair of semis just off camera to the left were built in 1904 apparently on the site of a very old house – possibly the Heath's oldest. Built by Ithell, a family member lived in the Heath House half and the other half – Woodbank – was rented out to his son-in-law plumber Frank Morris. The shop in the centre of the photograph is covered on page 164. Even though the Heath was now well established with some new properties, some dwellings were in a poor state. A valuation in 1932 on the old end two cottages stated them as very poor and with no artificial lighting.

The Upton Heath Men's Institute which originally faced up Long Lane was formed on 31st December 1907. The site was given by Sir John Frost, and the foundation stone was laid by the Duke of Westminster. The building was erected for use as a reading room and club to be used by men of the farming, artisan and industrial classes resident in the Township of Upton. It was stipulated that the building was not to be used for *'religious instruction or religious meetings'* or *'the promotion of party politics whether Parliamentary, Parochial, educational or otherwise'*. There were further restrictions on *'the sale of intoxicating liquor'* and on *'gambling'*. The building was used for civil defence purposes during WW2 but returned to recreational use in the 1950s. Today it is known as the Guides HQ (see page 197).

The new Congregational church, shown here, was built in 1900. Upton Heath now had the feel of a village centre with pub, shops and other community facilities.

Two significant properties were built on Long Lane in the early 1900s – both on the site of the former brickyard. The 1872 OS simply shows a field but by the 1898 survey there was a brickyard with kilns and a clay pit filled with water. The Mount was built on the site of the actual brickyard for local cattle dealer Tom Hinde. His slaughter house was built further back behind the other major

building – the Children's Cottage Home – just off right - which still stands with its commemorative plaque.

The Mount was later acquired by auctioneer Leonard Wright until c1937, the Hindes having built a smaller house alongside. The Mount was used by the military during WW2 and was bought by auction in a poor state c1948 by Alfred Halliwell using the land to the side for his building business as shown above. Finally the Mount was demolished in 2000 and the current McArthur & Stone residence built.

Shown on the OS maps as 'The Children's Cottage Home' the characteristic building with its decorative rounded gable ends was built in 1900 as one of six such homes in the Chester area. It was built when public care of children rested with Poor Law Guardians but closed c1920 when this care passed to the County Council who operated under a different policy. Memories of this home are that it was a happy and friendly place under the long-serving matron Miss E M Flook. The children (who were possibly only boys) wore a uniform which

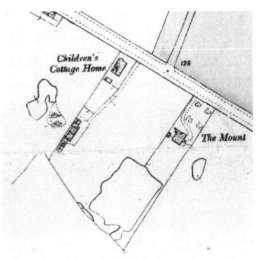

Reproduced from the 1911 Ordnance Survey Map

was not much different from that of the local children with whom they mixed.

After the closure, the house lay dormant until 1930 when it was, in part, rented out to the Coventry family and upstairs as offices for the County's Roads & Bridges Dept. under district surveyor Basil M Trew. By 1972, it was used by the County for its Probation Service but is now in private ownership as a consultancy business.

The era of building large country houses had now gone but established roads near other properties were desirable sites for housing in the early 20th century. In 1904 a few properties were built near to the existing Upton Park on its road in from the Mill. One larger Edwardian house was built on the southeast side of Mill Lane complete with a tennis court in its large back garden.

In the early part of the 20th century leading up to the Great War, Upton had taken on board many of the signs of town living. Mains water had been available since around 1890 and some main sewers were in place. During the 1917 prevalence of epidemics, the Upton Council was seeking to persuade the owners of cottages still on privies to convert to water closets. Traffic was increasing considerably partly due to Upton roads being the link between the Birkenhead road and the Warrington road. There were frequent calls for respraying of the roads due to dust from the heavy traffic. Crosville was operating a bus service from Upton but the fares, suited to the long distance through traveller, were seen as expensive to those only coming back from Chester.

Throughout this early 20th century period however, Upton life was still influenced by the handful of gentlemen from the big houses or the farms. They often acted like squires, running the Council and holding village events in their

grounds. This continued after the Great War with traditional country pursuits such as shown here from the early 1920s. The pack is believed to be the Royal Rock Beagles and is accompanied by the young Dutton brothers – Thomas Piers and Leonard Parker Dutton.

The Upton Trust set up by Potts and acquired by Owen

The character of a large part of Upton – the golf course and its surrounding area – originates from the establishment of this Upton Trust.

This aerial photograph – with acknowledgements to Fotocraft – was taken over 50 years ago, but except for its foreground & background, is little changed.
Mill Lane/Heath Road runs left to right across the photograph.

Charles Potts - Solicitor and Clerk to Cheshire County Council - had acquired the land bounded by Mill Lane / railway / Upton Lane / Church Lane as well other land outside this enclosed area. As covered on page 64 he had acquired Upton Bank and had bailiffs farming some of his land.

In 1871 he established in his will an 'Upton Trust' placing a restrictive covenant on the use of the land. This was a fairly common practice in the Chester area where the gentlemen of the City wanted to ensure quality developments. For several decades the trust was held by the Potts family with the pasture land rented to local farmers.

The only sale of any of this land before 1920 was a conveyance in 1896 to the London & North Western & Great Western Railway. The extent of this is not known.

In 1920 Trustee Hubert Potts sold land to the Brewery extending their land around The Brewer's Arms and then through the 1920s, sold a few plots to build affluent detached properties in prime roadside positions. The Gerrards had a large house with tennis courts built on the corner of Upton Lane & Liverpool Road. Rebecca Potts had a house – the last one before the railway bridge on Mill Lane. Another example was Glendales built in 1925 for John Glendale Lightfoot. His father John had been Sheriff of Chester in 1898 and was in the grocery & provisions business as well as mining interests in Glendale California. He had been living at the Gables in Upton Heath but acquired a field know as 'Cross Croft' from the Potts Trust. After some land exchanges Glendales had large grounds and stayed with the Lightfoot family until 1947. It is remembered as the home and surgery of Dr. Benjamin Carr for many years around the 1960s after they too had moved there from 'The Gables'.

Reginald Potts – the next generation - had succeeded Charles as Clerk with Chester Borough County Council and lived at The Dale. The Potts family had long since sold 'Upton Bank' – now known as 'The Oaks' – with a few acres of surrounding ground. In 1931 Fred Owen acquired the Oaks estate and then in 1934 after the death of Reggie Potts he acquired the remaining part of the Potts Trust – understood to be the land shown here.

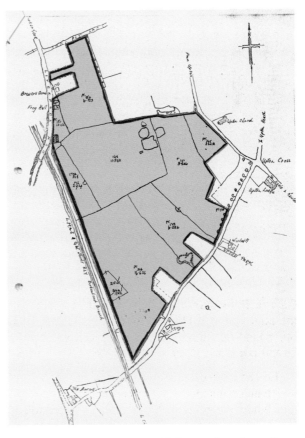

Fred Owen (who is covered on page 267) not only bought these 57 acres but acquired the ownership of the Trust and hence control of the restrictive covenant. Clearly a shrewd businessman, most of the cost of this acquisition was on mortgage from the previous trustees. After selling parcels of land for housing development along the periphery he was soon able to clear the debt.

Squires – a local builder – had started buying some Mill Lane sites from Potts and continued doing so with Owen until much of that side of Mill Lane was built. A drive was left – shown on the 1936 OS - to access a small sandpit. This is only noted today by the shape of the back gardens.

Fred soon set up the Golf Club and was renting them a 9-hole course within months of acquiring the land. The rest of the land which included Bridge Farm was in use by both David Davies who leased the Bridge Farm buildings and by the Inglebys. By 1935 the course had extended to 15 holes although still subletting to David Davies as pastureland until 1939. The Club was also gradually leasing more of the Oaks . Fred Owen built on a few of the plots bordering the golf course. One of these, Linksmead on Church Lane, he made his own home. The development of Linksway was started and before WW2, properties were complete on the east side and in the vicinity of Bridge Farm. By 1937, Fred Owen had acquired the Upton Lawn estate which was leased for farmland. This enabled him to extend the golf course across the road and have further valuable plots for housing along the periphery – see chapter 9. Although some of the former Upton Lawn estate returned to agricultural war use, it is understood that the greens were retained. The Golf Club was seen as offering recreation and relaxation during the troubled wartime period.

Developments during the 1920s

This was an affluent period but only a few houses were added. These were fairly substantial homes built on desirable sites alongside existing roads – either singularly or as two or three. Upton Rise and its neighbour were built off Mill Lane in c1927 as were Eardisley & Cedar Croft on the northern corner of Upton Lane and Liverpool Road. These were for the Cooper and Hinde families respectively. This junction was giving great concern to the Council over road safety and they took the building as an opportunity for improvements. Other properties were added on the Upton Park arm off Mill Lane.

Demand for services was growing but the village was still under the control of the ten or so 'local barons'. When the Upton Council had an opportunity in 1919 to attend a conference on electrical services they concluded that the Council *does not wish to entertain the bringing of an electrical supply to Upton'*. Nevertheless the supply did come soon after and one of the houses being built in Upton Park - Rhosilli - had electric lighting, when built in 1923, but also had a back-up of gas. All very new, the electrical switches operated sideways. Interestingly the only electricity pole discussed in the Council, as raising concern, was the one at the Upton Park / Mill Lane junction. The Council pressed to get the services of a fire brigade, especially when they realised that their RDC taxes were funding the use of this service elsewhere. They also pushed for a railway station at Upton, possibly because several councillors actually worked in Liverpool or Manchester.

By 1922 Upton had 39 gas street lights and even by 1930 more gas lamps were being added where an electrical supply was not nearby. Conversion to electric street lighting was deemed too expensive and was delayed until post-war with the diminishing service of the local Gas company. Increasing standards of hygiene were important and rubbish collection (known as scavenging) came in during the mid-1920s although there was concern on the council over linking this charge to the Rateable Value ' *should only be paid for by those using the service'*. They still saw the eradication of privies and connection of WCs to main drains as being the key hygiene need. The various pits around Upton were being used as tips and this was raising concerns. In the mid-1930s crickets were becoming a big problem in the Sandpit Lane tip. Smoke was another nuisance with complaints about excessive output from the Mental Hospital in 1930. Staff at the hospital required local housing and the 1926 Upton Council was pressing for additional housing to meet this need. The growing Upton Heath population was stretching demand on the water supply and a water tower was built c1930

Traffic was an increasing problem and by 1926 there was a proposal for the Moston Road extending Long Lane to Moston and thereby creating a ring road around Upton. One implication of this was that the new road would pass through a field behind the Institute that Sir John Frost had made available to the children of Upton as a playing field. A long process over many years then started with Frost seeking to acquire an alternative playing field that could remain 'in perpetuity' for the children of Upton.

The Chemistry Pits Play Area

Various sites – all generally in the area of the final site – were suggested, offered or declined. The Council minutes imply that Sir John Frost was getting very agitated by this. He had agreed to sell his land for the Moston Road route for the sum needed to acquire this play area. It is understood – but not confirmed – that part of his desire for this play area was in memory of a daughter lost in childhood.

The ground was eventually bought and appears to have acquired the name 'Chemistry Pits' because it was 'by the chemistry pits' which was the name given to the area behind the Heath Cottages (see page 78). The site has had a difficult history from its beginning with poor drainage and being seen as a rubbish dump. In 1938 cinders were spread presumably because of the poor drainage. On another occasion mowing was not possible and grazing sheep were introduced.

The Council minutes frequently cover the need for repairs to the swings and the problem of keeping the area purely for the reason it was intended. Darlington, the local blacksmith, had to carry out repairs and Mrs Metcalfe complained, in 1939, of the swings squeaking badly. Boundary fencing was erected to prevent Mr Lawson of Longfield Avenue from trespassing by using it as a throughfare.

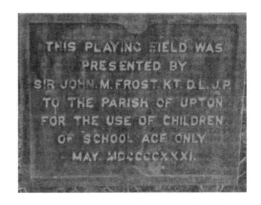

The plaque pictured here is the original which is now missing. Today's Parish Council is planning to erect a similar replacement as part of the recent refurbishment to the field.

The Upton Council Minutes for the immediate pre-war period indicate concern for recreational activities and the need for more suitable public ground. In earlier times landowners had made ground available for such use but this was declining as land was being developed towards suburbia. Playing fields were being built over. Up to WW2 the cricket ground complete with pavilion was to the east of Demage Lane and is remembered now by the name Willow Close, given to the post-war development on its ground. Football was played on the field later used for Daleside but this was a cattle field which rather hampered the standard of matches. Nevertheless some cine footage remains in the archives. The main recreation ground of today – off Wealstone Lane (see page 118) – Ben Roberts' small holding (shown below c1912) was still rented out for agricultural land.

From 1928 Upton had the facilities of the Village Hall (Chapter 12) but the 'local barons' continued to be a major part of community life with popular garden parties held in their grounds. This photographs records an event held at Upton Lawn

Some other 1930s building developments built on existing roads

The little old cottages, to the east of Upton Farm, were demolished and a Council Yard established. Shinn built some houses on the north side of Upton Lane and lived in one of these himself before moving to Upton Farm post-war. A few properties were also built on the lower end of Demage Lane. On the golf course side of lower Heath Road, a few properties were built in the late30s. The rest of the road up to the Wheatsheaf corner was tree-lined and undeveloped until post-war (see aerial photograph page 92).

Long Lane developments after establishing the A41

The Moston Road was constructed in 1932 and this encouraged development on Long Lane. It is understood that the railings shown here were removed during

the war. The Long Lane shops can be seen. Working from the garage (see page 159), the shops are remembered as follows –

The Post Office & Newsagents run by the Bradleys (see page 159).

Furleys Electrical shop (see page 163).

Florists / Garden shop.

Fish & Chip shop run by Mr Smith during the war period and later by ex-military men Reece & Barnes before Doug Hughes and later the Moseleys.

Bakers & Confectioners (Delice?).

General Provisions Wholesalers run by Mrs Roberts.

Across the entrance of Marina Drive was the Pharmacy run by Mr Taylor and then Miss Henshaw's Wine shop (later Irwins).

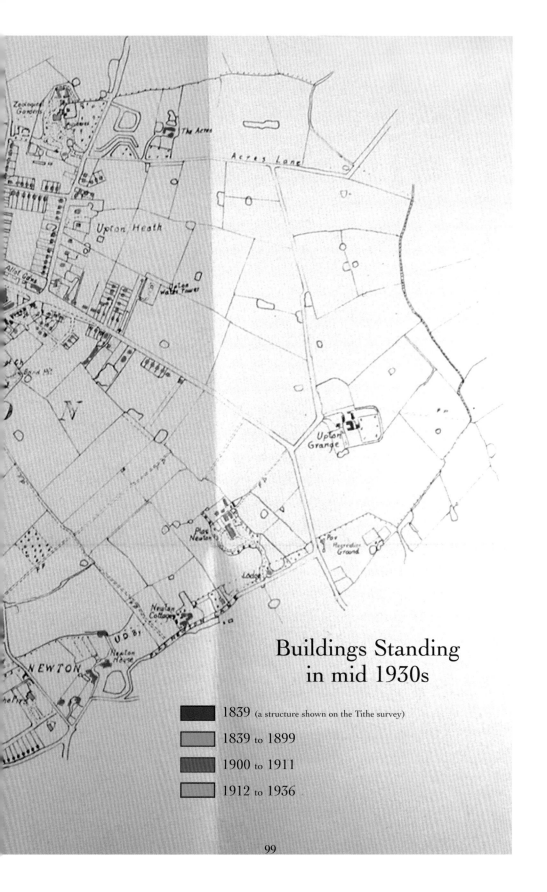

Buildings Standing
in mid 1930s

1839 (a structure shown on the Tithe survey)

1839 to 1899

1900 to 1911

1912 to 1936

Housing estate development from the mid-1930s

The depression must have decreased the wealth of Upton's 'barons' as well as the absent landowners – principally Egerton. There may be many factors why land became available and why a demand for housing was deemed to be growing. Certainly in the Upton area, several housing estates were started in the mid-1930s, building off new roads cut into green fields.

Kingsmead

This was developed by Mr Cottle and Peter Cooper believes it was possibly named after Cottle's prep school on the Wirral.

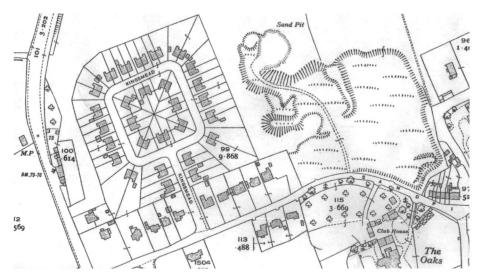

The Kingsmead cul-de-sac estate – in the northern corner of Liverpool Road and Upton Lane – first appears on the 1936 Ordnance Survey Map

The fields known as 'Long Croft' and 'The Dale' had been leased by the Egerton estate to Richard Ithell. By a 1927 mortgage we know that Richard Ithell still had the sandpit area but Long Croft and the Dale fields were now tenanted by Arthur Hinde. In December 1933, Egerton sold some 7 acres to the Surbiton Development Co. Ltd of London. This sale gave access from Sandpit Lane (now Upton Lane) to develop a fairly typical 'mid-1930s' quite suburban housing estate. Kingsmead's builder was Mr Morgan who also built similar properties at a similar time (1934/5) on Liverpool Road opposite the Frog. Morgan himself lived opposite the Frog. The 1935 Ordnance survey shows the estate complete nestled between the declining Darlington's smithy business and Richard Ithell's sandpit which was also nearing the end of its days. The properties were apparently a mix of owner occupier and rental at this time with more take-up on the freehold post-WW2. Indications are that the properties fronting onto Upton Lane were sold as plots to other builders/owners.

Oakfield estate

When George Mottershead bought Oakfield in 1930, this former part of Roberts' Oakfield estate was already earmarked for housing development which then started in the early 1930s. The zoo bought strips of land along its boundary to prevent bungalows being built around its Lodge. Oakfield Drive had been built as a public road c1912 linking Caughall Road and Flag Lane (the former link lane having been absorbed within Roberts' Oakfield estate). In 1913, T A Rigby of Upton Heyes had acquired the land south of Oakfield Drive from Roberts. At some 13 acres it had acquired the name of 'The Cricket Ground' and leased initially to Darlington and later to Fred Davies of Damage Farm. In 1931, Liverpool architects Brown & Sanders acquired the land from the executors of the Rigby estate and housing development started shortly after. This early photograph records the northside of Oakfield Drive showing the access into Oakfield Avenue. The 1936 OS map shows much of the estate as built and with partly-built Oakfield Avenue named as Oakfield Crescent. By 1933 the Council was agreeing to an electric street light on Oakfield Drive. The 1938 Council Minutes record house numbering concluded for Flag Lane, Oakfield Drive and Oakfield Avenue. It is understood that Danny Jones built at least the bulk of this estate. Endsleigh Gardens was then developed from c1938 and was being occupied by 1939. Developed under the 'Cheshire Investment Trust' the name 'Endsleigh Gardens' was requested by Mr H W Stacey.

Meadows Way area

In the mid-1930s the area enclosed by Demage Lane, Moston Road, Upton Lane, the penfolds and the Heath back gardens was still open pastureland and the village cricket ground complete with pavilion. In the late 1930s house building was underway with each end of Meadows Way and all Walnut Close built before the war suspended further construction. The road was named 'Meadows Way' in memory of Sir John Meadows Frost and the cricket ground appears to have been remembered by Willow Close built post-WW2.

Upton Heath (West of Caughall Road)

The new Arterial Road led to considerable housing development besides the Oakfield estate. The exhibition house, shown here copied from the original publicity, can still be recognised on Caughall Road.

3-bedroomed semi-detached properties were available as outright purchases or for a deposit and a weekly rent

They offered –

drawing room, dining room and kitchenette.

electric lighting and gas boiler.

coal and undercover washhouse.

garages were available at an additional cost.

The agents were Curlender of Liverpool.

Alwyn Gardens had just been started at the time of the 1936 Ordnance survey. The entrance on to the main

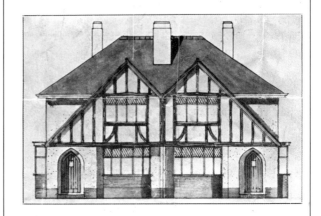

EXHIBITION HOUSE

ON SITE.

DECEMBER 1st—15th, 1934.

(Open for Inspection WEEK DAYS and SUNDAYS).

Crosville Bus Service from Chester Cross to Upton Village.

"ALBERVILLE ESTATE"

STOKE WERVIN ROAD, UPTON VILLAGE,

Near CHESTER.

road and the first properties on the northern arm are shown. By war-time, Alwyn Gardens was complete and the Acres Lane development had started (see page 124), allowing re-housing for those in poor Upton village centre cottages that were being demolished. The land had become available from the Egerton estate and acquired by P Curlander (Chester) *'for the building of private properties only and with a sale price no less than £550'*. This restriction was later reduced down to £450. The properties were initially a mix of owner occupier and rental, having been acquired by investors from Liverpool.

Curlander had started building along the south side of Acres Lane but this was suspended with the war. When they restarted in 1946 the properties were in great demand due to the post-war restrictions on building.

By 1936, Brooke Avenue had been completed except for the far end which was built post-war. The name 'Brooke' comes from the developer who used Danny Jones as his builder.

Stanton & Egerton Drives area

The area bounded by Mill Lane, the railway, Bache Drive and Park Drive was all former Dicksons nursery ground which they were looking to sell as early as 1925. They, too, established a restrictive covenant to maintain a minimum standard of building. By 1930 the land was owned by The Newton and Upton Land Company Ltd and appears to have been sold to various builders. In 1934 at least some of the Bache Drive area land was acquired and developed by Hoole builder, Rowlands. Stanton Drive (see page 9) was built c1937 by local builder George Morgan, who lived on the Stanton Drive/Rosewood corner.

Delvine Drive

Eddy Jones built the north side of Delvine Drive in 1939, not building his own property at the end of the cul-de-sac until the immediate post-war period. The south side, completed post-war, is understood to have been by another builder.

Upton Drive / Liverpool Road area

Peter Warrington recalls the story of how his uncle called into the Egerton Arms one evening c1930, to be told by the owner publican that he was selling former nursery land to the north of the pub. Warrington concluded the deal that evening and his company then built Bache Avenue and the first few houses up Liverpool Road from the pub. Liverpool Road development was continued north by Heywoods during the mid-1930s. Also in the mid-1930s, Capstick & Owen acquired and built on the rest of this ex-nursery land - the wedge between the railway and Liverpool Rd. While the 1936 OS map shows only a few houses on Upton Drive nearly all the rest were completed, along with the Bache shops, before the outbreak of war. Post war, when it was possible to start building again, they completed the last few, including Beechway, at the far end and Pine Gardens, all before 1950.

Wards shop alongside the Egerton Arms, 1940s

The first shop, after the Egerton Arms, was Williams newsagents which was soon taken on by Wards, as featured in the previous photograph, relocated from Liverpool Road. The baker/confectioner was Miss Miffans followed later by Yoxhalls. The greengrocers was Hanlons and then followed the chemists, initially Lanceleys later Gittins. Finally a grocers initially run by the Wilsons and then by the Stears. The Post Office was still across the road with Miss Nixon (see page 165).

Capstick & Owen also acquired Dicksons' Stanton House estate and started building in the grounds. Before building was suspended by the war, only the first few properties on The Croft had been constructed.

Life in the immediate pre-war period

Much of the land was still being farmed especially around the boundary of the village. Fred Davies continued farming out of Demage Farm until his death in the mid-1940s. Within the village, Powell of Upton Farm had pigs in the former penfolds and was slaughtering and processing, selling pork pies and black pudding.

With a steady growth in the population, several issues were being addressed by the Parish Council – then under the chairmanship of Richard Ithell and vice-chairman Frank Morris. Bache was amalgamated into Upton-by-Chester and for the first time, Public Indemnity insurance was adopted for Parish Council ground. Land was for sale and the Council was encouraged to acquire some for both recreation and for allotments. While the new Moston Road had encouraged considerable development in the northern part of the Heath, there was now concern about traffic dividing the community. The 'Upton Ratepayers Association' was requesting a Caughall Road by-pass. Some development was clearly slower than expected – the Council sent a letter to the Ministry of Health complaining about lack of progress by contractors on the Acres Lane development. Meanwhile the Parish Council was still meeting in the schoolroom but had acquired better seating for their meetings.

Dicksons nursery had largely become waste ground offering children a play area. Remnants were harvested – either children scrumping from the orchards or

families of the previous nursery workers still managing to grow and gather a few crops. This view spans from the Upton Park Avenue of trees to the left and Newton's Rose Cottage, at the cul-de-sac end of Well Lane , to the far right.

CHAPTER 8
Military & Wartime Activities during the 20th Century

Military bases are sited according to their strategic and tactical needs but personal desirability of the precise location often plays a big part. Upton had many large houses built during the 19th century and these became available and suitable as military headquarters and for military hospitals. Government House along with Upton Lodge became the official residence of the General Officer Commanding Western Command and his immediate staff. Oakfield (the Zoo) along with Moston Hall and the Deva hospital all became wartime military hospitals. Other large houses took on other functions during wartime and barrack huts were built in their grounds. Although the losses of local soldiers killed in action was greater during WW1, nevertheless, WW2 was closer to home - involving the community to a greater extent. The proximity of Liverpool and the presence of major fuel stores probably contributed to the extent of the Ack-Ack activity and to several recorded bomb drops within Upton and the surrounding area.

Government House & Upton Lodge

During the Great War the Royal Flying Corp (predecessor to the RAF) took over Dorin Court (see page 68) as their Group HQ. In 1920 the house and grounds were purchased by the War Department from Lieut. Colonel Gossage. Upton Lodge was then bought by the War Department in 1927 as an extension to the facility. The Upton Council minutes for 1927 record General Butler GOC Western Command living at Upton Lodge and War Office permission being sought to move their hedge back 20ft, all as part of making the Upton Cross crossroads wider and safer. While Gen Jackson occupied Government House, the Lodge was used as residence for the Chauffeur, the Dispatch Rider and other military staff but was mainly the offices as used by Jackson's ADC. Jackson retired before the outbreak of war and then the dual site became the official residence of the Major General Chief of Staff Western Command. This led to an impressive list of GOC's with their

An unknown German POW in the grounds of Government House during WW2

personal residence shifting from Government House to Upton Lodge. Residents included Generals Butler, Elliott, Horrocks, Templer and possibly others. As a major military residence during WW2, several distinguished guests are recorded. Princess Mary was a guest for a while. Her Lady-in-waiting was reputed to have taken Princess Mary's ration book to the Bache grocery store. During a visit by Field Marshall Montgomery the village school had difficulty getting the boys to attend in case they missed the opportunity of seeing 'Monty'.

In 1948 Gen. Horrocks relocated to new Government House at Eccleston Hill Hall and Upton's Government House became known to the Army as Old Government House and was converted into three flats for officers. Despite being remembered as a beautiful house with oak panels and sweeping staircase - it was demolished c1970 and the new building retook the original name of Dorin Court before recently becoming Weal Stone House. In the 1950s six married quarters were built in the grounds with more planned but not built. By the 1970s these were abandoned derelict squatted and vandalized. In 1983 the houses were sold with preference going to service personnel and the final link with the military broken since the local Council had already acquired and demolished Government House. Only the front boundary brick wall of Government House remains.

Other military sites around Upton

Further southeast along Wealstone Lane was 'The Firs'. This was another example of a 19th century gentleman's country residence used during the 20th century as military offices and barracks. Demolished in the early 1980s the memory is retained through the name Horrocks Road. According to records with the 'Firs School' – nearby Heywood Lodge was taken over by the military during WW2 and used for both an Ack-Ack headquarters and for ENSA as a training ground for military entertainers. A parade ground was established on the former tennis courts – now the school playground. The huts, later used by the Firs School, housed Italian POWs. The Italian POW presence in the village is well remembered. One task they undertook was to improve the bank alongside the Moston Road built some ten years earlier.

Ack-Ack guns and/or search lights were located on the top of the rise were Weston Grove now runs. The army huts in the area of the Weston Grove shops were later used for Polish families, immediately after the war. The Divisional H.Q. of No. 26 Fire Fighting Area, Liverpool, had a staff of forty based in the house and grounds of Upton Grange (now demolished) on Church Lane. This service began as the Auxiliary Fire Service in 1940 and was nationalized in August 1941. Extension huts within the Church Lane grounds were built in 1942 and used until the end of the war. An Ack-Ack gun on this site is well remembered by the Church Lane residents of the time. Some of the huts were dismantled and used by the scouts and other local organisations but the sites of these huts can still be seen on the 1956 OS map.

Around Acres Lane and Oakfield

This northern area of Upton Heath has seen military activity during both World Wars. The Acres was used as a Remount School during WW1 and horses were stabled in Oakfield's extensive stables. Prior to WW2, the Cheshire Yeomanry used Martin's Riding school. In 1939, Martin accompanied them to Palestine.

During WW2, a heavy Anti Aircraft battery known as H25 was set up to the north of Acres Lane. Early radar was reputedly used – taking the form of a large rotating cross carrying dipoles. The 71st Cheshire Home Guard HAA Battery was formed in April 1943. 'A' troop under the command of Capt. S H Woodiwiss supported H25 from its HQ at The Mount on Long Lane. American servicemen – mainly engineers in training for the invasion - are remembered as being there although the site is often refered to as 'the Polish Camp'. This relates to the immediate post-war period when Free Polish troops were sent there after duty in Italy and the site became a medical camp with military doctors and dentists. With reference to the late 1940s aerial survey photograph on page 124, the gun emplacements and the military huts can be clearly seen above the overlayed 'ACRES LANE' marking. The sites of the huts and of the gun emplacements can still be seen on the 1956 OS map. Even into the 1960s, local children continued to play in the underground passages. To the untrained eye, no indications remain in place today.

The fuel depots were largely located just to the north of Upton and supplied from Shell at Stanlow. The Royal Army Service Corp provided the guard and various outposts are remembered. These supplies were part of the PLUTO (PipeLineUnderTheOcean) fuel supplies for the D-Day invasion and beyond.

Once into the 1960s most traces of war-time activity had gone but the air raid sirens were still used for a while to warn of animals escaped from the zoo – which did happen but only post-war, despite wartime concerns.

Wartime Army Hospitals

During both wars local facilities were used as military hospitals. Moston Hall, Oakfield and the Deva were all used – the railway serving as useful transportation. Huts were added in the grounds to extend the facilities as shown here at Oakfield during WW1.

Lady Arthur Grosvenor instigated the hospital at Oakfield gaining it the name of 'Lady Arthur's Place'.

One fund raiser for Oakfield was through the sale of 'Birthday Books'. These contained photographs of the patients and staff at Oakfield – see some featured here – and each day was accompanied by a quotation.

One such quotation from Sister Allwood ran

'When the war is done
we'll recall the fun
The fun that conquered the pain -
For we'll owe a debt
(and we'll not forget)
To the jokes that kept us sane;
How the wounded could laugh
and bandy their chaff,
And kick up the deuce of a row !
....It may be, in peace,
when the sufferings cease,
We'll be sadder, aye sadder,
than now.'

And from a patient –

'When troubles arise,
promptly sit on 'em'

The following photograph shows injured WW1 troops on a day out at the Mill.

The Dale Barracks

The Dale barracks opened in 1939 for the 22nd Cheshire Regiment and Manchester Regiments. During the war the Machine Gun Training Centre relocated from London and the Office of the Commander of the Royal Engineers (Mersey District) was established. Post-war the Dale was a Primary Training Centre. In 1949 the Queen visited the Queen's Bays and in 1950 the King visited the Royal Dragoons. In 1956 the current building, used today as the Officers' Mess, was a secure asylum with the remainder of the barrack buildings converted to house patients as part of the hospital. The current sports/playing fields held some 29 Nissan Huts and 8 H Blocks again all part of the Moston Hospital. In 1987 following a major rebuild, the military hospital role was replaced with the 1st Battalion The Kings Regiment moving in to provide a Home Defence. In more recent times regular Infantry Battalions have used the Dale Barracks as home from which they can be rapidly deployed to 'Hot Spots' around the world. Married quarters are provided and many of the children attend the local schools. Also on the site – Fox barracks – is the local HQ of the Territorial Army.

The Memorial to those of the Upton Community lost in two World Wars

'Lest we forget' - this photograph records the dedication by Bishop Mercer in 1921.

The following local names are remembered on Upton's War Memorial –

1914 - 1918

James Anderton; James Benson; Archibold Buck; John Cash; Charles Coppack; George Crosby; Donald Cowie; Philip Evans; Laurence Frost; William Hancocks; Charles Harding; Francis Hodgson; William Joseph Hughes; Lewis Reginald Hughes; Thomas Knowles; Ernest Ley; Harry Lloyd; Roland Logan; Townshend Logan; Arthur Morris; Helenus Robertson; George Simpson; John Sturman; James Cecil Williams; John Williamson.

1939 - 1945

Samuel Brough; William E Farley; Stanley Formstone; William S Green; Roy C Hitchen; John B Hughes; Thomas Pleavin; Norman Rowlands; Percy E Williams.

A very thorough account of establishing Upton's War Memorial has been retained in the Upton War Memorial Committee Minute Book archived with the CRO – it is summarised here.

Although a memorial had already been created in the Parish Church, a public meeting was held in the Schoolroom on 21st March 1919 where it was decided to erect a village memorial. Sir John Frost of Upton Lawn, who was currently the Mayor of Chester, offered to donate land opposite the Wheatsheaf. However it was felt that this was not a central site. A site near Upton Cross was later preferred and Sir Philip Egerton was approached to donate land on the corner where it now stands. Sir Philip Egerton had lost two sons in the Great War and although they were not Upton men they were added to the Upton memorial in recognition of the gift of the site. The Celtic Cross of Darley Vale stone was the original design although varieties of cenotaph, obelisk and column were all actively debated before it was adopted. Mr Tyrer of Plas Newton had offered £100 and the community raised sufficient monies to fully complete the memorial as well as establishing a trust for its upkeep and a donation to the Royal Infirmary. The original idea was for the Parish Council to be the trustees but it was then decided to sign this over to the Charities Commission.

By the late 1930s, the site was neglected and the British Legion were offered an insufficient sum to reinstate it. However, after WW2, an envelope appeal funded the refurbishment and allowed for a further stone to add the names of those who fell in this conflict. This second dedication took place in 1948 and involved the military commanders of Western Command. By 1957 the growth of the village and the resulting traffic required road improvements. Warringtons, who were developing the land behind the memorial, agreed to allocate some land so that it could be moved back to where it now stands. In 1997 the County Council carried out a major refurbishment of the memorial and site and the 1922 Trust was wound up.

Remembrance of post-WW2 military conflict

The only Upton road name commemorating a lost military life is Moorhouse Close. *'Lt. Anthony Moorhouse died heroically during operations in Suez 1956'*

Community activities and experiences during WW2

Many local people were members of one or more of the voluntary Civil Defence organisations – whether uniformed or not. Others were involved in either 'digging for victory' or 'cottage industry production' or in 'raising funds' or in 'blood donations' all for the war activities. 'The WI Book' was written shortly after the end of the war and records some of the extensive local involvement. The following pages record two of the formal group photographs with lists of names.

The ARP outside St.Mary's village school in 1940.

From left to right

Back row - J G Kirkland; F Smith; G Woodworth; A R Brockley; C L Jeffery; A H Martin; S Wilson; C Bennett; W J Scarff; R E Oney

3rd row - W Jones; W H Gregg; C H Moors; W O Hughes; W S Reynolds; S K Thompson; Capt. R L Sadler; W Hird-Jones; C Smith

2nd row - Insp. Crosby; P C Wakefield; N E Mills; S Moore; F R Derry; A Halliwell; F G Clarke; A C Phillips; J H Moss; G H Reading; A Hirst; H Griffiths, Insp Foley

Front Row - J G Williams; F W Hooper; E Bancroft; H D Bell; W Paul; A J Warner; E T Wilson; J E Owen; F Stanley; F L Odel

The work of the A.R.P. (Air-Raid Precaution) started many months before the outbreak of war. Classes were held in the village school, and many adults were instructed and trained in various branches of First Aid including methods of dealing with gas warfare. When war was declared, the Men's Institute at the village crossroads became H.Q. for a mobile First Aid unit. This was under the direction of Mr. Chew, who organised A.R.P. work for Chester and Tarvin Rural District Council and for Hoole Urban District Council.

This mobile unit consisted of a fully-equipped travelling van. About sixty men and women from the village staffed it via a rota. These consisted of nurses, ambulance men, light rescue squads, messengers and drivers, all supported by a doctor attached to the section. Whenever a call came through from the Central Control at Hoole, our mobile First Aid unit was ready to help. When the main buildings of the Barrowmore Sanatorium received a direct hit from a bomb in 1941, causing many casualties, the Upton unit was the first on the scene.

Civil Defence Personnel 1942 comprising several organisations such as the Red Cross

from l to r (no definition of abbreviations offered – since none known)

back row - Parker(FAP) Sadler(M) Swaisland(MD) Denning(FAP) Smith(FAP) Hugh Pratt(FAP)

3ʳᵈ row - Jim Harrison(FAP) Parry(MD) Harrop(FAP) Marchant(MD) Smith(FAP) Sutton(FAP) Cresswell(FAP) Leales?(FAP) Davis(FAP) Lightfoot(FAP)

2ⁿᵈ row - Chimes?(FAP) Oswald(MN) Collins(MN) Boughly?(MN) Griffiths(MN) Woodcock(AD) Dandy(AD) Bradbury(AD) Fruan?(MN) Braham?(MN) Wilson(Tele) Cassady(FAP)

front row - A.Chimes?(MN) Pearson(ML) Musgrave(AL) Rev.TOCEast(FAP) Dr.Whitlaw (i/c Mobile Unit) Samuel(GL) Pat Clay(TN) Matthews(TN) Lloyd(DL) J.Davies(DAL) Lilian Pratt(AD) EADavies(MN)

In January 1941, Mr Hugh K Frost J.P., presented a mobile canteen to the A.R.P. section. Staffed by Upton helpers, this canteen served throughout the war, including service in the Liverpool blitz. After its wartime duties, in May 1945, it was presented to the City of Chester Cadet Welfare Committee. When the war ended, the Upton A.R.P. unit was thanked by Mr. Herbert Morrison for all its valuable work.

In August 1939, a branch of the Women's Voluntary Service (W.V.S.) was formed in Upton by Mrs. Epton. Their first task was to make preparations for dealing with the evacuation of schoolchildren from Liverpool. The Golf Club House was taken over as a school. W.V.S. members made over one hundred straw palliasses, then set to work to clean and clothe the children. Homes were found for them all among the inhabitants of Upton, and some of these children became so attached to their war-time homes and foster-parents, that they remained in Upton after the war was over and a few of them became officially adopted.

Many members of the W.V.S. were also doing A.R.P. and Red Cross work. From the day the Moston Military Hospital opened, Upton W.V.S. supplied voluntary staff to assist with meals seven days per week. Some members worked in the Hospital library, and when an outbreak of 'flu' occurred, voluntary staff were supplied to help in wards and kitchens. The W.V.S. made over 160 camouflage nets in preparation for D-Day. The Village Hall was used during the day for this task – becoming a canteen and leisure centre during the evenings (see also page 116).

A Voluntary Aid Committee was also formed, composed of members of the Parish Council, the Women's Institute and the W.V.S. Every Christmas each local person serving in the Forces received a parcel of food, knitted comforts and money. The knitting party made over 5000 garments in six years for the Services and for children from occupied countries.

At the end of the war, Lady Reading wrote personally to Mrs Epton, as W.V.S. leader in Upton, to thank the group for all their war work, and to congratulate them on their wonderful effort.

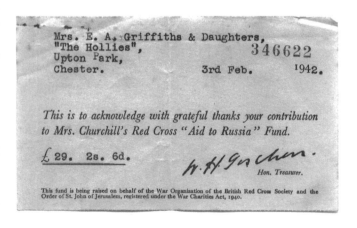

Mrs. E. A. Griffiths & Daughters,
"The Hollies",   346622
Upton Park,
Chester.   3rd Feb.   1942.

This is to acknowledge with grateful thanks your contribution to Mrs. Churchill's Red Cross "Aid to Russia" Fund.

£ 29.   2s. 6d.

Hon. Treasurer.

This fund is being raised on behalf of the War Organisation of the British Red Cross Society and the Order of St. John of Jerusalem, registered under the War Charities Act, 1940.

Mrs. Griffiths received a personally signed letter from Clementine Churchill and the receipt, shown here, for her collection effort during the war. The National Savings Group was formed in June 1940 and had collected £56,887 by its cessation in July 1946. During Victory Week in April 1943, £13,000 was raised in Upton, more than five times the target figure. Children bought Savings stamps and most of the community was involved in fund raising.

Air Raids

Air raids were expected in WW1 and by 1916 emergency measures required a significant reduction in Upton's gas lamp street lighting from nearly 40 to only 5 with reduced hours. At this time no air raids actually reached our area but by WW2 it was a different story. Many air raid shelters were built but only one – on Demage Lane – is still known to exist today.

Several bomb drops are remembered. One fell on the Golf Course by the 9th Tee and the following extract is from the resident of 114 Upton Drive writing the next day – 27 April 1941

Last night the sirens went at 10.30pm as we were returning home so we hurried back picking up a strange man to shelter in our house because the raid was so bad. We also called for the lady next door and she came in. We just had time to put up the blackout, light the fire and the next we knew the house came in. It was over before we knew what had happened and all we were thankful for was that we were all safe and sound. The four of us spent the night in the scullery with no light but the gas fire on and never did the hours seem so long. The all-clear went at 2 a.m. and we had to wait until 5 a.m. to see the damage in daylight. A quarter of an hour after the bomb dropped the warden came and told us the crater was 30 foot deep and 50 foot across and was by the fence on the golf course by the railway lines. When we did see the damage it was heartbreaking but we set to and got to work. Ours is the worst in 20 - 30 houses. We can't sleep in the house it isn't safe. We got the windows boarded up and the demolition squad put tarpolein over the roof. I'm afraid that if we get anymore gunfire the lot will come down. We did order the sweep for May 12th but we don't need him since the lot came down.

One bomb caused a breach of the canal and on another occasion a run of three bombs landed in the fields of Demage Farm. Had a fourth bomb been dropped it could have been a direct hit on a fuel reserve but in practice the three bombs only succeeded in splattering the cows in mud. Sheila Hooper recalls a direct hit on a house in the Moston area near the Moston Garage.

Village Hall use during WW2

With so many billeted soldiers in the area, the Village Hall served to provide some of their evening entertainment. Dances were held and many soldiers attended including Americans and other nationalities. During the day, the hall was used to make camouflage nets and it is understood that considerable local voluntary effort was employed. During autumn, local people had the opportunity to bring in their local stewed fruit for the canning facility that was on offer. There were a fair number of fruit trees in the area and this facility was heavily used at 1p a can.

Elephants displaced by the war given zoo sanctuary

At the outbreak of WW2, two Asian cow elephants, Molly and Manniken, were part of Dourley's Tropical Express Revue - a German-Argentinian concern - travelling around Europe. The elephants became stranded in Northampton and were offered to the Government for work in the forests. The Forestry Commission's rules made no provision for the employment of elephants and their plight came to the attention of Ralph Marshall, a theatrical agent. George Mottershead agreed to them joining his zoo and they were transported to Chester by train. Locals recall them being walked through Upton to the zoo accompanied by their Singhalese mahout, Khanadas Karunadasa. Sadly, Manniken was in poor condition and died shortly after her arrival. Post-war, anti-tank

blocks and pill boxes were used to construct a new elephant house and many locals recall their childhood rides on Molly (see page 273).

The aftermath

Rationing continued into the 1950s. A ration book – deposited with the Local History Group – records that T C Garner was entitled to a special cheese ration.

In 1951, a party of German visitors was present at an Upton Parish Council general meeting to study our local Government *'in action'*.

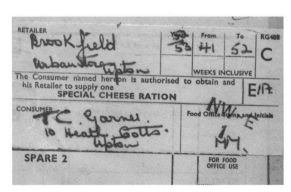

CHAPTER 9

Developments 1945 - 2005

In line with much of Britain, this period saw dramatic growth in house building. The demand overcame difficulties with ground conditions - ponds were filled, undulations levelled and streams drained into underground culverts. Most of the former agricultural and nursery land within the ring road became available for house building. Today, we have reached the point where Upton is now part of Chester's suburbia and there is little available ground remaining for residential development.

Several new housing estates, cutting into former fields, were underway when the war effort suspended housing development. In the immediate post-war years rationing and building licences restricted the continuation of developments such that only modest size houses were initially allowed. By the late 1940s the maximum floor size was increased and other restrictions relaxed. By the 1950s development was well underway. The war and food rationing had taken some land back into agricultural use but other areas lay waste with no take-up since the demise of Dicksons nursery. Much of the land was still in the beneficial ownership of the Lord of the Manor – Sir Philip Grey Egerton – at the time of his death in 1937. His Upton land had been heavily mortgaged and the aftermath of handling his estate started the mass sale of Upton land to building developers – with some conveyances completed during wartime. Arthur Hinde was farming in the Dale area. Lloyd-Jones still occupied Newton Cottage on

Plas Newton Lane (shown here), and farmed the land spreading over the Style (or Stile) fields towards the Village Hall. Frank Hinde was farming just north of Lloyd-Jones. The latter two saw fit to sell up from farming in the 1950s - the large estates were underway.

The first few years after the war

The late 1940s were years of 'getting back to normal' during 'ration conditions' before modern developments got underway in the 1950s. Some building did soon restart. One such case was to extend the cul-de-sac of Woodlea Avenue, named by the builder's wife, Mrs Morgan, due to the small run of woodland as shown on the 1936 O.S. map. Similarly Capstick & Owen continued with Upton Drive. A few one-off properties were built such as one in Upton Park built by Frederick Oldham – very much limited in size due to the post-war restrictions.

One minor new building, remembered nostalgically by some, was a shippon built on Ben Roberts' smallholding on the site of the former tennis court and pavilion, where the teen shelter now stands on Wealstone Lane playing fields. This was built immediately post-war with the help of local children who shifted the bricks and were then rewarded with pony rides.

Other haunts for children were the various derelict sites. The former Dickson's home of Stanton House had been owned, since the 1920s, by the Rev. Algernon Ernest Grimes – a former Head of the Kings School - and used as a small private prep school until the mid-1930s. By the late 1940s it was derelict with cellars that offered a play area for the children.

The post-war new thinking started with a Council decision to finally convert all the gas street lights to electric (most recent lamps on the new roads were already electric). Councillor Furley (see page 163) convinced the Council to use 100 watt lamps rather than the lower power initially proposed.

The 1936 Ordnance Survey shows allotment gardens behind the Men's Institute. These were privately owned and by the end of the War are understood to have become overgrown resembling an orchard. The Horticultural Society supplied names of residents requiring allotments and one proposal was for the letting of the old orchard at Upton Heyes. However it appears that Upton never acquired Council allotments and the few private ones were absorbed for housing development. The private allotments, mentioned above, became Endsleigh Close in the 1990s.

In 1948 a talk was given on 'The Welfare & Social Facilities for Old People' but not until 1953 was a committee set up to organise 'The Upton Old Friends Association', able to look after the welfare of the elderly. What became of this Association is not known but it may have been influential in the fact that the RDC built housing suitable for the elderly in the early 1960s.

As the population grew and land was being developed for housing, concern was expressed for more recreation areas and the Cheshire County Playing Fields Association was viewing possible sites in Upton. The Parish Council was still struggling to find a suitable building for a library. They had been offered a former wartime military hut but declined. Some of these were however being used for other leisure activities such as the scouts & guides.

Meanwhile many of Upton's residents still looked out on rural scenes – with cattle in the fields and agricultural events such as the annual gymkana for the Upton & District farmers.

UPTON AND DISTRICT FARMERS'
Agricultural Show & Gymkhana

.•. FIRST PRIZE .•.

Whit-Monday, May 17th, 1948

Awarded to .... No. ....

Judges ....

Shire horse 'Dawpool Trooper' with Charlie Howell of Dawpool Farm Thurstaston.

Post-war creeping ribbon developments and strategic planning

Fred Owen had been selling plots around the former Upton Lawn estate. The village folklore tells of the cash offers being £500 a plot and £750 if bordering the golf course. The houses along the west side of Heath Road were completed around 1949, preserving many of the Upton Lawn boundary trees, although some had to be felled. With Deeside Sawmills relocating to Mickle Trafford (see page 162) the rubbish tip on the Heath Road / Upton Lane junction opposite the Wheatsheaf was filled in; allowing property development bordering onto the golf course to continue round into Upton Lane.

Much of this early post-war housing development was on a small scale, building on individual plots and gradually extending recent pre-war roads. The post-war period, however, was a time for Cheshire County Council to look strategically at developments. This 1945 proposal shows the shaded possible development areas as well as the hatched existing or committed developments . It seems to have responded to traffic concerns in the Long Lane / Caughall Road area, pushing the greenbelt further out to the north-east. Interestingly, the Plas Newton estate provided a green belt wedge between Upton and Newton. By the early 1960s this idea had been dropped.

A 1945 Cheshire County proposal

1951 saw the Festival of Britain celebrations (see page 182) and a spirit of optimism for the future. Flowering trees were donated by various village organisations and planted on the grass verge between Upton Cross and the Village Hall. Flower beds were planted on vacant spaces on Long Lane corner.

The new school – initially known as Upton County Primary - was built in 1951 to a modern style and using redundant wartime materials such as aluminium which converted from aircraft bodies to windows. As well as catering for the increasing number of children, demand was growing for the new school to offer a range of evening classes.

Upton County Primary School during its 1951 construction –
see also page 242

Much of the expansion in housing was either in extending or completing the small estates that were started pre-war, or in ribbon development along the established roads. The bungalows, built by Warringtons in the mid-1950s, on the east side of Heath Road, were set well back due to proposals to make the road into a major through route – possibly even dual carriageway. This also explains the well set-back Wealstone Lane properties, built early 1960s, since this road was also part of main through route proposals. These Heath Road and Wealstone Lane properties enjoyed a few years of looking out, over their back gardens, at corn fields from which foxes would be disturbed at harvest time. The Wealstone Lane properties, from Upton Cross to approaching Weston Grove, had very high Witch Elm trees that were lost c1980 to Dutch Elm decease.

October 1963 – *aerial photograph with acknowledgement to the former 'Krissair of Leeds'*

Council housing & sheltered accommodation development

Upton's first council housing development started just pre-war in the Acres Lane area of Upton Heath. Immediate post-war RAF survey photography shows the Caughall Rd houses between Acres Lane and Greenfields as well as the Acres Lane crescent. Greenfields however was only marked out roads. The crescent on Acres Lane – now a filled-in 'green' – was a deep sandpit used by local children for play and the annual bonfire. Chester Rural District Council (CRDC) had acquired this land pre-war from the Egerton estate and by 1949 they had built Greenfields and improved access by widening the roads. Greenfields was able to house those families temporarily using the war-time huts near Weston Grove.

The Council's next area of development was the land generally defined by the boundaries of Marina Drive, Newhall Road and Plas Newton. The boundary between the CRDC and Chester City ran through this – broadly Cornwall Road and north of it being CRDC and to the south Chester City. The CRDC side was refered to as their 'Upton Estate' and on completion amounted to some 100-150 properties. The City side was refered to as their 'Plas Newton Estate'. Aldford Road crosses this boundary and the change in housing style can be detected.

For the 'Plas Newton' estate, work started around 1959 with Bolesworth Road, Dunham Way and Chirk Close. Newhall Road followed with some 2-storey blocks of flats and garage blocks. The full Plas Newton estate was planned to comprise 160 dwellings of various types with 100 garages. By 1965 there were ten roads – besides those mentioned above, this gave – Peckforton, part of Aldford, Shipbrook, and Shocklash. Handford Road has a large 3-storey block of flats shown here shortly after being built.

Newhall and Bolesworth are on the right of the picture. Clearly the naming convention was after local villages. Newhall Road was initially a cul-de-sac off Plas Newton Lane and the buses were provided with a shale turning area at its cul-de-sac end.

The early 1960s 'Upton estate' built by the CRDC was of a slightly smaller size. Building began at the southern end of the private housing which had started pre-war. By the late-1950s, Weston Grove was complete – having initially stopped at the southern boundary hedge just past the 1954 short stub cul-de-sac of Cornwall Road. Woodlea Avenue was

similarly extended south and at the southerly end the houses were allocated for Deva hospital staff (shown here as new builds c1964). Cornwall Road with Dorset Road and the rest of Aldford Road were all completed in the early 1960s.

To the north-west of Weston Grove the early 1960s CRDC estate encompassed Dukesway, Queens Crescent and Marl Heys – the latter for elderly citizens. To the north of Marl Heys is a land locked area of approximately 1 acre which was transferred from the CRDC to the Upton Parish Council in 1968. The area still maintained by the Parish Council is simply grassed over and with pedestrian access from Marl Heys.

Newhall Road generally followed the route of the old 'stile path'. The route of this footpath from the Village Hall to Weston Grove can be seen on the 1963 aerial photograph (pages 122/123). This aerial photograph clearly shows the extent of the development at this time. The Dukesway & Queens Crescent area is understood to have been started by Rody's in the mid-1950s but continued by Halliwells. The photograph shows that by 1963, Warringtons had extended and developed the once cul-de-sac Weston Grove. Although the Westlea school had been built, the Cornwall Road /Aldford Road estate was still fields. It is understood that Shones of Buckley developed this area shortly after the aerial photograph.

Following the 1974 reorganisation of local government, these estates passed to the City Council and then after the 1980s 'Right to Buy' Act several properties passed into private ownership. On 27th November 2000 the Chester & District Housing Trust – a not-for-profit company – took over the Council's stock of property which by this time had reduced to about 50%, although a lower proportion of the houses and a higher proportion of the flats. The Deva hospital had built some 10 houses for staff on the north side of Deva Lane and these passed to the Council following a policy change. David Rooke of the Housing Trust has provided much of this information on their current and former properties.

In the mid1960s the City Council built 'Weal Stone' providing simple sheltered accommodation of a bedsit with bed, chair and wardrobe. In 1975 Appleton House, accessed from Appleton Road, opened as a new Children's Assessment Centre. This provided education as well as '30-bed' accommodation. By the mid-1980s it had become a Local Children's Centre eventually closing as child care policy changed. By the 1990s both properties were demolished and Bellways built Arradon Court and Bretton Close – named in accord with Upton's new French twinning. The field at the back of, and attached to, Appleton House had become known as the 'Donkey field'. The Council retained this piece of 'land locked' ground and it has become a small public area and fenced-off wild park area.

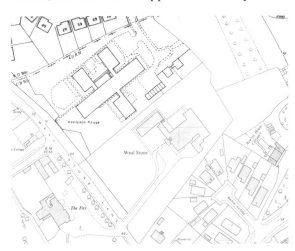

This marked up map, preceding the later Arradon Court/ Bretton Close area, shows Appleton House and Weal Stone to the east of lower Wealstone Lane. Base map – 1967 Ordnance Survey – Reproduced by kind permission of Ordnance Survey. © Crown Copyright NC/04/100035349. Marked up to show Appleton House by Chester City Council

Cheshire County Council were running the former Newton House as a care home for the elderly but by the late 1980s closed and marketed it in the belief that it had outlived its purpose. It was acquired by Chester City Council who after consideration of refurbishment decided to demolish it for purpose-built sheltered accommodation with a live-in warden. As part of the former Newton House estate, Tiverton Close was developed at around the same time, 1992, as sheltered accommodation under the wing of Newton House. Around 1972 the CRDC built Arderne House (Arderne is a famous mid-Cheshire family name). This provided 22 bedsit flats with a warden's accommodation and a communal lounge. After the 1974 reorganisation of local government this passed to Cheshire Council and subsequently to CLS – County Lifestyle Services – a not-for-profit company. Weal Stone House (previously Dorin Court) was built on the site of Government House (see page 68) and is also now with CLS. At the same time the Council acquired some of the former MOD land behind Government House and decided to build Deans Close (named after the Dean family of Upton Mill) as Council property. In 1981 they built eight flats with the four ground floor flats intended for those unable to climb stairs. Most of the flats are now under the control of the Housing Trust as sheltered accommodation with warden visits.

The 'back-of-school' Sand Pit

The brickyard behind St.Mary's school had closed before the 20th century. Folklore tells of the discovery of good sand when dogs were seen digging out the rabbits. By the 1930s it had become a working sandpit and in the 1950s Warringtons had an extraction contract with the owners, Capt. & Miss Gardner. As a good red sand, suitable for bricklaying and plastering, it supplied Warringtons for much of their operations. There were three levels – the lorries would park at one level and the sand manually shovelled in from the level above. Apparently no mechanised shovelling was used. Locals recall the Sand Martins in great abundance. In filling was started around 1957, apparently using blast furnace dross from Shotton Steel Works. This process lasted for about a year. By the October 1963 aerial photograph (page 122), not only had the pit gone but other ground had been levelled off ready to build the Warrington estate and extend Marina Drive.

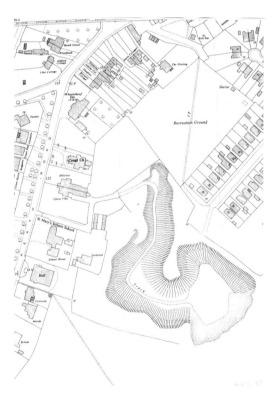

Reproduced from the 1956 map
by kind permission of Ordnance Survey
© Crown Copyright NC/04/100035349

Warrington's Upton Cross estate

The October 1963 aerial photograph (pages 122/123) shows the extent of the land, to the west of Weston Grove, acquired by Thomas Warrington & Sons of Ellesmere Port from the Egerton estate. In the immediate post-war years, Warringtons had many Council contracts around the Chester area but did not start building in Upton until the mid-1950s. After early 1960s planning consent they started the private developments on both sides of Weston Grove which now linked to Wealstone Lane.

Development on the Cross Green side started first with some properties occupied in the early years of the 1960s. The shops were built on Weston Grove which meant the loss of a familiar sight of a Romany caravan parked there. The first shops are remembered as –

Yorks Self-Service, Ashe & nephew, Nicholsons – Butchers, Chemist, Lloyds

Bank (opened Apr 65) Ladies Hairdresser - Raymond & Jason (opened Sept 65) and later Newsagents – Lewis

As seen in the aerial photograph both the Westlea school (see chapter 16) and the Clinic – shown here - were built by the mid-1960s.

Newton's northern estate

This area – formerly Dicksons Nursery – was initially named the Upton Park Estate when development started in the early 1950s. This site entrance was off Dicksons Drive, near the footbridge, looking towards Park Drive. The site plan reveals the extent of this first development even though the detail cannot be read.

Before the builders, Spinks & Denning, started on this estate in the early 1950s, the Newton housing on Dicksons Drive ended at the footbridge. Shepherds Lane was a short cul-de-sac accessed from Dicksons Drive. By the mid-1950s Park Drive was complete and renamed Rosewood Avenue. Thornton Drive was a track providing the boundary of the development. Whitby and Pensby Avenues were complete. Kirby Close and Ellesmere Avenue were nearing completion. The northern end of Dicksons Drive had also been completed with Caldy and Bidston Closes.

Well Lane gave access to Rose (later Dawpool) Cottage. As shown, in this winter scene, the footpath then circled the cottage and continued west to Dicksons Drive.

By the early 1960s, Spinks & Denning had completed Thornton Drive and Neston Drive along with Neston's cul-de-sacs – Gayton, Denhall and Moorhouse. Finally, Shepherds Lane was linked to Well Lane with Dawpool and the Menhuin building.

All this land was previously the showgrounds and greenhouses of Dicksons Nursery – see pages 152/154. The name change of Park Drive to Rosewood Avenue appears to remember the nursery but most of the other names have drawn on Wirral villages. This nursery land was well served with streams and springs - all needed to be diverted and controlled before the whole area became a building estate.

The two photographs show some culvert work taking place in the early 1950s. Residents recall a major collapse in the 1960s which resulted in Neston Drive being closed for several months.

The railway line is seen in the background with the Garth Drive area behind.

The last Dicksons Nursery feature, from their spectacular landscaping (see page 152), was the famous 'Marble Arch'. It had been reduced from its 12 foot height during war-time, down to being suitable as a seat. No doubt much of the marble was dispersed to the private gardens gradually being created in the area. The photograph, from the early 1950s, shows Olive and Jennifer Fox sitting on the remains of the arch. Francis Fox is responsible for most of the post-war period photographs of this area.

Train derailment of the early 1950s in northwest Newton area

A significant goods train derailment in the early 1950s was a major talking point at the time and is still well remembered.

The resulting fire drew the attention of the local children. This photograph shows the housing spreading up towards Upton from Newton. The lamppost is on the lane linking Stanton Drive with Dicksons Drive. The derailment is believed to have occured near the end of Caldy Close.

Appleton Road development

These fields on Upton's southern boundary, were previously farmed out of Newton but by the late 1800s had become part of Dicksons Nursery. Post-WW2, they were scrubland until taken up for development in the late 1960s. Development was started by Truebond with the first Appleton Road occupants moving in by the end of the decade. The rest were completed in the early 1970s.

Daleside/Sandpit/Lawn/Grange

This late-1940s RAF aerial survey shows the extent of the development.

Apparently the Potts estate still owned the sandpit and some surrounding area including at least some, of the Dale Cottages. Daleside was built in 1953/4 by George Morgan on farmland for Viggor Estates Ltd. He also built in the lower area of the pit but building initially kept away from the sandpit cliff edges. Later the pit was filled in and eventually building allowed so that by 1963 the area had been totally built over with St. Christophers Close. The lower grounds of the Grange estate were first built over in the mid-1960s starting along Church Lane and forming Grangeside. The main house and out-buildings were demolished in the late 1960s and Nield Court built - named after the Grange's last private owner Sir Basil Nield MP (see page 66).

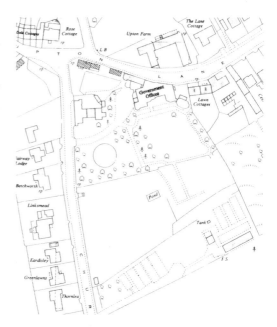

133

Upton Lawn was demolished c1970 by John Youdale; initially retaining the old snooker room used by gardener and ex-Everton player's wife, Audrey Heywood. The Coachman's House, shown here shortly before its demolition c1986, was by then in a derelict state. Its last role was as a store for an antique dealer.

Lawn Drive, Grangeside and Nield Court were developed by a number of different builders as plots were acquired – Youdale, Halliwell, Marshal Hudson, Wibly, Stewart Lee – to name but a few.

Windmill Rise, a small cul-de-sac off Heath Road, was built between 1962/4 by builders Norman Taylor & Sydney Addis on land purchased from Rev. Leslie Francis Harvey, who owned the Upton Cross estate at that time. The entrance can be seen on the 1963 aerial photograph – page 122.

Flag Lane South developments

John Youdale demolished Upton Manor in 1974 – the building having previously been set on fire. Developing the area attracted souvenir hunters from a wide area; quickly digging before the site was built over. Wheldon Close was built 1975/6 and named after the Rev. Wheldon Williams (see page 258). The Manor House (see page 39) had stood at the centre of the Close hammer head.

The Baptist church was built in the 1980s and the Smithy Court development followed after the blacksmith's had closed and been demolished.

The Plas Newton area (see also page 75)

This RAF aerial survey from 1945/8 shows that this area was farmed and apparently stayed that way, with cattle in the fields until Lloyd Jones abandoned farming around 1960. After completion of the Council estates (see page 125), further housing was built from the mid-1960s. By 1969, Boot the builders had completed St. James Avenue, circling Plas Newton. Arley Close was built by Percy Eden who had completed Tintern Avenue earlier in the 1960s.

The field to the west of Long Lane, opposite Plas Newton Lane, had become the Brookhirst Athletic Ground. The former Brookhirst Switchgear Company of Newry Park employed many people who lived in the Upton area. The 'County Officers Club' was built off Plas Newton Lane and now incorporates these sports fields, all under the name of the Cheshire County Sports Club.

The Beeches

The Shell company acquired the remaining Plas Newton estate (see page 75) including the main property and built accommodation along the drive for staff attending courses. By the early 1980s, they sold out to developer Christian Salvesen and builder Wainhomes began construction of The Beeches. Recently, the main house has been demolished and Bellways have built a block of apartments – The Court Yard.

The growth of community facilities in the 1960s & 1970s

The major growth in housing was accompanied by a range of new community facilities. More schools were built – see chapter 16 – and by the mid-1970s, the new High School meant that local children no longer had to be bussed out of the area.

By the mid-1960s, Wealstone Lane playing field was established. The football pitch was followed with a pavilion and then putting, bowls and the play equipment. Finally a new tennis court was built; the former pre-war one having been located where the teen shelter now stands. A new purpose built library was erected in 1969 on land adjacent to the playing fields. With a car park, this Wealstone Lane public facility became the main location for outdoor events – see chapter 13. Land acquired for Mill View school in the late 1960s, also allowed a Youth Club to be built – further adding to the community facilities of this area.

The Roman Catholic church acquired some land on Upton's southern boundary and resolving the necessary drainage issues, were able, by the mid-1960s, to build a modern style church - St.Columba's. Until it opened, the Village Hall had been used for their services – see chapter 12.

The Firs development on Wealstone Lane

The Firs estate is covered on page 72. As discussed on page 106, the estate had been acquired by the War Department and a large number of wooden barracks erected during WW2. Post-war the army built married quarters on Horrocks Road – named after the last General, the Commander-in-Chief. By the 1950s, the army appear to have abandoned the main Firs building and it stood empty, becoming derelict, until c1980 when it was demolished. Cllr Eric Gerrard had attempted to save it – suggesting that the Conservative Association acquire and restore it for their use. The site was developed in the early 1980s by Christian Salvesen. The planners, apparently, insisted on retention of the sandstone wall, wherever possible, along the frontage. One of the new roads is named Whitton Drive. This suggests that it may have been named after Delores Whitton, although this has not been confirmed. She was not Mayor of Chester until 1986/7 and did not represent an Upton or Newton ward.

Moston area

The Oakfield estate (page 69), established by Roberts, had included much of Moston. The area between Daleside and the Moston garage traffic lights, had passed to the Rev. Stephen Williams and was later acquired, in part, by Dandy for his nursery (see page 283). The field to the south of the nursery, known as *'Big Moston'* was acquired by Thomas Hibbert with an early 1900s building which was developed, becoming Hillcrest. This is best remembered as Brickland's pig farm. It was demolished in the 1970s.

Brickland's pig farm shortly before its demolition.
Acknowledgement to the unidentified aerial photographer.

The County Council Highways depot on Liverpool Road, opposite the Dale camp, had been used to dump wartime concrete debris and other material. No longer required by the 1990s, it was considered unsuitable for housing development and in 1997 it was decided to make a wildlife area of the available half acre. With volunteer help it became the first *'access for all nature reserve'* managed by the *'Cheshire Wildlife Trust'*. In 1998 a hedgerow was planted and a pond created. With its raised beds, access to all is much improved and further developments are in hand.

The Bache Supermarket

The area's most ancient site – the Bache Pool (see page 17) – remained generally undeveloped until the mid-1980s. Dicksons Nursery had acquired the land, cultivating up to the marshy pool edges. By the early 1900s, railway sidings had been built and various temporary buildings were gradually added – see page 143. In the mid-1980s, Safeway acquired the railway sidings area and built their initial supermarket which overlooked the scrubland and horse grazing field of Mr Godwin (see page 7).

The entrance to the former smaller Safeway store can just be seen in the far right of the picture and the Bache shops in the background. In the late-1990s, the supermarket was extended after acquiring Nixon's field and carrying out archaeological digs within the former Pool area – see page 25. The raised bowling green (see page 196) behind the Egerton Arms was removed in the 1990s and an hotel built.

With the new Bache roundabout (see page 9 colour photo), and Countess Way removing one of the last wild play areas for local children, the Bache area was dramatically changed during the last decade of the 20th century. Developments required extensive underground construction of water courses.

In-filling

Several small cul-de-sacs have been added as the housing demand has sought out any available land. Names are needed for these and occasionally the Council forget the origin of neighbouring road names. Hence the small cul-de-sac off Marina Drive (named after Princess Marina – icon of the age); has been named Harbour Close. Alas no mooring berths are available!

Finally two recent News items whose legacy lives on

A potentially very serious accident occurred in April 2001 when a double decker bus, carrying children to Upton High school, attempted to pass under the railway bridge on Mill Lane. The roof was torn off and the children suffered shock, bruising and whiplash. The 'Low Bridge' warning signs remain to this day.

A 2000 'Keep Upton Green' campaign was formed to fight proposals to develop part of 'Chemistry Pits' playing field (see page 95). Those supporting the development argued that developing a quarter of the site, for a sheltered accommodation scheme by the charity Scope, would fund improvements to the whole site and help supervise the vandalism problems. Those opposing the proposals, argued that this was a dangerous precedent as there was a shortage of open public land and the Council had an obligation to find the necessary funding for required improvements. The proposal was dropped and many site improvements made – the latest of which has involved local school children helping to plant a wild wooded area.

CHAPTER 10
Traffic

Growth of the traffic network – principally road and rail – not only provided easier access between the main centres of population but also put Upton within easier reach and as traffic grew placed a greater strain on our village lanes. Greater accessibility increased the desire to live here while working elsewhere. Although few in number, Upton businesses were able to trade more easily and further afield. The increase in traffic had a big impact on the rural village with speeding vehicles and dust creation on narrow, winding, unmetalled, country lanes. Amongst the changes would have been the arrival of newspapers on the day of publication and a daily mail collection and delivery service. The year 1851 saw the laying of a telegraph line alongside the railway, not just for railway use. It is not known if and when any Upton residents made use of this service. After 1939, the local halt at Upton, no doubt, encouraged the speculative building of houses for commuters.

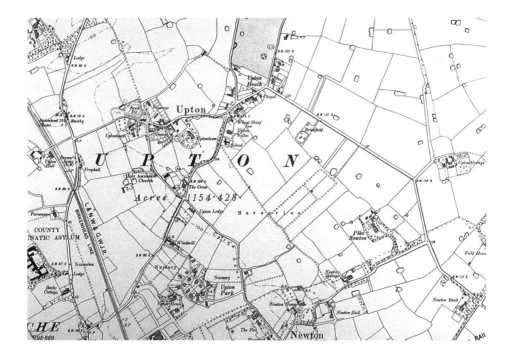

This map, reproduced from the 1898 Ordnance Survey Map, shows how the railway cut through the drive to Upton Hall but skirted Bache pool. The roads within Upton were merely narrow lanes and with no Moston Road the village suffered with much through road traffic.

The Main Road network

The Chester – Birkenhead road (Liverpool Road) through the Bache was turnpiked in 1787, with a tollhouse near its later junction with the present A41 at Moston and possibly another at the Bache. Prior to 1787 most of the goods would have been carried by packhorses and although the number of wagons increased, they generally averaged no more than 2.5 m.p.h. The stretch of Liverpool Road from the Bache to the Frog public house was made into a dual carriageway in 1968, with land being taken from the hospital side for the widening. Further north the line of the road seems to have been governed by the existing buildings, although some of the site of the former Brewers Arms now appears to be under the southbound carriageway, in front of The Frog public house.

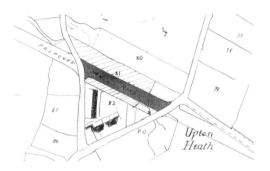

Upton's missing road link – from Long Lane to Moston – was proposed in the late 1920s. Shown here is the length from Caughall Road to Flag Lane and although the Institute is not shown on this sketch it was the reason for diverting the end of Long Lane and consequently creating the wide road at that point. It was constructed between 1931 and 1933. Prior to that, traffic coming along Long Lane would have had to turn into Heath Road and use Upton Lane to get to Liverpool Road and then continue onto Birkenhead. It was planned to make Wealstone Lane, formerly called Upton Lane, into a wide distributor road, generally of the same width as at its junction with Plas Newton Lane. This plan was dropped in the late 1970s. Plas Newton Lane, once winding around Newton Hall, was straightened and widened post-WW2. Numerous junctions have been widened – at Upton Cross this required moving the war memorial back in the late 1950s having previously taken 20feet from Upton Lodge, courtesy of the War Office. Probably the latest major roadworks was in 1992 for Countess Way which required major landraising and loss of a popular 'wild play' venue for local children.

Following WW1, traffic around and through Upton increased dramatically. Lorries returning from the war were adopted by various carriers mixing with traditional horse and cart. The more affluent moving into the area had their cars and this mix led to many accidents on Upton's narrow lanes and blind junctions. The local Council was frequently discussing the problems and acquiring land to widen roads and junctions. Traffic surveys conducted on the Chester – Birkenhead traffic passing through the Bache showed increases from around 3,500 vehicles per day in 1922 to over 8,000 by 1928 despite the improvements to roads around Queensferry meaning travellers to Wales did not have to come through Chester. After the Moston Road opened, the increased traffic caused such concern that by 1939 the Upton Ratepayers Association was calling for a bypass and this was incorporated in post-war plans (see page 120). The A41 dual carriageway near

Duttons Lane and the wider road north of Moston were seemingly part of plans to bypass up around the Zoo. See the 1945 Cheshire County proposal (page 120). In 1970 when planning the M53, proposals were made to terminate the motorway at the Duttons Lane/Long Lane junction, rather than off the Hoole roundabout. Well before all this, a proposal was made in the 1920s for a toll motorway between Birmingham and the Mersey running through Picton Gorse.

From Stage Coach to the Crosville Bus Service

It appears that in 1762 there were three stagecoach services per week, on alternate days, between Chester and Woodside, connecting with the ferry to Liverpool. It is thought that these services may have used the Liverpool Road route. By 1837 it was claimed by the promoters of the railway, that there were 22 coaches per day between Chester and Birkenhead, carrying an estimated 2,715 passengers per week. In addition a further 799 passengers made the journey in other 'cars'. In a last stand against the railway, 1840 saw a race between coach and train running from Tranmere to Chester. Despite being given a one-hour start, the coach lost.

From 1911 the Crossville Motor Company started routes running north from Chester passing through the Bache. The high cost annoyed local people but Crosville claimed they were taking seats from longer distance travellers leaving Chester. Direct services to Upton commenced in 1921 and by the late 1920s were running special late night services (2.00a.m.) to assist with Village Hall functions.

In the early 1990s the Park and Ride site was opened at the Zoo. Buses avoided the centre of Upton by travelling via Liverpool Road. An earlier plan for this scheme evisaged a tram service along Longlane to the disused Mickle Trafford railway line and then into the City.

Canals

The Wirral Line of the Shropshire Union Canal around Upton was originally part of a scheme to link the rivers Severn and Mersey, crossing the River Dee close to Crane Wharf. The section around Upton was begun in November 1793 and was in use by July 1795. Passenger and goods carrying on this part of the canal flourished. By 1810 'Express fly' passenger boats could carry up to 200 passengers, who could purchase, tea, coffee and refreshments on board. Tipping was forbidden.

Smaller vessels ran pleasure cruises along the canal for the same fares. Passenger services ended about the time of the opening of the railway. The cargo trade was however still buoyant with over 60,000 tons of iron alone being carried in 1838 before seeing a steady decline. By the mid 1930s it was much reduced and barges could not carry a full cargo due to the lack of dredging and maintenance.

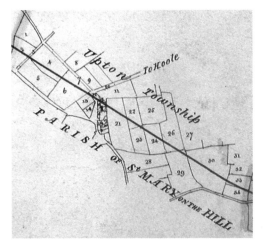

The canals as built, did not have a big impact on Upton but other proposals if adopted would have transformed it. The 1833 proposal shown here would have run through Upton Heath – through our current traffic light cross roads – on through the post-war Warrington's housing developments. Shortly before this in 1824 a proposal was submitted for a large ship canal linking the Dee with the Manchester, skirting north of the zoo. Finally as late as 1907 the Waverton Stoak Canal was proposed crossing the east of the parish. Today our only canal circling west and north offers a leisure route for boat, cycle and pedestrian.

Railways

The Chester & Birkenhead Railway Company was incorporated in 1837, with work commencing in May 1838. The Southern Section, from Moston to Chester, measured 5 miles 37 chains and the terrain made the works relatively simple. The major local task was the construction of the viaduct over the canal, at Moston. As the pace of work increased so did the workforce, which would have had to be accommodated locally. By April 1839, 447 men and 32 horses were employed on the Southern Section, increasing to 900 men and 40 horses by October. The final cost of the railway was over twice the original estimate.

For the construction of the line, Mill Lane had to be excavated a further two feet to allow vehicles to pass beneath the railway, whilst the "Turnpike" (Liverpool Road) had to be raised by 18 feet to pass over the track. Culverts were also required for Flookers Brook and the brook that flowed roughly along the line of Neston Drive and Ellesmere Avenue.

The Official Opening of the line was on 23rd September 1840 and saw the locomotive 'The Wirral' make the 50-minute journey to a temporary station in Brook Street, Chester. Initially the line was single track, but by 1847 much of the route had been doubled. Such was the growth in traffic that by 1902 four tracks were required, but the cost of duplicating the Moston Viaduct was too great so widening works ended at Ledsham. If laid, the extra tracks would have been to the west of the existing line, taking the land now occupied by the houses on the eastern side of Upton Drive as well as part of the site now occupied by the supermarket.

Only basic facilities were provided at intermediate stations. Amongst these was a cottage at the station, in Station Road, Mollington, which served Upton for many years. Upton obtained its own station when a halt was opened on 17th July 1939.

Upton Halt shown here c1970 was immediately to the south of the bridge where Liverpool Road passes over the line. Mrs. Bowker is remembered as the ticket collector for many years. The site was cramped and on the 9th January 1984 the new station at the Bache replaced it. The land used by the new station, and the adjoining supermarket, had previously been the local goods yard.

By 1885 about 22 passenger trains, ran from Chester to Birkenhead each day. There were many more goods trains than passenger trains. By 1890 about 27, coal trains, consisting of 20-25 eight-ton wagons, passed through Upton, each day. Other goods trains would be carrying manufactured goods, fertiliser, grain, flour and iron ore, from Birkenhead, with building materials and manufactured goods going the other way. Perhaps 190 trains a day passed through at this time. In the 1890s much of the GWR coal traffic was lost to coastal ships, which made the carriage of more parochial goods of greater significance and led to the opening of a small goods yard, at the Bache, on the 17th July 1911. The yard remained open for general goods until 2nd June 1969, and as a coal yard until 14th May 1972. As well as domestic coal, the goods yard would have imported building materials and exported farm and nursery produce. For a while, it appears the mail train also stopped here.

The entrance to the goods yard, off Mill Lane – photo early 1960s

A Chester bound steam train approaching Upton Halt about 1950

In the 19th Century there were several proposals for railways through Upton. These included - the Birmingham / Mersey Railway – proposed in 1824; the Chester Junction Railway - proposed in 1836 and the Birkenhead / Lancashire and Chester Junction Railway – proposed in 1844.

Running north to south these routes would have run where we now know as -

1824

Park & Ride Car Park;
Demage Lane;
East of Upton Lawns;
Gatesheath Drive;
Junction of Weston Grove with Wealstone Lane;
Mill View School;
City Branch (west of the Firs School);
Birmingham Branch (through Kingsway High School).

1836

St Christopher's Close;
Across the golf course;
Mill Lane/Delvine Drive junction;
Bache Drive;
The Wiend.

1844

Park & Ride Car Park;
NorthWest of Daleside;
Then 1836 route to join existing line close to The Wiend.

In the 1920s or 1930s, there may also have been a proposal to construct a commuter railway from the bridge over Mill Lane, towards the centre of the village. The route appears to have been along the northern edge of Mill Lane then to the rear of the houses. The length of the track is not known but it appears that the owner of the Cockpit refused to sell, causing the plan not to proceed.

Air

For the last few decades Upton has benefited from the proximity of two regional airports – Manchester Ringway and Liverpool Speke – both of which have developed in stages from the 1930s. However in the late 1920s, proposals were considered that could have made Upton to Chester like Speke, today, is to Liverpool.

The Chester Municipal Aeropark – on a 271 acre site bordered by Duttons Lane, Acres Lane, Caughall Road and Long Lane - was proposed 1929-31. Amongst the reasons put forward by Councillors for rejecting the plan were, that *'the imminent achievement of world peace would release RAF Sealand for civil use and that flying would never prove economic'*. Supporters of the aeropark still wanted the site acquired, just in case, claiming that if the proposal did not ultimately go ahead the land could be sold at a profit, particularly when the ring road was completed. Alternatively it could even have been used as a site for a Municipal Mental Hospital. Another major concern of the Council was the location of the water tower, then being planned. Chester Waterworks Company indicated that they would be willing to change the site of the tower to the junction of Duttons Lane and Long Lane if required.

Even though the aeropark was not built, air displays took place on the site in 1931 and 1933 featuring the Sir Alan Cobham Flying Circus. Amongst the various type of aircraft displayed were autogiros, a predecessor of the helicopter (shown here).

There were other notable aviation events in this period including a visit by the ill fated airship R101, which flew over Chester at 11.45am on 19th November 1929. It approached the city at about 1200 feet flying along Parkgate Road and in July 1932 the German airship Graff Zeppelin flew towards the city along Liverpool Road.

Much of the research for this chapter has been undertaken by Tony Barratt.

CHAPTER 11
Business & Employment

Today very few of Upton's residents have employment within the parish boundary; those who do are most likely to be 'working from home office' or in small local service supply. Upton has never had any large industrial employers but two of its sources of employment have been with us for a good while - the zoo and the hospital – although formerly as an asylum it existed quite isolated from Upton. The history of these two establishments is well covered in other publications but are summarised here for the completeness of Upton's history. The other large concern was Dicksons nursery which ceased in the early 1930s. All other businesses have tended to be small family concerns – many of which are covered within this chapter.

As a rural community, most employment before the mid-1800s was either in agriculture and its supporting roles or in domestic service. As the demand for farmland declined and the business gentry moved in, building large country residences, the number in domestic service increased considerably. These included grooms and gardeners as well as those engaged within the house. Those directly employed in agriculture as farm workers or agricultural dealers are not recorded in this chapter having been covered in earlier chapters. Similarly the publicans, clergy and teachers are covered elsewhere along with the history of their premises and organisations.

1841 was the first census to record individuals and their occupations. Over the period to 1901, the census records clearly show the gradual influx of those with occupations unconnected with agriculture. As well as the more well-off owners of businesses within the North West there was a steady increase of professionals and clerical staff and those associated with the 'new' industries such as the railways in the 1800s and the Merseyside industries in the 1900s. Initially this served to increase the demand for servants with many households having at least one servant.

By the beginning of the 20th century the community was very mixed with those in employment ranging from commuting professionals and retailers to the servants and labourers. While the rest of this chapter provides an insight into employment over the years it clearly has not been able to cover all types of employment. Those with extensive local community involvement, such as the local tradesmen, have been singled out. The advertisements within 'Church & Parish' – the magazine of the Parish Church – have been used as self-contained records of well-remembered local businesses.

The history for two of the three main businesses, as recorded here, have drawn extensively on original research carried out by others, namely Carol Coles for the Asylum and Dr Roger Wilkinson for the Zoo.

The Asylum and later the Hospital

The Cheshire County Lunatic Asylum opened in September 1829, under the auspices of the 1808 County Asylum Act. This allowed for Justices of the Peace to levy a county rate in order to establish asylums to accommodate pauper lunatics. The original building, still called 'The 1829 Building' consisted of a long front with two return wings. It was built on land purchased from the Egerton estate; the architect was W Cole Jnr and the contractor W Quay of Neston. It was built in brick with stone dressing. Around the front courtyard there were stables, repair shops and the mortuary. The basements in the front section of the building housed the kitchens, brewhouse, storehouse and laundry. In the central section of the house there were the offices of the doctor and matron and other staff quarters. At the rear were the exercise yards and well. The Asylum had accommodation for 90 patients, men in the south wing and women in the

Reproduced from 1873 Ordance Survey Map

north. The patients slept on straw bedding and used unbreakable bowls, horn feeding mugs and wooden spoons. To look after these patients there were 12 attendants and a matron – Mrs Bird – but no regular night nurse. The two doctors– L I Jones & Mr W Rose – were neither resident nor full time. Only in 1853 was the first full time resident Medical Superintendent appointed.

Throughout the nineteenth century the Asylum expanded in order to accommodate an ever increasing number of pauper lunatics. 'The 1829 Building' was extended and in 1896 a major building programme started which resulted in the complex known as 'The Main'. It included accommodation for 404 patients, attendants and administration blocks. In the early twentieth century further building took place which resulted in 'The Annexe'.

The Medical Superintendent had his own house and servants, the principle aspects of his job being concerned with the administration and legal aspects of the running of the Asylum. There was very little medical treatment available for mental illness except for sedatives such as bromide & paraldehyde. The assistant medical officers were principally dealing with the general health of the patients. Due to this lack of medical treatment the attendants were appointed principally for their practical skills such as farm work, carpentry, laundry, cooking etc. The

Asylum was as far as practicable a self sufficient organisation. Attendants were poorly paid and lived in with part of their pay consisting of free lodgings, food and laundry. The 1881 Census does not include any one on the staff with obvious links to Upton. By 1901, an attendant lived in one of the Frog Hall Cottages and a nurse in local lodgings. Edward Twist Jones of Upton Park was clerk to the Asylum during the 1920s & 1930s and the store keeper lived in Caughall Road. An inhabitant of Swindley's Row is recorded as having been the asylum gate keeper.

The 1829 Building – taken from the 1831 Hemmingway book 'The History of Chester'

The isolated and stagnant world of the Asylum was broken by the impact of the First World War on the British home front. The most immediate issue was the loss of male staff to the armed forces. This staffing crisis was aggravated by the fact that the Asylum had to accommodate patients from Winwick and imbeciles from the Chester Workhouse as these institutes were taken over by the Government as War Hospitals. The only solution was to employ more women and break the traditional practice of male attendants nursing male lunatics. During WW1 the Asylum ploughed up more of its land including some of the airing courts. A poultry farm was set up in some of the outbuildings at Bache Hall under the control of a Miss Hartley. Female staff and patients as well as male were employed on the land and the buildings deteriorated.

During WW2, the female section of the Annexe was taken over by the military for the nursing of soldiers. Conditions for patients improved from the 1930s with the introduction of occupational health schemes. The introduction of effective drug treatments during the 1970s meant that there was far less requirement to take people with mental health problems into hospital. 'Care in the Community' introduced in the late 1970s resulted in the gradual closure of the hospital. The 1829 Building is now the offices of Cheshire West Primary Care Trust. The provision of mental health care is by the Cheshire and Wirral Partnership Trust who have their clinics, offices and limited inpatient facilities principally in the Annexe. On the land between the former Asylum and Bache Hall stands the Countess of Chester NHS Foundation Trust - the principal provider of acute care for Chester and its environs.

George Mottershead's Zoo

The Zoo – governed by the North of England Zoological Society – is one of the largest zoos in the United Kingdom. It covers more than 100 acres, being just under a quarter of its total landholding which includes farmland. The austere economic climate of its early years prompted the zoo to create the innovative enclosure designs for which it became known. It has furthered its international reputation through its scientific and conservation work with numerous breeding successes. More than 1 million people now visit each year.

George Mottershead and lion clubs in the 1930s

George Mottershead's daughter, June, recounts how her father (shown here) was badly wounded in WW1 and was advised to work on the land until he was fit. From earlier experiences with a small zoo near Crewe, he founded Chester Zoo in the early 1930s purchasing Oakfield with under ten acres of land. He met stiff opposition from Upton Council who claimed '*it would be a serious menace to the whole neighbourhood*' In 1932 his animal collection formerly held at Shavington, which included a polar bear, a tapir, and a chimpanzee, were transferred to Upton. By 1934 it had a council chaired by Richard Blair Young. Mottershead served as director-secretary with his wife, Elizabeth, as catering manager; his father, Albert, as head gardener, and his older daughter, Muriel, as assistant curator. His school-age daughter, June, later proved to have a special interest in fish, perhaps promoted when an aquarium with six cold-water tanks was built in the wine-cellar basement of Oakfield and opened by Lady Daresbury in 1934. They remodelled the monkey house, added parrot aviaries and a penguin pool, and recorded its first successful hatching of a black-footed penguin chick.

Visitors were few and financial success still eluded the Zoo but it extended its landholding. Major benefactors including the Holt family shipping line and the Duke of Westminster gave help and collections of animals. A lion house opened by Lord Leverhulme in 1937 accommodated African lions. Mottershead asked the zoo council to consider a '*zoo without bars*', proposing to build a large, outdoor lion enclosure surrounded by 12foot high chain-link fencing.

Almost half of the council opposed this idea, fearing the lions would escape, and many council members resigned. Not until 1947 did Mottershead finally realise that dream.

During WW2 Mottershead had regular broadcasts on BBC's Children's Hour about his animal adoption scheme and the plan received much support. Animal numbers grew as they were evacuated from other zoos. The post-war period saw great success with expansion to 65 acres and 320,000 visitors by 1949 and association with names such as Peter Scott. The present aquarium, built by Fred and June (Mottershead) Williams, opened in 1952 and included the innovative feature of a roof tank with glass panels set in its base. This design allowed visitors to view fish from below and may be seen as a precursor to contemporary tunnel tanks. New visitor facilities included two cafeterias and a souvenir shop. The zoo's gardens became a feature in 1952, complementing the animal enclosures with flower beds, borders, rose and rock gardens, and shrubbery. P W Gallup, appointed the head gardener in 1953, oversaw the development of greenhouses and nursery areas to supply the zoo's rapidly expanding needs—some 80,000 plants being required for the summer bedding alone.

Aerial photograph of the zoo from the 1951 'WI Book'

Annual visitors had reached 500,000 by the mid-1950s when Demage Farm and the Riding school were bought. Linking the zoo across Flag Lane required the building of a footbridge. Mr Edge, who farmed Caughall Farm, rented the zoo a field for car parking until by the mid-1960s they had procured the farm, taking their land ownership to 330acres. The approximate 840,000 visitors in 1960 enjoyed the new Fountain Restaurant and Cafeteria, additional gardens, a pair of gorillas, and the new small mammal house. The present elephant house was built in 1961 as the pachyderm house; at the time it also housed rhinos, tapirs, and hippopotamuses. Construction work continued with the building of cafeterias and a souvenir shop in 1965, a cat house in 1966, and a jaguar enclosure in 1967. Visitor numbers peaked around 1.14 million in 1967. The small veterinary laboratory built in 1968 has recently been replaced by a modern veterinary hospital.

For his outstanding zoological achievements, Mottershead was made an Officer of the Order of the British Empire (OBE) in the 1973 New Year's Honours List five years before his death at the age of 83. A while later Dr. Michael R Brambell, formerly curator of mammals at London Zoo, became director of a zoo estate that now totalled more than 500 acres, including adjacent farmland, which was used to grow food for the animals. The present director is Prof. Gordon McGregor Reid.

The last three decades have seen more innovations with the penguin pool, the twilight zone walk through bat enclosure and the monorail – pulling back from declining attendance figures. Chester Zoo has won many other awards for its environmental contributions, for its famous gardens, for zoo business and marketing, and for education. Its crowning achievement at the end of the 20th century was being named Britain's Zoo of the Year in both 1998 and 1999 and gaining the Queen's Award for Enterprise in 2001. Upton abounds in stories of zoo animal antics – and these are covered in Tale Ends (page 291). One zoo  animal however made its biggest mark on Upton. The elephant is featured on the Upton crest and the most famous surely is Jubilee born in 1977 – shown here on his first birthday.

The zoo has acted as a major containment on Upton. By its acquisition of farmland in the days before Chester's Green Belt policy and planning regulations, it has prevented the potential urban sprawl northwards. In 1960 the zoo owned 8 private dwellings and this peaked at around 18 in the 1970s. These have been used for housing some of its staff while many others have had their own homes in the Upton area. Employment has risen as the zoo has expanded and today about a quarter of these live within the CH2 postcode area amounting to over a million pounds of annual salary. This helps quantify the expansion over the 70 years since Mottershead started with what appears to have been a family business. While most of the permanent and part-time staff now live within the Chester area, the zoo's international standing means that many others from around the world are here for various periods of time. The zoo's commitment to education has meant that many students have benefited from work experience and local schools have frequently been involved in visits and major events.

Dicksons Nurseries

At the height of their business around 1880 – Dicksons was very extensive covering much of Newton and the southern parts of Upton. While the main showground gardens were in Newton, the nursery is very much a part of Upton's history. The old maps and some of our current road names reflect that period. At first there were two businesses, which later became a limited company. Dicksons was probably one of the largest general nursery businesses in Great Britain. Their nurseries were reputed to have extended to over 400 acres in the Newton / Upton area and employed hundreds of local men and women. Due to the suitable conditions other nurseries have existed within Upton but Dicksons was by far the largest.

The story starts with two cousins, Francis R Dickson and James H Dickson, who moved here from Scotland c.1821 when they were aged 32 and 25 respectively. They married Chester sisters Selina and Lavinia Roberts and by 1836 had established their nursery and seed business. Although initially combined, the cousins eventually severed this partnership forming 'F & A Dickson' and 'James Dickson & Sons'. Francis and Selina settled in Upton House (later Upton Villa then Stanton House) while James and Lavinia built and settled in Newton Villa after acquiring more of the Kilmorey estate in 1845. The Upton and Newton Tithe surveys of c1840 show that the cousins between them already owned land stretching from Brook Lane to Upton's Mill Lane. The Upton Township Minute book for 1840 records them as claiming reassessment of Rateable Value on a property. James died in 1867 the year after Francis.

Their families were large and many family members became involved in the business. Employment seemed to draw largely on the Newton and Chester areas. In 1851 only one Upton resident – Charles Bebington - is recorded as a nursery labourer but by the 1881 census some addresses occupied by nursery managerial staff are given as Upton Nurseries and Nursery Cottages, located nearby to widow Selina's home of Upton House.

The second generation of the family business took it to the heights for which it is remembered and after the deaths of the two founders they combined to form a single limited company. A son from each founder went on to become the two key figures - Francis Arthur Dickson and George Arthur Dickson. They were both very successful businessmen and became Aldermen of the City and Mayors in 1870 and 1885 respectively. George was Hon.Sec of the Royal Agricultural Show in 1893 and was known in royal circles. Francis moved to Chester's Queens Park but other family members lived in Newton, Hoole and Upton. Newton Villa passed to William Dickson and eventually became the main nursery offices. George moved to Springfield in Newton and James from Upton Lodge to Brookfield in Newton - both Newton farmhouse residences that the family had acquired along with the local land purchases. They all had such large families that by the third generation the family was very extensive within the Chester and North Wales area.

The successful business occurred during the strong national interest in horticulture resulting from the explorations of the new plant hunters. The Newton part of the nursery show grounds was very resplendent at its height, with floral gardens and features. From the main entrance on Brook Lane, the long drive (now residential Dicksons Drive) was lined with red, white and blue flowers and what is now Sandon Road, lined was pansies. Newton Villa was a magnificent building and the gentry customers were received there as their carriages swept up the drive. There were extensive greenhouses and potting sheds as well as features such as the 'Marble Arch' - remembered post-WW2 as a ruin amongst the waste ground (see page 131).

The whole nursery area was reputedly never short of water with springs and brooks draining from the Upton Heath area. Dicksons appear to have managed these water sources with culverts taking them under the various lanes. Many of the greenhouses (especially on the Newton Brook side of the drive) had their own wells. One of the springs was horseshoe-shaped and produced lovely clear water. In the 1920s it was a watercress pond but now is under concrete at the junction of Thornton and Ellesmere roads.

Newton Villa (see also caption on next page)

The business appears to have been in financial difficulties by the beginning of the 20th century. They were selling off ground and the 1908 OS survey shows a considerable amount of housing development in Newton. There were attempts to sell land in Upton at this time but none was developed until the 1920s and then only for the land readily accessible and suitable.

From the 1920s the nurseries were closing down and were finally closed in 1933. The Chester shop continued for a further three years. Auctions and sales distributed many items such as gardening tools to locals and former workers. Several of these ran small businesses growing and selling garden products – many locals still remember produce stalls and seeing people harvesting from the abandoned grounds.

The business took a while to wind down during which Mr. Scarratt strictly policed the site from his cottage – the former time-office just inside the newly positioned main gate.

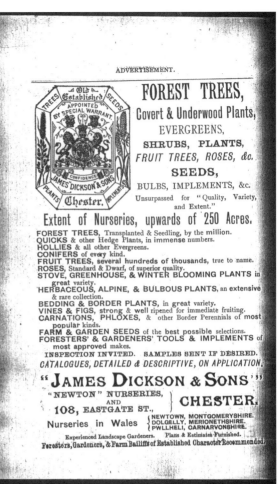

Besides supplying much of this history, both drawings are by Mike Hoddinott based on his memories of Newton Villa (previous page) and of Scarratt's cottage (above).

154

The 1951 W I Upton History scrapbook notes that Mr. Dickson used to drive his trap to the station every morning at 6 a.m., except Christmas Day and Sundays, to fetch the letters, of which there would be 800 - 1,000. In time, the nurseries had their own special post bag and postman. Well-to-do Welsh farmers apprenticed their sons to Dicksons in order to learn English while working. Finally they noted that Pedrog, a former Archdruid, had worked in Dicksons Nurseries as a young man.

Dicksons nurseries is still remembered today by those who played in their youth within the abandoned site. Some housing development within the Upton area started in the 1920s but much of the site stayed as waste ground until the extensive post war housing boom. This is all covered in chapters 7 &9.

Moston Nursery

From all accounts this was never part of Dicksons. Charles Dandy of Belmont Cambrian View, Chester, appears to have established the nursery post-WW1. It was then taken over by the Shenton family – Hilda Shenton recalls her memories in the Reminiscence Chapter (see page 283).

Peter Snelson

Peter Snelson (bn c1900) was a well reputed gardener through much of the post-war period and is remembered here through his 1956 advertisement. He had worked for the Beresford-Jones at The Heyes until Mrs. Beresford-Jones moved to Rose Cottage. Peter then established a nursery where the 'park & ride' is now sited on Moston Road. He was remembered for cycling to work each day from his home in Brooke Avenue and he built up a good reputation for roses. He was a well known member of the community and the business continued until his death in a car accident in 1971.

Deans Country Maid Bakery

Upton Mill is covered on page 46 – here we tell the story of Deans Bakery. Edward Dean had married Elizabeth the daughter of Mill owner and farmer William Carter. By the late 1870s Edward, aged around 40, was the miller and owner of the mill and was succeeded c1900 by his son Edward. Timescales of how the bakery business developed have not been deeply researched but indications are that early in the 1900s it was an established bakery with its own local outlet – shop being too grand a name since locals bought their bread and cakes through little more than ' a hole in the wall'. Apparently, in the early days, villagers would bring their dough ready to be baked into 8lb. loaves. Arthur Cooper recalls buying 'Chester cake' in the late 1930s which they nicknamed 'Tram Stopper' since it was a solid but tasty block of a mix of different cake bits.

In 1929 they built a new bakery and under the name Country Maid it served bread in North Wales and throughout the North West of England. After expanding with a modern bakery in Cardiff, by 1938 they had amalgamated with Allied Bakeries. Now under the management of the 3rd generation, Geoffrey Dean retired in 1950 and the Upton business was entirely wholesale with the bakery now in Saltney. Numerous stories abound from older residents of the bread baking smells and of buying bread direct from the bakery. They would bake overnight for a string of delivery wagons to leave early each morning. One appealing story tells of a wealthy but incapacitated lady customer, for whom they started ready slicing and wrapping the bread in waxed paper. Whether this is the actual origin of 'ready sliced' is unproven but clearly the product was the success story of Country Maid – see their 6-wheeler from the early 1930s.

How many local people were employed has not yet been identified but this photograph records Geoffrey Dean presenting Emily Griffiths with her long service award. Seated on the wagon is either a younger Emily Griffiths or Dorothy Cooper.

Rural crafts

In the 1800s there were a number of blacksmiths with the Darlington family being predominant. In their name for several generations, the last practicing family member died in 1941 and the forge and all its tools sold. The drawing shown here is their smithy – now demolished - on the Liverpool Rd alongside Kingsmead estate.

James Hayes blacksmith is recorded in the 1841 census probably operating out of the smithy understood to have existed on Upton Lane (then Smoke Street) just up from Upton Farm.

Before the WW2 JR (Dick) Jones had been looking for a site to set up a more modern blacksmiths with welding equipment and providing a variety of fabrication work. Eventually he settled on Flag Lane South, the site of the former coal merchant Enoch Davies, and built the workshop shown here. His two sons Bob and Bernard became

blacksmiths and later took on the business. They employed several local craftsmen over the years tackling work for the remaining farmers and jobs further afield. Amongst these were Tom Jones (no relation) who continued with traditional tasks such as wheelwright – putting the metal hoops on wheels – and shoeing horses. Barry Crump served his time here before setting up himself in Christleton. In the early 1990s the business was wound up and the equipment sold by auction. Tom had completed 23 years moving on later to work for his son Tom on the Sealand Industrial Estate. This Upton site is remembered by the housing development named The Smithy.

The 1850 & 1874 Directories record Charles Darlington as a Boot & Shoe Maker – presumably operating out of the building in Demage Lane opposite the Vicarage known as the Cobblers. In 1881, Frederick Jones of Cromwell Bank was recorded as a boot manufacturer but his premises not identified. The last cobbler, based in the building opposite the Vicarage, was Mr Peacock who as an old man was still working during WW2. The cobblers ceased after his death.

The 1851 census records a wheelwright - Thomas Knight – who by 1874 is recorded as both beer seller and wheelwright, located where the Wheatsheaf pub now stands. By the turn of the century Henry Griffiths had a wheelwrights shop on Long Lane. He is pictured here in the early 1900s with an unknown worker. The workshop, demolished c1996, stood where the entrance to Dulas Court now stands, and was used by his grandson upholsterer Peter Griffiths.

The 1841 census records Joseph Jones as a Carriage Proprietor and in 1881 William Smith as a Carter. Coal Merchant and carrier Enoch Davies is pictured here in the 1920s. He operated from Flag Lane South (site of the Baptist church) and was reputedly quite a character – generous and liked his drink. He collected coal from the Bache sidings. His son however bought a lorry and took on council haulage work.

The Garages

The three main road garages all started out in the 1930s as traffic built up and car ownership becoming more common.

Upton Heath Motors is believed to have been started by Mr Davies whose engineering business was on the other side of Heath Road. By the 1940s the Post Office and one or two petrol pumps were owned by Mr & Mrs Bradley. Mrs Bradley would serve in the Post Office and go outside to serve petrol when someone was at the pumps. Mr Bayley, Mr Taylor and Mrs Reece (who later became Mrs Burgess) bought shares in the garage in the late 1940s. Mr Jagger then joined the team and in 1959 took on Derek Ryder - a young keen enthusiatic worker. In 1960 Mr Jagger died and by this time his daughter Susie had married Derek. Together they ran the petrol station and tyre business for 36 years with Susie's brother Richard joining them later. Derek was tragically killed in a car accident in 1996 and their two sons - Geoff & Steve - who had come into the family business as teenagers then took over the business.

From 1962 to 1986 the Heath Motors workshop was taken on by Don Stacey, as shown here, who had previously been the mechanic at Moston garage.

The Bache garage was also originally operated alongside a Post Office business. Built in the early 1930s by Mr Nixon these pumps were only attended when a vehicle was waiting and there were no Post Office or grocery customers. With a milk road to attend to as well, the story goes that petrol service was rarely available in the early morning. Pre-war, the mechanic here was Mr. Gallagher who later moved to run his own business in Sandicroft.

Weston Grove garage was built in the mid-1960s, at the same time as the shops, and run by Derek Moffatt until the early 1980s. Returning to Upton in the late 1980s Derek took on the Bache workshop when the petrol station ceased and the forecourt became used by car sales businesses.

Mr Bocock ran Moston Garage when it was built c1932, shortly after the new road was completed. As this 1956 advert shows, Moston operated a car hire service while Davies had previously operated a taxi service from Upton Heath.

MOSTON GARAGE

:: For Service Repairs and Spares ::

NOW ENLARGED AND FITTED WITH
—— TIME SAVING EQUIPMENT ——

CAR HIRE - - - Telephone: Chester 2 1 9 5 1

Building & allied trades

The earliest identified named local 'builders' are William Bagley recorded as a bricklayer in the 1850 Bagshaw's Directory and a stonemason William Lewis from the 1851 census and 1874 Directory. Whether they worked on Upton properties is not known. The many local builders of later years are mentioned throughout the chapters covering the development of the area.

Plumber Frank Morris married into the Ithell family and lived in Heath Road. Very involved in village life and on the Parish Council - he is understood to have been a key figure in the mid-1930s celebrations. Both the Frank Morris and the Bob Jones adverts shown here are from 1930. Bob Jones died in 1995.

Besides the wheelwrights, the other early named joiners and carpenters are recorded c1850 as Samuel Davies and Joseph Jackson.

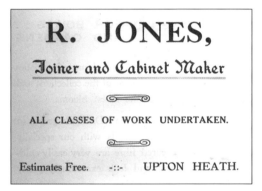

— IF IT'S PLUMBING, —
RING UP, CHESTER 1820.

Frank Morris,

PLUMBING ———

—— CONTRACTOR

UPTON HEATH, CHESTER.

Specialist in re-construction of
Bathrooms and Modern Sanitation.

HAVE YOUR PLUMBING DONE
: : THE "MORRIS" WAY : :

R. JONES,

Joiner and Cabinet Maker

ALL CLASSES OF WORK UNDERTAKEN.

Estimates Free.   -::-   UPTON HEATH.

and from 1956

Telephone : Chester 20061

J. LIGHTFOOT & SON

PAINTERS and DECORATORS

" DELAPRE "   DEMAGE   LANE,   UPTON - BY - CHESTER

CONTRACTORS to : War Office — Ministry of Works — Air Ministry — Cheshire County Council

Wilfred John had been making the wooden frames for the metal windows of 'Williams & Williams' of Grange Road Chester. The outbreak of war killed the market for housebuilding and John was forced into finding subsistence work. His machinery was initially stored in the Upton Golf Club until, through the builders 'Capstick & Owen', a potential site was found. This was the triangle of ground opposite the Wheatsheaf previously used as a tip. He was able to build a simple corrugated roofed wooden shack and produce field gates and potato boxes amongst other local requirements. Such was subsistence that his son Graham recalls his father delivering firewood in winter. The John family lived initially at 8 Bache Avenue then moving to 128 Liverpool Road opposite to the hospital. The firm's machinist - Horace Caroll - followed Wilfred John and settled in Upton. Eddy Edison became their apprentice working with three others. Post war an MOD depot at Mickle Trafford became available and Deeside Sawmills relocated.

The brickyards and sandpits would have employed labourers and work for carriers. The 1881 census records a Mr Thomas as a brickmaker living in the Heath cottages as well as naming others as bricklayers. A well remembered road maintenance and road sweeper of the 'between the wars' period was Abraham Woodward. On duty he was always seen wearing a bowler hat.

Workmen on the Capstick & Owen 'Upton Drive' site, mid-1930s

The many local builders as mentioned through Chapters 7 & 9 would have employed several local men. Arthur Cooper, shown here on the right, was an apprentice joiner to Capstick & Owen while working on Upton Drive. Behind them was the current site office that progressed up the road with the work. The old lorry, previously belonging to Arthur Jones, to bring gravel to site but with age stayed on site unlicensed as the site wagon. With labour on site they could always give a helping hand and on one occasion had to help Godwin's horse (page 7) out of the brook when it got stuck.

Furley's Electrical and later MacFarlanes

Arthur Walter Snead Furley and later his son - provided electrical services from the 1920s – opening their own shop on Long Lane in the early 1930s. Locals brought their accumulators in for recharging as well as buying the new electrical provisions. From his place on the Parish Council he assisted in Upton's take-up of this new utility.

Roy and Molly MacFarlane took over the shop in 1952, operating as their 1956 advert shows. They later expanded the shop with a 2nd floor for childrenswear. A very popular local couple, their 1987 retirement was marked with the celebration shown below. Derek Ryder of Upton Heath Motors is shown next to Roy.

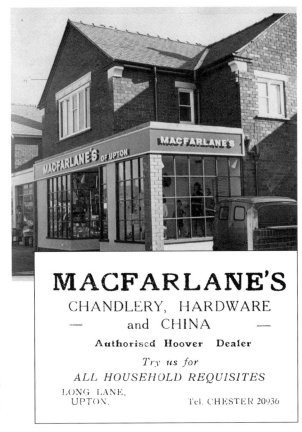

MACFARLANE'S

CHANDLERY, HARDWARE

— and CHINA —

Authorised Hoover Dealer

Try us for

ALL HOUSEHOLD REQUISITES

LONG LANE,
UPTON.   Tel. CHESTER 20936

The early shops

Located near the site of the current Bache local shoppers carpark, Nixons was a general provisions and grocers that also housed the Bache Post Office. It was trading back in the 1870s and was still in business post-WW2. Miss Nixon's father ran a milk business from here – later taken on by his brother-in-law Arthur Godwin. See page 271 and Eddy Edison's reminiscences (page 272).

Another early shop still stands on Heath Road but is now a private residence. Known pre-war as the 'Urban Stores' it was run by Mrs Saunders. From 1936 -1974 it became Brookfields and is shown here in the early 1960s. Built around 1900 it was owned pre-WW1 by David Watkin. He initially lived at Rose Cottage but later built a bungalow behind the shop.

The former chapel (see page 81) became a shop after the new chapel was built in 1900. Seemingly always a newsagents/confectioners it has been known as Jacksons for many years but was formerly Hammonds. During the 1940s it was run by the Masons and earlier in the 1930s it was the Heath Post Office prior to re-location onto Long Lane.

Mr Jones had a newsagents by The Frog pub during the 1930s to 1950s. Pre-war there were attempts to establish a Post Office but these failed. This advert is from 1966 shortly before the shop was demolished for housing.

Other local shops recalled through their adverts

From 1956

From 1980

And finally those in domestic service

For the period between the mid-1800s and the mid-1900s, the largest single group of employed females within Upton were those in domestic service. Inspection of the 19th century census records, show large numbers, not only serving the rich 'local barons'. In 1851, 11 of the 61 households employed a total of 16 female domestic servants. By 1900, the number of households with domestic servants had grown significantly. By the 1930s, the numbers were reducing to serve only the more comfortably well-off. Male servants tended to be grooms, gardeners and drivers. Most properties with larger gardens employed a gardener.

The following reminiscence is from Eunice Evans (nee Jones) born in 1916.

When I was 14 years old, I started in service for Mr and Mrs Wooliscroft who lived at Taluca, in Church Lane, and had a hotel in Chester. I had been recommended by their gardener, at that time, Mr James Stacey. My normal day started at 8am after I had cycled to Church Lane from our home, at Upton Grange Farm. There were no lights along Long Lane and one day, on the way home riding in the fog, I passed the farm and ended up, almost, where the Hoole roundabout is now. I wore a blue dress, white apron and cap and finished work about 2pm. If they had guests, I used to wear a black dress and white apron and would work until later in the day. My duties included cleaning, waiting, lighting fires, washing and ironing. Initially, my pay was five shillings. They treated me well and I am still in touch with the family

CHAPTER 12
Village Hall

A public meeting was called in the village school in May 1924 to address the need for a village community centre. Four and a half years later – on 8th Dec 1928 our hall was officially opened by Lady Grosvenor with virtually all of the costs met.

The Men's Institute (see page 89) was seen by some as serving this purpose with various plans of the Heath locality identifying it as 'Village Hall'. Also the village school – St.Mary's – had long served as a community centre for Upton but now the village expansion was rendering the school unsuitable and

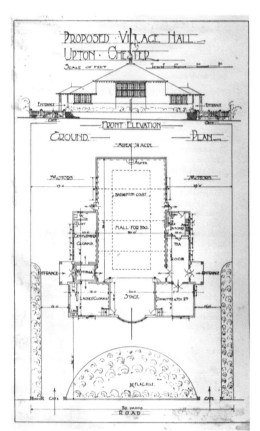

Headteacher Frank Hewitt was pushing for purpose-built premises. Other communities in the Chester area had their community centres and these had been visited by some of Upton's dignatories. 60 people attended this May 1924 public meeting in the school and a committee was appointed to make things happen.

Chairman H Beresford Jones
Hon.Sec. F Hewitt
Treasurer W Clayton

Committee Sir John Frost;
Mr.& Mrs Andrews Crompton;
Miss Clark Lloyd
Messrs Len Wright and R Ithell.

By October 1924 they had a report which was circulated and locally displayed calling for a public meeting to discuss. The report covered the purchase of the site; the plan of the proposed hall and the approximate cost. It stated that a hall was needed '*to meet the present day advancement of corporate life*' and also that ' *the latest methods of comfort and convenience was an essential*' and '*building on the best possible convenient site which would for all times provide a living representation of the present generation's effort to raise the status of the district and provide a centre for the uplifting of our younger generation*'.

A piece of land was identified *'to permit of posterity enlarging the building'* – this was ¼ acre adjacent to the St.Mary's school owned by Philip Grey Egerton who was known to have a soft spot for Upton. Records are quiet for 1925 and 1926 but perhaps much was happening behind the scenes. The only significant record is that in June 1926 a Garden Fete was held in the grounds of Upton Lawn – courtesy of Sir John & Lady Frost – which raised £138/2/6ᵈ for the building fund whose appointed trustees were H Beresford Jones; W Clayton & Mrs A Crompton.

By 1927 the project was underway. Sir Philip Egerton Grey had offered the land for the modest sum of £20 provided legal and boundary fencing costs were met. Formal plans were submitted in October 1927 by architect George Hutchins (tel Chester 26) with total project cost estimates of around £1900. At that time (October 1927) the fund held £407 plus promises of a further £300. An unidentified sporting friend of the village (believed to have been cricket captain Len Wright) had also promised £10 for every £100 raised before Christmas that year. There was now strong support across the village and a determination to raise funds before Christmas. The committee was much enlarged – adding H Griffiths; G Mason; Rev Sparling; Nield; Paterson; Haselden; K Tyrer; W Gray; Hylton Stewart; T Hinde; Brickland; H Cheers; Kinsey; Ingle; H Whaley; Garner; Hibbert and the Misses Newport & Wilson. By 25th October 1927 the shortfall was down to £800 and by 30th November to just over £600. Local joiner H Griffiths had donated a notice board.

1928 and building is underway

By June 1928, there were four firm builders' quotations. The fund stood at £1415 but with building quotations above the original estimate there was a shortfall of over £500. Builders offered reductions by using corrugated roofing rather than Brown Brindled asbestos tiles or using ordinary brick – interior whitewashed – rather than Brunner Mond brick. The committee strongly supported the project going ahead with the original specification. An entertainment sub-committee

was formed and in July 1928 a major community-wide appeal was launched. The siting of the village hall required a footpath diversion and this was duly approved on the 2nd July 1928. On 27th July Rev Sparling cut the first sod in a launch ceremony with Sir John Frost and other committee members joined by the architect G Hutchins and contractor A Shepherd.

There was a clear determination that the full community should contribute and the following appeal was put out showing donations to date.

UPTON VILLAGE HALL.

UPTON,
24th July, 1928.

DEAR SIR OR MADAM,

Opposite you will find a list of the subscribers to the fund for building the Village Hall with the amount raised to date which it is hoped will be of interest to you.

You will notice that the fund now amounts to the sum of £1382-8-1, and although this is short of the amount that will be required to complete the scheme, exclusive of the furnishing, by about £450, it has been decided to proceed with the erection of the Hall at once. The lowest tender amounting to £1690, has been accepted, and the work has been put in hand.

To mark the commencement of such an important undertaking, the Vicar of Upton, the Rev. Wilfred Sparling M.A., has been asked to inaugurate the work by cutting the first sod on the site and he has kindly consented to do so.

This ceremony will take place on Friday, the 27th day of July, at 6-30 p.m., on the site adjoining the Village Schools, and the Committee has much pleasure in giving you a cordial invitation to be present on that occasion in order that you may give your support at the outset of the scheme.

As the amount still to be raised (£450) is still very considerable the Committee, while thanking those who have given so generously, appeals to all for help in obtaining further subscriptions from their friends or from anyone whom they think might be persuaded to help so good a cause, as they feel sure there must still be many whom they have not been able to reach.

Subscriptions may be paid to the Hon. Treasurer, Mr. Wm. Clayton, either at the District Bank Chester or "Hill Crest" Upton, or the Hon. Secretary, Mr. F. Hewitt at the School House or any member of the Committee and will be duly acknowledged with thanks.

May we also take this opportunity of asking all those friends who have already kindly promised donations to pay them to the Hon. Treasurer as soon as now the building has been put in hand the money will be required.

Signed, on behalf of the Committee,

H. BERESFORD JONES, J.P., Chairman.
A. CROMPTON, Vice-Chairman.
W. CLAYTON, Hon. Treasurer.
F. HEWITT, Hon. Secretary.

Committee:

Mr. J. Brickland	Mr. H Griffiths	Mrs. C. Newport
Miss S. M. Clark-Lloyd	Mr. J. H. Haselden	Mr. C. Nield
Mr. H. Cheers	Mr. F. Hibbert	Mr. G. Paterson
Mrs. W. Clayton	Mr. T. Hinde	Rev. W. Sparling, M.A.
Mr. H. E. Crane	Mr. J. Ingle	Mr. E. Hylton Stewart
Mr. A. Crompton	Mr. R. Ithell	Mr. K. Tyer
Mr. J. D. Dutton	Mr. E. Twist Jones	Mr. H. Whaley
Sir J. M. Frost, J.P.	Mr. T. Kinsey	Miss M. Wilson
Mr. E. Garner	Mrs. G. Mason	Mr. L. Wright
Mr. W. Gray	Mr. F. Morris	Mr. W. Young

List of Donations towards the Upton Village Hall.

	£	s	d
Sir J. M. Frost, J.P.	100	0	0
Mr. H. Beresford-Jones, J.P.	100	0	0
Mr. A. Crompton, J.P.	100	0	0
Mrs. A. Crompton	100	0	0
Mrs. A. Tyrer	60	0	0
"A Sporting Gentleman"	50	0	0
Mr. G. Darsie	20	0	0
His Grace the Duke of Westminster	20	0	0
Mr. J. Soutter Clayton	20	0	0
Mr. and Mrs. Patterson	20	0	0
Miss S. M. Clark-Lloyd	15	0	0
Mr. C. Nield			
The Birkenhead Brewery Co., (per Mr. Harry Williams)	10	10	0
Messrs. E. Dean & Sons, Ltd.	10	10	0
Rev. W. Sparling, M.A.	10	0	0
Mr. W. Clayton	10	0	0
Mr. and Mrs. E. Garner	10	0	0
Mr. and Mrs. K. V. Trubshaw	10	0	0
Miss M. Wilson	10	0	0
Mr. Beavan...ulf	10	5	0
Mr. J. D. Dutton	5	5	0
Sir Chas. Cayzer, Bart., M.P.	5	5	0
Mr. A. K. Tyrer	5	5	0
Mrs. A. K. Tyrer	5	0	0
Mrs. W. Clayton	5	0	0
Mr. J. Brickland	5	0	0
Mr. Brickland (not received)	5	0	0
Mr. F. Hibbert	5	0	0
Mr. J. H. Haselden	5	0	0
Mrs. S. Haselden	5	0	0
Mr. W. Young	5	0	0
Mr. J. Schofield	5	0	0
Mr. J. Lightfoot	5	0	0
Mrs. J. Lightfoot	5	0	0
Mr. W. Gray	5	0	0
Mr. C. A. Earle	5	0	0
Messrs. Dicksons (Nurseries) Ltd	5	0	0
Mrs. C. Pearson	5	0	0
The Misses Egginton	4	0	0
Mr. C. Newport	3	3	0
Mr. and Mrs. J. T. D. Darbishire	3	3	0
Mr. J. W. R. Crompton	3	0	0

	£	s	d
Mrs. A. J. Baker	2	10	0
Miss I. Jones	2	10	0
Mr. E. Hylton Stewart	2	2	0
Mr. T. Gibbons Frost	2	2	0
Mr. and Mrs. S. Martyn	2	2	0
Mr. A. B. Coleman	2	2	0
Mr. J. Joseph	2	2	0
Mr. R. Ithell (Not Received)	2	2	0
Mr. and Mrs. Woolliscroft	2	2	0
Col. R. A. F. Hobbs	2	0	0
Mr. T. Burgess	2	0	0
Mrs. Parry, Mrs. M. Parry and Miss G. Parry			
Capt. E. Hylton Gardner	1	10	0
Mr. C. Blandford	1	1	0
Mr. F. H. Garland	1	1	0
Mr. H. T. G. Edmonds	1	1	0
Mr. F. Morris	1	1	0
Mr. E. Twist Jones	1	1	0
Mrs. G. Mason	1	1	0
Mrs. B. Newport	1	1	0
Miss E. Ithell (Not Received)	1	1	0
Miss N. Darlington	1	0	0
Mr. S. Oldham	1	0	0
Mr. J. McKay	1	0	0
Mr. W. Partington	1	0	0
Mr. J. Saunders	1	0	0
Mr. J. Grayson	1	0	0
Mr. and Mrs. Slack M.	0	10	6
Mr. H. Griffiths	0	10	6
Mr. T. Kinsey	0	10	6
Mr. J. Ingle	0	10	6
Mr. E. Branson	0	10	6
Mr. W. Corfe	0	10	6
Mr. J. S. Buxton	0	10	6
Mr. F. Hinde	0	10	6
Mr. E. Burgess	0	10	6
Mr. R. Smethurst	0	10	6
Mrs. J. E. Duff	0	10	6
Mrs. W. Phillpot	0	10	6
Mrs. and Mr. P. Snelson	0	10	0
Mr. and Mrs. E. Hughes	0	10	0
Mr. H. Whaley	0	10	0
Mr. P. Wall	0	5	0
"A Friend" (Per Mrs. J. Schofield)	0	5	0

	£	s	d
Part Proceeds, Fete, Upton Lawn, 1926	138	2	6
Raised by Lady Frost—Tombola and Sale of old Silver	79	5	6
Raised by Mrs. H. Beresford-Jones—Pantomime, 1927 and sale of photographs, May Day Festival 1927	26	2	10
Raised by Mesdames W. Clayton & Grimes—Dance	10	1	0
Raised by Mrs. T. Hinde—Dance	6	11	6
Raised by Mrs. E. Stacey—Home made shawl	6	6	0
Raised by Upton Heath Women's Institute	69	5	1
Raised by Upton Women Unionist's Association	51	7	0
Raised by Upton-by-Chester Cricket Club	7	0	0
War Stock dividends and Bank Interest	4	0	8
Total to date	£1,382	8	1

The 'Declaration of Trust' to the 3 trustees is dated 23rd August 1928 and states the plot as 1200sq yds. With the building underway and further funds needed, a major social fund-raising event was held on Wednesday 19th September 1928 – a Gypsy Fair held in the grounds of Upton Lawn.

The 1928 Gypsy Fair

Frank Hewitt surrounded by –

His wife and the Mrs Ingle, Newport, Moore, Williams, Branson, Hinde, Gray & Horswill. Also the Misses Wilson, Griffiths, Smethurst, N&K Jones, Parry Mousedale Evans & Hinde.

The village hall was completed before the Official Opening Day but this allowed a major Chrysanthemum Show to be staged 'in the new Village Hall' on Tuesday 27th November. The event raised £338/19/0d for the building fund. Admission was 1/-d before 4.30pm and 6d from 4.30pm until 7.30pm.

The Official Opening Ceremony – 8th December 1928

This was a formal orchestrated ceremony with Lady Arthur Grosvenor unlocking the doors as an official opening. Although many dignitaries had sent their apologies nevertheless the event was attended by key civic, church and military names accompanying the committee. The vicar – the Rev. Wilfred Sparling – spoke from his long experience of the village saying that *"such a building was most desirable and would be chiefly used for recreation and amusement – they should remember that these things, if not taken to excess, were good for them spiritually as well as bodily"*

With a further £100 from Mr Tyrer only the final 10% of the total cost was now outstanding. The full Board of Management stood at 40 members involving most of Upton's wealthy but also drawing on the community as a whole. The ceremony was followed with entertainment by a whist drive and a dance led by the Carlton Band. Local resident Frank Whaley recalls his part in the entertainment as a small boy and Frank was also a star guest during the Hall's 75th anniversary celebrations in December 2003.

Besides the donations, nearly half the cost was raised by events from cricket competitions to fetes, dances, sales and money raised by various groups. One major group was the Women's Institute, seen here outside the hall shortly after it opened.

Events in the early days of the Village Hall

In these days the Hall was claimed to have capacity for 400 and it is understood to have had electric lighting from day one. The stage was a key part of these early days with concerts and dance bands. The committee minutes archived with the CRO not only cover the management of the hall but are a good scrapbook of the various programmes – some of which have been reproduced here. Worthy of note is the frequency of dances where a Crosville Bus had been arranged to leave the Hall at 2 a.m. returning to Chester via Newton.

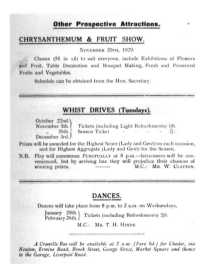

THE VILLAGE HALL, UPTON.   WEDNESDAY, APRIL 9th, 1930.

POPULAR CONCERT

☙ PROGRAMME ☙

PART 1.

1	Overture	...	"Raymond"	*Thomas*
			THE ORCHESTRA.	
2	Song	...	"Love the Jester" ...	*Montague Phillips*
			MISS IVY KEITH-HILL.	
3	'Cello Solo	...	(a) Nocturne	*Trowell*
			(b) Orientale	*Cui*
			MR. S. ENNION.	
4	Song	...	"Fisher Lad" ...	*Maud Crafke Day*
			MISS EVELYN KEITH-HILL.	
5	Selection	...	"Spring Song" ...	*Mendelssohn*
	Intermezzo	...	"Billet-doux"	*Werner*
			THE ORCHESTRA.	
6	Song	...	"Romance from L'Eliser d'Amore" ...	*Donizetti*
			MR. HOWEL DAVIES, L.R.A.M.	
7	Duett	...	"Still as the Night" ...	*Carl Bohm*
			MISSES IVY AND EVELYN KEITH-HILL.	
8	Selections	...	"Dance of Spirits"} ...	*Gluck*
			"Easter Melody" }	
	...	...	"Czardas"	*Michaels*
			THE ORCHESTRA.	

INTERVAL.

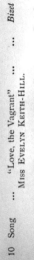
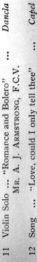

PART 2.

9	Three Dances	...	"Henry VIII"	*German*
			THE ORCHESTRA.	
10	Song	...	"Love, the Vagrant" ...	*Bizet*
			MISS EVELYN KEITH-HILL.	
11	Violin Solo	...	"Romance and Bolero" ...	*Dancla*
			MR. A. J. ARMSTRONG, F.C.V.	
12	Song	...	"Love, could I only tell thee" ...	*Capel*
			MR. HOWEL DAVIES, L.R.A.M.	
13	Concert Waltz	...	"Liebstraume"	*Ertl*
			THE ORCHESTRA.	
14	Song	...	"Villanelli" ...	*Eva dell Acqua*
			MISS IVY KEITH-HILL.	
15	March	...	"Old Comrades"	*Teike*
			THE ORCHESTRA.	

GOD SAVE THE KING.

Leader of Orchestra : MR. A. J. ARMSTRONG, F.C.V.
Accompanist : MRS. R. L. LLOYD, A.R.C.M.
Conductor : MR. H. E. CRANE.

W. F. Hewley, Printer, Chester.

The Village Hall as stand-in for other facilities

During WW2, the Hall was used as both store and workshop by day and to entertain the troops by evening. With the post-war boom in community growth the Village Hall was called on to provide many services which subsequently acquired their own premises. The building was effectively 'squared off' adding rooms that significantly increased the storage and allowed for modernisation of the heating via a boiler room.

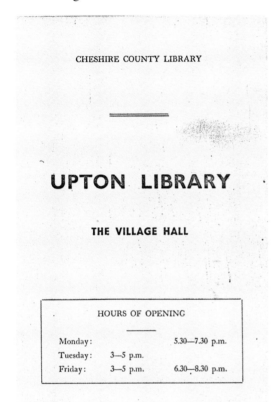

CHESHIRE COUNTY LIBRARY

UPTON LIBRARY

THE VILLAGE HALL

HOURS OF OPENING		
Monday:		5.30—7.30 p.m.
Tuesday:	3—5 p.m.	
Friday:	3—5 p.m.	6.30—8.30 p.m.

Those born during the post-war period would have been weighed regularly in the Baby Clinic in the days before the Weston Grove Clinic was built in 1969. Similarly the Upton branch of the County Library was built on Wealstone Lane in 1969. Prior to that it was housed in the Hall and apparently run, in the early days, by the W.I.

With St.Mary's school next door, the Hall served as their main hall for gymnastics as well as concerts and health screening.

Roman Catholic Mass was held regularly before St. Columbas was built in the mid-1960s. They had a regular attendance of around 50 each week with a priest attending from St.Werburgs and Eddy Edison as an altar boy.

The mid-1960s was again the period when Upton's youth acquired their own premises. Before the Church Hall was built the Village Hall was their only venue which they used for their many and varied events. This photograph from the early 1960s shows Gail Davidson and Eileen Keen serving refreshments after a dance event.

Private functions have also been held over the years – this 1934 event is believed to have been the first wedding reception.

The happy couple were Gertrude Mary Cooper and Edward Ken Davies.

Management & upkeep of the Hall

The Hall is managed by a set of Trustees, drawn from the community, who follow a policy of regular maintenance and refurbishment while retaining the period look. After the wartime period, however, the Hall was in a poor condition with complaints being made to the Parish Council. A new maple flooring replaced the pine floor, damaged after years of military boots. The solid fuel heating was replaced with oil. One reminiscence recalls the post-war refurbishment with the community doing the painting – ladies on the lower levels and men on the upper.

The 1955 extension had been dedicated to the memory of Martha Wilson who was chairman 1936 – 1945. Under Nancy Turton's chairmanship in the early 1980s, the frequently leaking roof was reslated after fund raising events and with community sponsoring of £1 a slate. For the last 15 years Norman Draper has been responsible for the building and has carried out a number of refurbishment projects including heating modernisation, kitchen upgrades and a major reorganisation of the toilet facilities, keeping the building up to date and catering for the disabled.

While many members of the community have served the Hall for a few years, others have helped and supported for many decades. The photo below marks the retirement of J W (Bill) Roberts after some 30 years of service as Secretary. Bill is seen receiving an envelope from Miss Hoole. Chairwoman Molly Bradbury and Treasurer Brian Constable can be seen between them. Also shown - progressing up the stairs – Leo Jackson; Kay Joseph; Alan Bisson; Doris Pearce; Shiela Garston; Nancy Turton; Gwen Griffiths; Mary Thompson; Biddy Barnett From far right progressing inwards - Hughie Pratt; Frank Hewitt; John Ross; Les Vincent; Joan Jones.

By 2000 there was concern that the Monica Sparling garden in front of the Hall had been left to get into a poor state. It was refurbished in the autumn of 2001. Secretary Geoff Newton located the great grandchildren of Rev. Wilfred Sparling, inviting them to a rededication of the garden set for 13th July 2002. The day was a success with a choir from Upton Manor school and a tableau history performed by the Upton Brownies.

The 75th Anniversary celebrations on 7th December 2003, saw the public launch of a major refurbishment project to further local pride in the facility for the early 21st century. To be completed by the 80th Anniversary, the project has been named Project 4-SCORE. Plans have been displayed in the hall and fundraising is well underway.

CHAPTER 13
Upton Celebrates

Occasionally, celebrations are planned for the whole village community. In the past these truly involved the full community although much less so since the mid-1900s. Such celebrations have generally been triggered by either a major national occasion or by a landmark in Upton's own community life. Coronations and Royal Jubilees have traditionally provoked such community celebrations and their success has often inspired periods of annual events and revival of past customs. Garden parties, shows and fetes from the days when Upton was a smaller community were previously held in the grounds of the various large houses until adequate communal halls became available. An early annual event was in May with the crowning of the May Queen who then processed round the village followed by dancing round the maypole and sports held in various fields or suitable large estate grounds. This chapter looks at village-wide celebrations – roughly in chronological order – from our earliest records through to recent times.

Our first recorded festivities were on the occasion of the celebration of Queen Victoria's Golden Jubilee in 1887. The parish festivities started on the morning of 23rd June;- *'A very hot and fine day'*. The festivities began with a service in church to which nearly the whole parish came, men, women and children – *'of all ranks'*.

A procession was formed headed by the Band of the Earl of Chester's Volunteers, and they marched to the church in the following order –

Band Banners of Upton
Oddfellows

Girls   Boys   Women

Upton Oddfellows with
insignia

Men   Churchwardens and
Sidesmen and finally the
Festival Committee.

PROGRAMME.

1-0 p.m.—A Procession will be formed in the Cricket Field and march four abreast, headed by the Band of the Earl of Chester's Rifles, by way of Smoke Street to the Church. The Committee hope that all the Parishioners will join in the Procession.

1-15 p.m.—A Thanksgiving Service will take place in the Church.

2-0 p.m.—The Procession to be re-formed and march by way of the Cross back to the Cricket Field. Those invited to dinner to break off at the Schools.

2-15 p.m.—Dinner will be served in the School-room to the Workmen resident in the Parish.

4-0 p.m.—A Substantial Tea will be served in a Marquee on the Cricket Field to all Women and Children resident in the Parish.

5-0 p.m.—The following Programme of Sports will commence and will be conducted as under :—

Clerk of Course.................Mr. E. Dean, Junr.
Starter...........................Mr. E. T. Logan.
Judge.............................Mr. C. H. Ashton.

1st.—5-0 p.m.—Race for Boys attending School. 200 yards.
First Prize, 2s. 6d.; Second, 1s. 6d.; Third, 1s.

2nd.—5-10 p.m.—Race for Girls under 14. 100 yards.
First Prize, 2s. 6d.; Second, 1s. 6d.; Third, 1s.

3rd.—5-25 p.m.—Race for Boys under 17. 300 yards.
First Prize, 5s.; Second, 3s.; Third, 2s.

4th.—5-30 p.m.—Treacle Bun Race for Boys attending School.
First Prize, 1s.; Second, 6d.

5th.—5-45 p.m.—Flat Race for Single Men. 200 yards.
First Prize, 10s.; Second, 6s.; Third, 4s.

6th.—6-0 p.m.—Sack Race. 100 yards.
First Prize, 5s.; Second, 3s.; Third, 2s.

7th.—6-15 p.m.—Flat Race for Married Men. 200 yards.
First Prize, 10s.; Second, 6s.; Third, 4s.

8th.—6-30.—Three-Leg Race. 100 yards.
First Prize, 5s.; Second, 3s.; Third, 2s.

9th.—6-45 p.m.—Flat Race. Half-a-mile.
First Prize, £1; Second, 10s.; Third, 5s.

10th.—7-0 p.m.—Obstacle Race. Half-a-mile.
First Prize, 10s.; Second, 5s.; Third, 2s. 6d.

11th.—7-15 p.m.—Tug of War. Married *v.* Single. 12 Men a side.
Prize, £1 10s.

12th.—7-30 p.m.—Pig Hunt for Women only.
Prize, the Pig.

8 p.m.—Distribution of Prizes.

CONDITIONS.

The Committee reserve the right to alter or withhold any Prize if they consider there are not sufficient Competitors.

All Competitors must be residents in the Parish of Upton.

The Judge's decision in all cases to be final.

All entries must be made in writing to Mr. T. Wickham, Upton Bank, or Mr. T. Dickenson not later than Nine o'clock on the night of Wednesday, June 22nd.

Committee of Management:

THE VICAR	Mr. E. A. DICKSON	Mr. C. TOWNSHEND
Mr. T. W. THOMSON	„ G. GREENHOUSE	„ G. A. ABELL
„ E. DEAN	„ W. SHONE	„ W. HOLLAND
	„ J. DICKENSON	

Hon. Treasurer..................Mr. B. C. ROBERTS.
Hon. Secretary....................Mr. S. J. CARR.

In Church Lane the procession was met by the surpliced choir, the Chaplain to the County Asylum and the Vicar of Upton. The church was *'crowded to excess'*. After the service the procession re-formed and returned to Mr. B. C. Roberts' field. The men sat down at 1 p.m. to a dinner in the schoolroom, while at 4 p.m. the women had a tea of a very substantial character in a marquee erected in the above field. Athletic sports and dancing were carried on until the evening. At 10 p.m. a bonfire was lit, rockets and fire balloons were sent up and coloured lights were lit. The National Anthem was frequently sung during the day and the company dispersed about 11 p.m.

'A highly successful day's holiday'. Arrangements were carried out by a committee of parishioners and the whole village took part.

In the 1897 Diamond Jubilee there were rejoicings similar to the festivities of ten years earlier. This time, however, we learn that dinner was provided for the men in the schoolroom, and tea for the women and children in the afternoon. There were *'sports for the men and dancing for the young men and maidens'*, finishing up with a bonfire in the evening.

Again in June, 1911, at the Coronation celebrations of King George V and Queen Mary practically the whole village went to church. This time the proces-

sion was formed at the school and they marched to church, headed by the Boy Scouts. The children were each given a New Testament, *'a coronation cup and two pence in the new coinage'*. As on previous occasions there was a dinner at 1 p.m. for the men, followed by sports, while at 4 p.m. the women had a *'knife and fork tea'* and at 5 p.m. came the children's turn. The festivities were held at Upton Lawn which was illuminated, and ended with a display of fireworks. The photograph shows Walter Cockram's home in Upton Park being suitably decorated with patriotic flags. Several Cockram photographs have been used in this book covering the early 1900s.

In 1919 the Upton Council discussed the Peace Celebrations and agreed to a sum of £5 to provide a tea party for the 120 children with a further £2 for sports prizes. Deans handled the catering supplemented with 3 gallons of Ithell's milk.

In the days of the smaller community there were real *'village weddings'*. In June 1904, when the eldest daughter of Mr B C Roberts was married, the village was decorated with bunting and arches. The whole village was invited to the celebrations. The children were given tea and entertained with hobby horses and swings. The rest of the village then had a tea with dancing to follow.

The Rose Queen Festivities

The earliest photographic record (above) of Upton's Rose Queen parade is from 1929 although it is likely that the event dates from very much earlier. The photograph below dates from 1933 taken in the grounds of Upton Lawn – a frequent venue for such community events due to its magnificent grounds.

The photograph below is understood to record a 1940s Rose Queen event, after which it appears there was a lull until the 1953 Coronation celebrations.

Further national occasions from the mid-1930s

A £50 precept provided tea and treats with a children's souvenir for the 1935 Jubilee celebrations. Two years later the coronation of King George VI again saw village celebrations. Frank Morris organised tea for the children and buffet teas in the evening for the older folk. No longer were the sexes segregated for these festive meals. The over-60s were given tea or tobacco, and a bank book and £1 deposit was given to the oldest and youngest parishioners respectively.

The 8th June 1946 was chosen to celebrate the peace after WW2. Again the Council allocated funds - £124 this time – for games, sports and light refreshments. No definite photographs have been identified; however this vicarage garden party may have been part of the celebrations.

The Early 1950s

The early 1950s saw three major occasions – each celebrated with significant events involving the whole community – Festival of Britain in 1951; the Coronation in 1953 and the parish church centenary in 1954.

Festival of Britain Week was celebrated with entertainments for all ages – as can be seen in the programme below. It is interesting to note that the '1951 WI History of Upton' records that

'to-day there are more attractions outside the village and less general participation in (village community) affairs'.

BRITISH LEGION
UPTON-BY-CHESTER BRANCH

Festival of Britain Week

2nd to 7th July, 1951

Souvenir Programme

Price Threepence

. . . *PROGRAMME* . . .

Monday, 2nd July

Grand WHIST DRIVE
in THE VILLAGE HALL

Commence 8-0 sharp.   Admission 2/-

NUMEROUS AND VALUABLE PRIZES

Tuesday, 3rd July For Children only

MARIONETTE SHOW
(Kindly given by Mr. NIXON)

Interlude by VINCHENTO, Entertainer and Mystifier

in THE VILLAGE HALL

Commence 6 p.m.   Admission Free

For Adults only (over 16 years)

MYSTERY NIGHT
in THE VILLAGE HALL

Any time after 8 p.m.   Admission 3d.

Wednesday, 4th July

OLDE TYME DANCE
in THE VILLAGE HALL

Music by JACK PARR'S BAND

Dancing 8 to 11.45 p.m.   Admission 2/-

Thursday, 5th July

Festival WHIST DRIVE
in THE VILLAGE HALL

Commence 8-0 sharp.   Admission 2-

NUMEROUS AND VALUABLE PRIZES

Friday, 6th July

St. Matthew's Concert Party

(SALTNEY FERRY), present "HAPPY DAYS"
A Review of Music, Laughter and Charm

in THE VILLAGE HALL

Doors open 7-15   Commence 8 p.m.   Admission 2/-

Saturday, 7th July

CHILDREN'S SPORTS—(see back page)

CARNIVAL DANCE
in THE VILLAGE HALL

Music by "THE ARCADIANS"

Dancing 8 to 11.45 p.m.   Admission 2/-

Queen Elizabeth's Coronation in 1953 was marked with village events following the formation of a committee comprising amongst others – the Joseph sisters; the Burgess brothers; Rev Wheldon Williams. One outcome of their plans was to revive the Rose (or May) Queen tradition.

The Coronation Celebrations Committee decided that the Rose Queen should be selected by auditioning to find the local girl who could best recite the speech originally made by Queen Elizabeth on the occasion of her 21st Birthday. Her retinue were then chosen from a draw. The first crown, which was quite heavy, consisted of a metal frame made by Mr Ernie Lloyd and covered with masses of little pink rosebuds by Kay Joseph. The train was made from pink furnishing velvet - quite an achievement because it was not easy to get suitable fabric at that time.

Smaller communities within the growing village organised their own street parties – see colour photo on page 9 and the organising ladies below.

The next year – 1954 – marked the centenary of the parish church. This was a major event and as the following programme shows set out to involve the full village community. A large marquee was set up in a field off Heath Road with the scouts sleeping in it overnight acting as nightwatchmen. One decision of the organising committee under Rev. Wheldon Williams was to continue the recently revived Rose Queen ceremony and procession. This started a tradition of the church's annual Rose Queen that has continued through to the current day. At first the Rose Queen and retinue were chosen from girls at the large Sunday school. Loyalty and good attendance were the criteria and everyone enjoyed seeing the delightful way the successive Queens and their retinues behaved with such dignity and really entered into the spirit of the occasion. Latterly the Guides have supplemented the numbers.

CENTENARY FESTIVAL CALENDAR

SUNDAY, MAY 30th.

8-0 a.m. Holy Communion.

10-45 a.m. Matins and Sermon. *Preacher*, The Vicar.

3-0 p.m. Service for Freemasons—In the Marquee.
Preacher: REV. W. WILSON, Vicar of St. Andrew's, Crewe.

6-30 p.m. Festal Evensong—In Marquee.
Preacher: CANON S. J. MARRIOTT, Sub-Dean of Westminster Abbey.
Mr. Basil Nield, M.B.E., Q.C., M.P., will take part in this Service.

MONDAY, MAY 31st (Day of Consecration of Church).

7-15 a.m. Holy Communion.

7-15 p.m. Short Service in Church with Procession and Festal Evensong in Marquee.
Preacher: CANON S. J. MARRIOTT, Sub-Dean of Westminster Abbey.

8-30 p.m. Play "Everyman"— Admission 2s. — in Marquee.

TUESDAY, JUNE 1st.

7-15 a.m. Holy Communion.

7-30 p.m. Social Gathering of all Parishioners.

WEDNESDAY, JUNE 2nd.

7-15 a.m. Holy Communion.

10-15 a.m. Holy Communion—Mother's Union.

8-0 p.m. Centenary Parish Dance—In Village Hall

THURSDAY, JUNE 3rd.

7-15 a.m. Holy Communion.

7-30 p.m. Celebrity Concert—in Marquee
Artistes:—
EIRWEN JONES, *Soprano*
JEANETTE THOMPSON, *Contralto*
WALTON PRITCHARD, *Bass*
DEVA LADIES SINGERS
CHESTER MALE VOICE CHOIR
Chairman: ALD. MRS. L. BROMLEY-DAVENPORT, J.P.
Admission 2s.

FRIDAY, JUNE 4th.

7-15 a.m. Holy Communion.

6-30 p.m. Senior Children's Centenary Party—In Marquee.

SATURDAY, JUNE 5th.

7-15 a.m. Holy Communion.

3-30 p.m. Kindergarten Children's Centenary Party — in Marquee.

SUNDAY, JUNE 6th (Whitsunday)

7-0 a.m. Holy Communion.

8-0 a.m. Holy Communion.

10-45 a.m. Matins and Sermon. *Preacher*, The Vicar.

11-45 a.m. Holy Communion.

3-0 p.m. Children's Service—In Marquee

6-30 p.m. Festal Evensong—In Marquee.
Preacher: LORD BISHOP OF CHESTER.

The Carnival years 1977 - 1980

1977 marked the Queen's Silver Jubilee – the first major royal event for 25 years to be strongly supported throughout the country – and the first with Upton now significantly grown and part of Chester's suburbia.

An organising committee was formed in October 1976 chaired by Eric Gerrard with Secretary Ailsa Clegg and Treasurer David Clegg supported by Len & Betty Holland. They had ambitious plans and a determination to involve the whole village community. A target was set to raise funds of £2000 – enough to present each child with a commemorative mug and to hold a carnival complete with a procession. Fund raising events were many and varied with dances, weekly coffee mornings and a grand draw. With village traders providing prizes, this latter event raised over £300 - the main prize going to a person from South Wales.

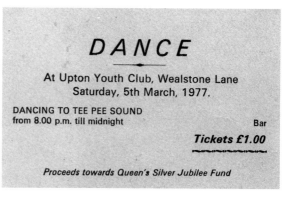

Eager to revive past traditions they noted that for the 1937 coronation – the oldest villager and the first-born baby were presented with special momentos to mark the day. Articles in the local press were used to track down the oldest villager – eventually locating Mrs 'Granny' Brough.

As Jubilee day approached various local organisations and residential areas were holding their own events. The Cotebrook Drive Street Party was the first in Chester – and choosing an early date, gave them the benefit of glorious weather which wasn't so available on the actual Jubilee Day. Flags & bunting were stretched around lamp posts & trestle tables were covered with yards of white paper decorated with the children's designs of crowns & Jubilee messages. One of the organisers - Mrs Jean Demack -commented that *"all the food had been eaten - including the huge Jubilee Cake made by a resident - and that there had been real community spirit."*

A plan for the residents of Lawn Drive, Penfold Hey and Upton Lane to have a party in the grounds of the demolished Upton Lawn had to be abandoned because of bad weather, so it was held in the Church Hall instead. After a Musical Parade by the children there were party games, a table tennis tournament and a special tea. Pets (including budgerigars) had been invited and they too had refreshments.

Celebrations Programme

1.45 p.m. Procession of Floats

Route:—

Upton High School (grounds)
St. James' Avenue
Weston Grove
Gatesheath Drive
Heath Road
Upton Lane
Church Lane
Upton Cross
Wealstone Lane playing field (Pavilion car park)

Participants (accurate at time of going to press):—

Army Vehicles
Boys' Brigade Band
Upton Royal British Legion
Upton Acresfield School
Upton County High School
Upton Manor School
Upton Mill View School
Upton St. Mary's Infants' School
Upton Westlea School
United Reformed Church
Upton Parish Church
Upton Girl Guides and Brownies
Upton-by-Chester Scout Group
Chester Vintage Car Club
Henley's of Chester (Rolls-Royce)

All participants gratefully acknowledge the generosity of companies who have loaned vehicles

3.00 p.m. Official Opening by the Right Worshipful the Mayor of Chester

ORDER OF EVENTS
(approximate times)

3.15	Judo Display
3.30	Country Dancing—Westlea School
3.45	Beer Race—local public houses
4.00	Fancy Hat Parade—under 5-years-old groups
4.30	Physical Education Display—Upton County High School
4.45	Sword Dancing ⎫ Upton Manor School
	Morris Men ⎬
5.00	Tug-o'-War—teams of eight
5.30	Barbecue Cooking—Scouts
6.00	Brass Band Recital—Cheshire Constabulary Brass Band
7.30	'Last Orders'
8.30	Youth Disco—venue: Upton Youth Club (price 40p)

OTHER ATTRACTIONS

Stalls
Side Shows
Bar
Refreshments
Finals of Tennis and Bowls Tournaments

The village-wide Carnival took place on Saturday 18th June 1977 and was very well supported. The day started with a procession including 20 floats (see page 8 colour photographs) and took a route along St James Avenue, Western Grove, Gatesheath Drive, Heath Rd, Upton Lane, Upton Cross and Wealstone Lane to the car park on Carnival Field (Wealstone Lane Playing Fields). Granny Brough rode in a Rolls Royce with floats from local schools and churches as well as businesses and organisations such as the British Legion.

Cllr Eric Gerrard and Mayor Shiela Garston with 'Granny' Brough

Upton resident Mrs Sheila Garston was the Mayor of Chester at the time and she officially opened the Carnival at 3pm. Teams from the Wheatsheaf Inn carried off major prizes in the Beer Race and the tug of war. A newspaper reporter wrote - *'The normally reserved village of Upton let its hair down as crowds lined the road to wave on the grand procession'*.

Upton Parish Council attended a special service on the following Sunday. At the United Reformed Church there was a Family Service - a re-enactment of the Coronation, ending with a hearty rendering of *'God Save The Queen'*.

Another Jubilee event was the Grand Field Day & Donkey Derby held by the High School at the County Officers Sports Club field. There were many stalls and sideshows and the High School Band gave its first outdoor performance all helping raise funds towards a new minibus for the school. The children of Upton Manor School were presented with their Jubilee Mugs by Mr John Ross as Chairman of the Governors. Nearly *£500* was raised at the *'Jubilee Jaunt'* and £300 of this was presented to the Jubilee Committee.

Festivities continued into July with a Gala Day at the Upton Youth Club in Wealstone Lane. As well as displays by local musicians the day had a strong football link. Former England Manager Joe Mercer attended and visitors were invited to *'score a goal against Chester F.C. Ace – Grenville Millington'*. The police even competed in a soccer special against the girls.

The Carnival clearly renewed a strong community spirit and enthusiasm that enabled the event to become an annual occasion for a number of years. In practice the 'Summer Carnival' survived through until 1980 – each year being self funding from prior fund raising and ticket sales. Without supporters to run future events the Carnival fund wound up and the remaining £400 donated to the Village Hall Re-roofing fund.

The 1979 event took on a nostalgic theme of 'through the ages' and was attended by the Duke and Duchess of Westminster as well as Chester's MP – Peter Morrison. The procession of floats was led by the Chester City Band.

Recent years

The Parish Council organised a Family Fun Day in 1994 to celebrate the centenary of Parish Councils. The Clerk - Andy Reilly – handled the organisation with Brenda Southward entering into the spirit of the event as seen here in her clown outfit.

The Queen's Golden Jubilee was not celebrated by village-wide activities, however many specific local communities held their own events, including street parties.

For the new Millennium, 'Churches Together in Upton' worked with the Parish Council to organise a summer celebration on Wealstone Lane playing field. This free event was funded jointly through the Millennium Lottery Fund and the Upton Parish Council. Local churches, schools and organisations provided entertainment with bands, choirs, comedy and numerous stalls. The day was well supported, across the community, despite the wet weather.

As this book goes to press arrangements are being finalized for Upton's first Music Art & Literature Festival with a theme of 'Upton Yesterday & Today'. Events spread over March & April 2005 should showcase much of the current local talent while reminding people of their local heritage.

CHAPTER 14

Leisure Activities

It is surprising how many activities there are in Upton; the residents are obviously an interested and interesting population. On the following pages is information on groups, both past and present. Without doubt there are many more activities that are not covered here and as things are learnt of them they will be added to the growing collection of Leisure Group information. The groups listed are in chronological order.

Bache Golf Club

The Bache Golf Club came into being on 24th May 1901 with a 6 hole course on land owned by Mr Ithell, a farmer, of Upton Hall. The land was adjacent to, and just north of the County Asylum. The club's stay there was short and in 1902 it moved to the Bache Hall Estate which was centred on Bache Hall. The Hall and land was then tenanted by Major MacGillicuddy, an Irish landowner, who was one of the founders of the Club.

Records show that in 1909 the men's entrance fee and subscriptions were both set at two guineas and the ladies at one guinea. This is the earliest reference to a ladies section at the club. Green fees at that time were 1/- per day; the Hon Secretary's fee was £25 and the auditor's was 2 guineas.

FIFTY YEARS AGO

(Extract from the "Cheshire Observer", 1st June, 1901).

NEW GOLF CLUB.—At a meeting held on Friday evening it was decided to form the Bache golf club, to play on the lands of Upton Hall farm. The club, in these present early days, is an unpretentious affair—it is only a six hole course—but the links are accessible to Cestrians, and the undertaking will doubtless, thrive and grow.

In 1910 when Major MacGillicuddy was elected President of the Golf Club rumours were circulating that the Bache Hall Estate was to be sold to the Asylum Committee. He thought a sale was unlikely but promised he would do all he could to protect the interests of the club. Fears of a sale became justified when a proposed sale was advertised to be on 8th June 1910. The club was naturally perturbed and set up a sub committee to watch developments. There followed much negotiating and activity about where would be suitable for a new golf course. Early in 1911 the first reviews of possible sites commenced; these sites included areas in Lache Lane; Butterbache Farm, Huntington; Eaton Road, Eccleston; and land in Bumpers Lane, off Sealand Road which was the preferred site. Unfortunately hopes for this site were dashed when the Medical Officer for Health in Chester declared that under the Public Health Act *"No concourse of people numbering 150 could be held within half a mile of a smallpox hospital"*, at that time Sealand House (now the Mulberry Centre) was such a hospital. Following this declaration the sub committee had to start their search for land anew.

In July 1911 the sub-committee reported that negotiations with Butterbache Farm had started again and at a subsequent meeting with them, mention was made of a site at Brewers Hall Farm, Curzon Park. It was suggested that the committee walk over the site.

A special meeting was convened for 25th July 1911 and the committee reported that the site had been thoroughly inspected. The total acreage was 107.5, part being under Lord Howe and part under Great Western Railway Company (G.W.R.) at a total rent of £188 per annum. The Chairman stated that he had knowledge of 'certain gentlemen' who were desirous of taking the land to use as a private golf course, and they wished to assist the Bache Golf Club. The minutes of the meeting noted that *'The suggestion did not meet with approval'*. The sub-committee entered into negotiations with Lord Howe and were granted a lease of 14 years at £200 per annum, for the 25 acres of G.W.R land which they believed they could purchase for £60 per acre. However early in 1912 Lord Howe stated his intention to sell his land, although he expected to get £5000 on the open market, he would let the Bache Golf Club have it for £4000. Following negotiations a price of £3750 was accepted and on March 20th the sale was agreed.

A special General Meeting of the club was held on 27th March 1912 at Clemences Café, Northgate Street. The meeting resolved that a) the sum of £4,500 (£3,750 purchase price + £750 course preparation) be raised by £2500 mortgage and £2000 from members. b) A company, to be known as *'The Brewers Hall Estate Company'* should be formed to buy the land and let it to the Golf Club Committee.

The original Pavilion

At a meeting on 23rd September 1912 it was decided *'To play the final match on the Bache course on Saturday 5th October 1912 between teams chosen from members over 40 and members under 40'. 'The winning team to provide supper on the night of the match and the losing team to provide liquid refreshment'.*

The move from Bache Hall to Brewers Hall Farm went ahead during the winter of 1912/13. In January Mr A Hornby resigned as Secretary of the Bache Golf Club and Mr Edward Andrews was appointed with an honorarium of £20 per annum. Mr F Small was appointed House Secretary with an honorarium of £15 per annum.

Following a meeting in February 1913 the club adopted the title of Curzon Park Golf Club. Most of the portable assets were moved to the new site in early 1913 - including the pavilion, where it gave good service for many years.

Football

Upton St Mary's Football Club successfully applied for membership of the Chester & District Football League for the 1910/11 season. Their first recorded match was against Buckley Old Boys on 3rd September 1910. They showed up well in their first season and on 5th November 1910 much to the delight of their supporters they beat Ellesmere Port Vics 3 -1 in a closely contested match, at Upton, to go top of the division. However this proved short lived and by the end of the season the club handed in their resignation from the league and disbanded.

In 1919 Upton St Mary's Football Club was reformed and applied once again to join the League. Interest in the football team was considerable. The committee had been strengthened by the addition of three new committee members and it was hoped that the playing strength of the club would also be strengthened as several members has been demobbed after service in the forces during the First World War. However a series of defeats left the club third from the bottom of Division 2. The report of one game in the Chester Chronicle highlighted the problems *'What is the matter at Upton? Pull yourselves together. Petty differences do not lend themselves to unity. It is only the combined efforts of players and committee that brings success. We shall be pleased to learn about your rehabilitation'* This very public rebuke seems to have had the desired effect. In their next game Upton St Mary's beat local rivals Christleton 3-0.

For the next few seasons St Mary's was in and out of the league until the end of the 1930/31 season when they resigned and disappeared from the football map altogether.

The idea of Upton Athletic initially came into being in the mid 1940s on the Community Playing Fields at the top of Heath Road which was known locally as Frost's Field (or Chemistry Pits). Mr Gordon Beck, a Chester estate agent, who lived in Endsleigh Gardens, and whose son played football with a group of others, presented them with a football kit – blue shirts, white shorts and blue socks and Upton Juniors was created. They played matches against similar teams as themselves from the surrounding area and it was people like Cyril Wheelton, Jim McDougall, Jim Watts and Eddie Roberts provided the serious direction and purpose which began to take Upton Juniors forward.

Upton Juniors, made a successful application to join the Chester Amateur Soccer Association League (known locally as the C.A.S.A. League) and they began the 1949-50 football season in Division 4 of the C.A.S.A. League which catered for teams under the age of 15.

The team began the season playing its home games on a field on Wealstone Lane, where the Library and the Medical Centre stand today. The land was owned by Mr Ben Roberts who had a small holding in Wealstone Lane. He allowed goalposts to be kept in his sheds and used to mow the pitch with a mowing machine pulled by a tractor Most of the time the team arrived at Wealstone Lane changed ready to play but from time to time it was arranged that they would change in the Village Hall and walk down to the Wealstone Lane pitch from there. On those occasions the team felt like a proper football team with its own changing facilities. Their first game on 10th September 1949 was against the Y.M.C.A. when the home team had a resounding 9 - 2 success. It was a marvellous start to the season but Upton Juniors found it difficult playing against well established sides. They won just four more games to finish tenth in the league.

c1948
E Cook, J Paddock, E Leach, K Ravenscroft, K Wheelton, G Gaskell
B Jones, P Webster, J Dentith, D Gaskill, M Sidwell.

In the 1950-51 football season Upton Juniors, now in Division 3 continued to progress. Thanks to Cyril Wheelton and Jim Watts the team had developed to such an extent that they went through the 1951-52 season winning every match and the league. *'Mr Wheelton was very strict; he would remind the team that under no circumstances argue with the referee, if the referee's decision was disputed a player could end up being sent off for dissent and that would mean playing with a man short'*. In 1952 the all conquering Upton Juniors reached the final of the C.A.S.A. League Cup.

The season 1961-62 was, from the opening day's fixtures on 26th August, a catalogue of misfortune, calamity and disaster for Upton Athletic. The club had problems arising from the uncertainty over the date that the new playing field at Wealstone Lane would be ready and a growing inability to raise a team to meet its commitments in the Chester & District League. Players became disgruntled and disillusioned. The result was that these players left the club to play for other teams. In the August, just before the start of the 1962-63 football season, Upton Athletic informed the Chester & District League that the club was unable to carry on in Section B and as a consequence they were tendering their resignation from the league. Sadly the dream that had first surfaced on Frost's Field in Heath Lane in the 1940s was now no more than a set of statistics consigned to history.

Upton Athletic 1958 -59   with Manager Cyril Wheelton
S Worrall, B Williams, R Purvis; B Ducworth; E Woodcock; K Wheelton..
T Johnson; R Pleavin; N Jones; R Bradley; T Woodcock.

Following the demise of Upton Athletic the next football club to emerge was Upton Athletic Association Football Club. Founded in 1962 the idea came from the Parish Church Youth Club leader Arthur Formistone and the Rev Perris Williams a curate at the Church of the Holy Ascension. *"Before a match we used to change in the garage of the house on the corner of Wealstone Lane and Weston*

Grove. The house was owned by the father of John Iles who played for the team.....it was really quite convenient!!"

Mr Denham, Mike Denham's father, managed to get hold of a large wooden hut which he thought would be ideal for the teams to change in. It was rumoured that the hut was one which was surplus to requirements on the Dale Camp. Approaches were made to the Chester City Council who agreed to provide a base for the hut, which was then duly installed.

"The hut was a huge improvement on the rather cramped conditions of Mr Iles garage and further more it was actually on the Wealstone Lane playing field. The hut was also useful as it served as a storage depot, between matches, for the goalposts, the goal nets, the line marking machine, the bags of lime for the line marking machine etc. As a result the hut acquired a unique atmosphere all of its own".

The exploits of the team had come to the attention of the selectors of the Chester FA Youth Team. Ken Hughes and Peter Futcher were selected for the team which enjoyed a run to the semi finals of the Cheshire FA Youth Cup. The team's success also attracted the attention of those scouting for league clubs.

Gareth Hughes and Stuart Crawford were invited to trials at Arsenal Football Club in London. They spent a fortnight rubbing shoulders with many of the club's international stars but at the end of the fortnight they were, according to Stuart Crawford, *"Thanked for coming to Arsenal for trials and wished the very best in their future careers...and that was it"*. Graham Futcher, who played for the Chester & District Youth team in the 1968-69 season, became the first player from Upton AA to sign for a League club, when he signed for Chester.

On 28th April 1973 the club played from its new home at the recently opened Pavilion on the Wealstone Lane playing fields. The move by Upton AA to establish its base at the new Pavilion was at the instigation of Reg Bedford who played for Upton AA and was a youth worker at Upton Youth Club. However, to meet the higher standards of playing and changing facilities demanded by the West Cheshire League, the club moved again to the County Officers Sports Club, in Plas Newton Lane.

The first of Upton AA Football Club's annual Sportsman's Dinners was held on the 25th February 1989 to coincide with the club's 25th anniversary year. The former Manchester United manager Tommy Docherty was the guest speaker and for the eighth year running a pre-season friendly match with Manchester United was organised, for 11th August 1989, to take place in Upton. It was a gesture of friendship from the Old Trafford club that they agreed to play the game in Upton to mark the 25th anniversary.

In 2002, forty years after the club was founded, Dave Iles, John Iles, Reg Bedford, Jimmy Dutton, Mike Denham, Derek Johnson, Chris Nevett, Graham Nevett, John Williams and Ian Caveney (players from the early years) rolled back time under the watchful eye of referee David Berry to take part in a commemorative 5 a side football match.

Paul and Ron Futcher

The Futcher family home was, and still is, in Upton. Whilst at Upton Secondary School both boys were selected to play for the Chester Schools under 15's and the Cheshire County football teams. In 1972 both Paul and Ron were nominated for the Chester Observer sponsored 'Chester Schoolboy Footballer of the Year'. It really was no surprise that the two Upton boys signed apprenticeship forms for their home town football club.

As Ron and Paul made their league debuts for Chester City in the 1973-74 season, their promise was recognized by Luton Town FC manager Harry Haslam. In August 1974 he signed Paul for £100,000, a record British transfer fee for a seventeen year old. Later in the summer Harry came back to Chester to sign Ron, so re-uniting the twins.

Paul & Ron at their league debut with Chester City

In the summer of 1978 their continuing development on the football field saw them sign for Manchester City for a total transfer fee of £425,000.

Upton Junior Football Club

In 1993 Upton United Junior Football Team's first official match was against local rivals Upton Villa, a club based at the Dale Camp. This match is memorable for one thing, the weather. Monsoon would be a good description. During the season of 1994 the team started to use the field at Upton Manor School to hold their practices and matches.

The move to Upton Manor coincided with the purchase of their first set of portable goal posts and nets. Every Saturday morning an army of parents would move the goals from the school store, across the pitch and struggle with the jig-saw-like contraption. During 1999-2000 the Under 14's played at Chester's home ground in Bumpers Lane, the Deva Stadium, when they were in the Subsidiary Cup Final. Since 1998 the club had grown at some pace with boys and girls playing in both the Chester and Ellesmere Port Leagues with teams ranging from under 6 through to under 17 years of age.

2002 was a significant year for the club with the merger of Upton United & Upton Villa to form Upton Junior Football Club. Their base is currently at The Dale Camp, where they meet every Saturday during school term 10 - 12 noon and the club has established itself as one of the major centres in Chester for football with nearly 270 children playing for the club.

The Bache Bowling Club.

The Bache Bowling Club came into being in 1912, shortly after the Northgate Brewery built a bowling green in Mill Lane behind their Egerton Arms public house. Some of the directors of the brewery were among the first members of the newly formed club, which leased the green from the brewery for an annual rent of 1/-. In those early days the green was accessible through a small orchard, which made it a wonderful setting. Some years later the orchard was forfeited to make room for a car park.

Not much is known about the early life of the club except that it was a thriving and popular one. In 1949 the membership stood at 38, 1954 saw them join the Chester and District Bowling League and by 1963 when membership was 42 they supported an 'A' and 'B' team; subscriptions at that time were £1.15.0. and club rules stated that *'The club shall consist of not more than 65 members'*. It was also in the 60s that they were promoted to the top division of the league.

However things were to change. In the early 1980s the Greenhall Whitley Brewery (formerly Northgate Brewery) announced their intention to close the green to create a beer garden. At a committee meeting held in March 1983 it was agreed that the club secretary would arrange a meeting with the brewery manager as soon as possible and an alternative venue for their matches should be looked for. The next committee meeting announced that the brewery would allow the club to carry on using the green for the rest of that season, while planning permission was applied for.

In October of that year hopes were raised when the planning application for the car park and beer garden was refused by the City Council. However, the brewery informed the club that the Bowling Green would be required for its own use and so, notice to quit was given on 17th October 1983. With hopes of retaining the green dashed once and for all, the club's priority was to find another location. The tenancy agreement was due to end on 1st May 1984 so until that time the club still had exclusive use of the Mill Lane green. At a meeting with brewery representatives, it was agreed that after 1st May the club would still be able to use the green on Mondays and Thursdays for their league matches but for any 'social bowling' agreement must be sought from the landlord. It was agreed that the bowling club would maintain the green for a period of 12 months and there would be no charge made for the club using it.

The new system continued, satisfactorily, until May 1989 when once again the Brewery applied for planning permission to build an extension to the pub. This time the extension was to be a 28 bedroom unit. Although, as before, the application was refused, in October 1990 the brewery wrote to the club informing them that the green would be closing at the end of the month. Again the other local bowling clubs were approached to look into the possibility of sharing facilities. Fortunately Upton Parish Council was willing to allow extra use of the Green on Wealstone Lane so negotiations were entered into, with the Royal British Legion, who also used it.

An amicable arrangement was reached and although they had to drop down to one team only, The Bache Bowling Club had found a new home and to date continue to play in the Chester and District Bowling League.

Guiding in Upton

Monica Sparling

The 1st Upton Brownie pack was started by Miss Monica Sparling (daughter of the first Vicar of Upton) in 1919 and has never closed. Guides started just a month later.

After Miss Sparling, Guiding in Upton became almost synonymous with the Joseph family. Kay Joseph assisted Monica with the Brownies and it was only natural that she took over in 1929 following Monica's death. During the 39 - 45 war, although Guides did much collecting of waste paper, rose hips etc. the company in Upton closed for a while due to difficulty in recruitment. In 1945 the movement started up again with just 3 guides and Alix Joseph as captain. Rangers, the senior section, started in

1956 and Rainbows, the most junior section, more recently in 1987. There are now 3 Guide Companies, 4 (+ 1 in Mollington) Brownie Packs, 2 groups of Rainbows and 1 Ranger Unit.

The Joseph connection with the Guiding movement only died with Alix's death in February 2000. However its continuity is assured as the dedicated leaders at all levels maintain the spirit of the movement with selfless care. Meeting places have included the Vicarage attic, a classroom at St Mary's School and the Scout Hut. The Scouts had an ex-army hut from Moston and Guides were to have another but it was rather decrepit, the ends didn't fit very well and it finally blew down in a gale!

Finally in 1956, thanks to the good offices of Canon Wheldon Williams, guiding in Upton was able to take over the Men's Institute building on the corner of Caughall Road. It had been used as a Civil Defence headquarters and was in a frightful condition. After 2 years of hard work by Guides, parents and all and sundry, it was officially opened in 1958. In 1964 the camp room was added. Since then it has had some excellent refurbishment including a new kitchen. Adequate heating was installed, as members froze for many winters and there were no such things as thermal underwear then. The garden/play area was developed as a memorial to Kay Joseph in 1972.

Camps have been many and varied in rain, wind and sunshine, with wonderful hospitality from our hosts. There have been visits from cows, sows and piglets, a pack of hounds and countless dogs. The sight of guides leaving Upton in a furniture van packed to overflowing was common in Upton for many years until furniture vans were no longer considered desirable transport.

Leaving for camp in the furniture van

Guides have camped at home and abroad, including U.S.A., Mexico and the Far East and have enjoyed hospitality within families as well as attending International Camps.

They have also helped to make the new County Standard which replaced the old one as Cheshire Guiding became so large that it had to be divided and much work was done at Wakefield Grange (Alix Joseph's school). There have been numerous pageants for which costumes were made and the Trefoil Guild, which is for retired or non-active Guides, has made many panels for display; one of which, representing Chester, is on display in Guide Headquarters.

Cricket

The Cricket Club was originally formed by Mr Horace Whaley, Mr Len Wright and Mr Harry Griffiths who had the unstinting support of Rev. W Sparling.

The first field they were able to use was on the site, owned by Mr Fred Davies that is now Endsleigh Gardens. Len was generous enough to pay for the construction of a pavilion and each Friday evening an attempt was made to mow the grass in the small area where the wickets were due to be pitched and the larger weeds and thistles were cut, but the outfield remained untouched except by cows; the fielders not only had to watch out for prominent tussocks but for large cowpats generously distributed around the pitch! Indeed, it was not unknown for fielders to have to run round a cow when taking a catch, for though the herd was shooed away when matches began, it usually tended to drift back.

After tentative beginnings in 1923, The Rev. W Sparling accepted the position of Chairman, and, subsequently, President and along with Horace Whaley, Len Wright and Harry Griffiths the club players consisted of young Upton men; Sam Broster; Harry Venebles; Tom Garner the lanky wicket keeper, Peter Snelson the slow bowler and Walter Woodward a fiery and erratic demon bowler. Upton Cricket Club had a full fixture list for 1924.

During the next few years, the club prospered, a roller was bought and used energetically before, during and after the match and a committee of ladies led by Emily Griffiths and Mrs Williamson began to provide teas for the players and visitors.

By 1928, the club was going from strength to strength. The arrival of two capable cricketers, Herbert Schofield and Frank Hewitt, the local schoolmaster, enabled Upton to enter the popular Boughton Hall 'knockout' competition. Boughton Hall was the rich, semi-professional club which played a sophisticated standard of cricket and worked hard in popularising the game.

When the cricket pitch land was taken for housing in the late 1920s the club moved to Demage Lane, to a field owned by Sir John Frost, where they stayed for many years. John Crompton, a new recruit to the club, paid for a new pavilion to be erected. This move meant that they could practice several nights a week on a field that was regularly mown and they didn't have to compete with the cows. John Crompton's participation also enhanced the prestige and the finances of the club. On August Bank Holiday in 1930 and 1931, many people of the village turned up to enjoy full day matches when a large marquee was hired and erected for a festive mid-day lunch and some good cricket was enjoyed. Both days were gloriously sunny and the players in their white flannels made an attractive English scene on the ground which was surrounded by splendid trees.

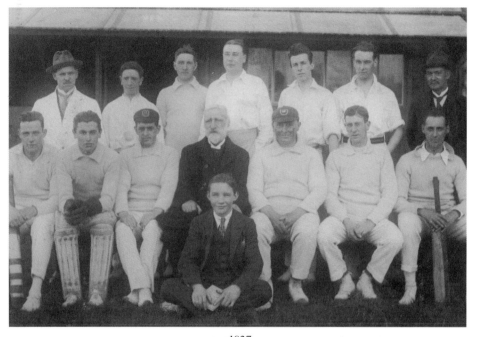

c1927

Rev. Sparling (centre front) with the team, sitting to his left, Horace Whaley and to his right Len Wright and Harry Griffiths

The improved standards of the Club enabled the team to challenge stronger opponents from further afield, and occasionally, a special away match would be organised and bus hired so that families could also attend. These were enjoyable outings which became wonderful family picnics.

The club continued to prosper until the outbreak of WW2 when, due to the players having other priorities, it disbanded.

The Women's Institutes

Upton Heath WI

On 12th May 1926, the Upton Heath Women's Institute met for the first time in the Chapel schoolroom, under the presidency of Mrs Crompton. From then meetings were held monthly, though the venue was changed in January 1929, to the newly opened Village Hall. Indeed, one of their first community efforts was to help in the raising of funds for the building of the hall. The membership steadily increased from 48 in 1926 to 220 in 1936. The latter was fixed as the maximum membership.

The Institute has taken part in all the various aspects of Institute work and has a large variety of interests; exhibitions of handicrafts and produce are held from time to time; exchanges of letters and gifts link the Institute with those in New Zealand and Canada. Social events include an annual outing, a birthday party and Christmas festivities. In 1951 the Institute marked its quarter century by having a cloth embroidered for use at meetings. It was made from a hand-woven linen sheet over one hundred years old and donated by a member. To mark the Coronation of King George VI a seat was donated to the village and placed at the junction of Heath Road and Long Lane. The

Institute joined in the scheme for planting flowering trees along Heath Road to mark the Festival of Britain. The Choir which took part in the Chester Music Festival in 1951 won the first award for large choirs and received a silver cup.

The war activities of the Institute were very wide in scope including A.R.P., Ambulance, W.V.S., Evacuation Scheme, camouflage nets, fruit canning etc. Of special importance were two activities, the knitting party and the National Savings Group. The former made about 5,000 garments in six years for the Services and children from occupied countries. A penny-a-week scheme, organised to buy wool, realised £213-10-0. The latter, formed in June, 1940, collected £56,887 until its cessation in July, 1946. In addition a market stall was opened in June 1944, and members also undertook the distribution of pies under the Ministry of Food scheme for rural areas. In six years a quarter of a million pies were sold and the total profit of £450 was partly given to charities and partly made available for village and institute needs.

In 1965 the membership stood at 207, of which 5 were founder-members. To celebrate the Institute's golden jubilee, the president Miss M Claxon represented Upton Heath branch at a Royal Garden Party.

This branch of the W I closed some years ago.

Upton Cross WI

Upton Cross WI was formed in 1953 as an offshoot of Upton Heath WI who had capacity membership. In November 2003 Upton Cross WI celebrated its 50th Birthday in true golden style with a dinner & entertainment.

Meetings are held on the second Wednesday of each month (except August) when a wide range of speakers entertain members with demonstrations or talks. A competition on the theme of the evening is held for which a prize and points are awarded. Points are added together annually to determine the winners of the two Cups presented at each AGM.

Daffodil bulbs were planted at the Village Hall to celebrate the Queens accession to the throne. Assistance was given at the re-dedication of the Monica Sparling Garden Ceremony in July 2002. Embroidered kneelers have been made for both Parish Church and Chester Cathedral and regular stewarding and flower arranging is done at both venues. Constant assistance is given to ACWW (Associated Country Women of the World). Coins are collected annually for a National donation to be given, to benefit less fortunate people overseas with for example, the building and maintenance of water supplies etc.

Denman College at Marcham in Oxfordshire is the WI's own residential life-long learning centre and Upton Cross offers a bursary each year to enable a member to take up a course of her choice. The 60 strong group is also active in other ways, with a long standing bowling team and rambling section.

In 1965 Miss Willett represented the branch at the Royal Garden Party to celebrate 50 years of the Women's Institute.

Doreen Luke, Mary Thompson, Beryl Parkinson, Wyn Beckett,
Helen Bebbington, Josie Coates and Flo Webster

Deva WI

In an endeavour to involve patients at the Deva Hospital a special WI was created there in November 1960. It was quite an exceptional branch because of the fact that most of the members were patients and ran successfully, for many years.

Staffed mainly by local volunteers, who formed a committee, meetings were held on Hospital premises. Doris Harrison was the 1ˢᵗ President and later Betty Tushingham worked tirelessly for years.

In addition to meetings, patients were taken for days out, birthdays were marked and they were given an annual birthday party with some guests being invited. Fashion shows were held at the hospital which were very popular. The Committee Members and some of the patients modelled the clothes from the hospital shop.

In June 1965 a meeting was held in the gardens of the Manor Hospital, Great Sutton, where they heard of the experiences of their representative at the Royal Garden Party.

Due to hospital constraints this branch of the WI closed some years ago.

Miss Nickson's Riding School

The Riding School was opened in 1932 by Mr H. C. Martin on land that had been part Mr B. C. Roberts' Oakfield Estate. On leaving the zoo area the school then moved to Heath Road, just behind St. Mary's School. In April 1939 the riding school was taken over by Miss Betty Nickson who ran it successfully for many years.

Along the quieter roads of Upton, strings of youngsters could often be seen walking one behind the other, many of them on their own ponies. Day rides were available and weekly riding holidays for children and adults were a popular occurrence. Pupils were prepared for show rings, including the jumping category and were often successful.

THE UPTON RIDING SCHOOL.

UPTON, CHESTER.

RIDING TAUGHT IN ALL ITS BRANCHES

JUMPING A SPECIALITY . . . .

GOOD HACKS FOR HIRE AT 5/- PER HOUR

SPECIAL TERMS FOR REGULAR RIDERS . .

H. C. MARTIN, Proprietor.

Ponies and horses would also be supplied for other events such as local fetes, where children loved to ride them, also for film promotions when the animals would be taken to the Odeon or Classic cinemas and on one occasion two horses were taken to the Plantation Inn, Chester to be photographed with cabaret performers on their backs.

Royal British Legion

HIGHEST AWARD FOR TWO LEGION MEMBERS

Club Ceremony At Upton-By-Chester

Mr. Clay

Mr. Pearson

The Royal British Legion was created, initially, by Lord Haig, for ex-servicemen who had been disabled in the First World War. The idea was to make poppies, to sell; not only to commemorate those lost in the war but to raise funds for the welfare of those who had returned disabled. There are two sections to the Legion; the club, which acts as a social centre for recreation of the branch members, and the branch, which takes care of the welfare of its members by raising funds to support them. The Royal British Legion in Upton was established in November 1933. One of its four founding members - Frederick L'Anson Morris was honorary secretary from 1935 - 1950 and is commemorated on a plaque in the clubhouse.

Newspaper cutting included in
'The WI 1965 Book'
Newspaper and date unknown

As they had no premises of their own at that time, their first meetings were held at the Men's Institute (now the Guide HQ) in Caughall Road. Later they had the use of rooms in other premises, where they could put up two snooker tables which were to move into the hut when it was built.

In 1946 the group was able to buy a plot of land in Heath Road, from a local farmer, for the princely sum of £400. The members cultivated the land and grew vegetables which were sold locally, and eventually this provided the funds to build their own club house. Built in the 1950s, the club house was officially opened by Sir Frederick Lister, first national chairman of the Legion. The opening ceremony parade was headed by the Band of the Cheshire Yeomanry which marched through Upton.

The structure consisted of a tin hut used by the members as a games room. Later as funds dictated, the tin was replaced by brick. Although the original clubhouse remains, it was incorporated into the newly extended building in the 1960s, which was approximately half the size of the building we know today. When the concert room was extended to its present size it was commemorated to Thomas Nichols B.E.M. who was honorary secretary of club 1970 - 1985. One of the rooms is dedicated to Jim Pearson, who was a relentless fundraiser for the legion.

Many groups use the friendly facilities of the Upton clubhouse, such as the Dunkirk Veterans; the Royal Corp of Signals; Royal Military Police Association and Chester and North Wales Long Service Medallists. In the early days membership reached a massive 1,400 and the rules of the organisation were that at least 60% of membership should be ex-service personnel. This rule has been relaxed more recently and the club welcomes all new members.

The women's section of Royal British Legion was created in 1925, and in Upton in 1949 when Mrs Jones was chairman, they, too, used to meet in the Guide Hut on the corner of Caughall Road. Once the new building was up and running in Heath Road the section was only too happy to hold their meetings there.

Dramatic Society

The original Church Choir Drama Group

The dramatic society began in 1934 when a new Vicar arrived in Upton and put on a play 'The Farmer's Wife' using members of his choir. When Rev. Gardner Brown left the Parish, his successor was not particularly enthusiastic about amateur dramatics so the choir members branched out on their own and created

Upton Dramatic Society. In those days the group membership was restricted to Upton residents only, so did well to survive. The society closed from 1940 - 1949, but soon re-established itself post war.

'Tilley of Bloomsbury'
1935

In the early days there would be one production at Christmas and it was quite a social event. Before the war people attending would wear evening dress, all the ladies in the cast received a bouquet and the front of the stage would be elaborately decorated with flowers. There was always a last-night party which would continue into the small hours of the morning. Later the group started to produce 2 plays each year.

'A Harvest Home'
an annual
production

The producer for some years was Mrs Gladys Mitchell (producer for Chester Operatic Society) until her death, since when the group have had a number of producers from its own ranks.

Some notable members of the group were Miss Beryl Nield (sister of Judge Basil Nield); Sheila Garston, former Mayor of Chester; Hugh Lloyd of TV fame, and many promising young actors who went on to greater things.

The society has continued to entertain audiences twice a year with comedies and thrillers, raising thousands of pounds for various local charities.

Upton Golf Club

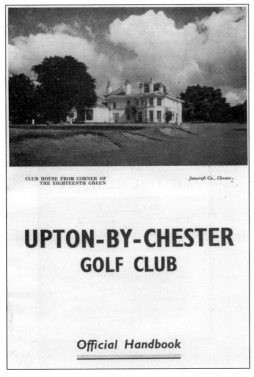

CLUB HOUSE FROM CORNER OF
THE EIGHTEENTH GREEN

fotocraft Co., Chester

UPTON-BY-CHESTER
GOLF CLUB

Official Handbook

Upton Golf Club was founded in July 1934 when Mr C J F Owen of Upton purchased 'The Oaks', owned by Mr Andrews Crompton, a cotton broker and land owned by Mr Charles Potts; all for the princely sum of £4,500. He later acquired the neighbouring estate of 'Upton Lawn', then owned by Sir John Frost of Frost Flour Mills.

Having an area that totalled 65 acres, Mr Owen called together a dozen of his colleagues and friends and the beginnings of the original 9 hole golf club was formed. Nine circles were mown as the greens on the grazing land (roped off against the cattle), plant pots used as holes and garden canes as flag sticks. The inaugural meeting of the club, when Mr C E Nield was elected to the chair, was held at 8pm on Tuesday July 3rd 1934. Mr Owen (Vice Chairman) offered the meeting access to the course, parking for members cars in the yard and the use of certain outbuildings of The Oaks as a temporary club house. Mr G A Samuel (Hon. Secretary) reported that he and Mr Owen had mapped out a possible 9 hole course and had estimated that expenditure during the first year (1934) would be £30 and £150 for the following year.

He also announced that 60 people had expressed an interest in joining and suggested, for the period ending March 1935, a subscription of one guinea. The meeting agreed that a club be formed and called the Upton by Chester Golf Club and that a joining fee should be levied as soon as the membership reached one hundred.

By August subscriptions had risen to 210 and as plans were in the pipeline to extend the course to 18 holes, a temporary limit of 250 members was agreed with boarding school boys being granted partial membership at 10/6^d pa. It was agreed to open the course for play on 4th August with green fees being fixed at

1/6^d for 18 holes (2 rounds of 9 holes). Mr Basil Nield was elected as Captain, with Sir Charles Cayzer Bt. MP, as President (1935-1940).

Mr J W (Bill) Davies and Mr T E (Eric) Par, professionals at Rhuddlan and Blacon Point Golf Clubs respectively, agreed to give advice on the course lay-out. Bill was also coerced into giving golf lessons and agreeing to stock and run a golf shop. He was appointed club professional at a wage of £2.5.0 which he held until November 1964, when Mr Peter Gardner took over until his retirement in February 2002. The current professional is Mr Stephen Dewhurst.

Soon after the club's formation Mr Owen purchased a number of large stone blocks from Mold Prison, which was being demolished, and created a golfers shelter that stands today near to the 12th tee. Up to the early seventies, players reached the 18th tee by ascending a series of stone steps (bought by a member and brought to the course). These were the very steps which led to the gallows at Ruthin Jail.

Due to the increasing demand for membership it was decided to make the course 18 holes. Extra land was offered by Mr Owen to allow the extension, provided the club paid for clearing the land. The new course layout was planned by Mr J E Hassall, the eminent golf architect, who mapped out an 18 hole course of some 4400 yards, the work being carried out during the winters of 1935/36 and 1936/37.

Further land was made available by Mr Owen, in September 1935. This allowed two, of the existing 18 holes, to be transferred across Church Lane, thus lengthening the course to its present 5810 yards.

In 1936 the Club was elected to membership of the L.G.U. (Ladies Golf Union). Entrance fees were set at one guinea with the first subscriptions two guineas. The acquisition of 'The Oaks' as the new club house with its billiard room and ballroom took place shortly after.

To mark the official opening of the new course an exhibition match was arranged for May 8th 1938 to include Percy Alliss, Alfred Pagham, (1936 British Open Champion), Bert Gadd (1933 French & 1937 Irish Open Champion), John Williams and of course the club professional Bill Davies.

In February 1940 the Club tragically lost its President, Sir Charles Cayzer, in a shooting incident at his Scottish residence. Mr Basil Nield, the 36 year old son of Mr Charles Nield of Upton Grange, became the club's new president.

In December 1942, the club was visited by a sub-committee of the Cheshire War Agricultural Committee and agreement reached that the 2nd and 3rd fairways be cultivated in 1943 for either oats or wheat, thus the course was restricted to 16 holes temporarily but remained open. It was frequently used by H.M Forces. During the war, part of the clubhouse was surrendered for use as a school for evacuees from St Patrick's Catholic Elementary School in Liverpool. In 1948, as food was still in short supply, approximately 12 acres were grown and cut for hay, following instructions from the Cheshire Agricultural Executive Committee.

Club members in 1951

Following Fred Owen's death, after World War 2, the Golf Club membership became a Limited Company to own and run the club; Bill Davies died in 1978 after spending his retirement in a cottage on the course near to the Clubhouse. The cottage was demolished in 1992 to create a small car park.

Mothers Union

In Upton the Mothers Union began in the 1930s when Rev. Sparling was Minister. The group continued to meet in the Vicarage, under the leadership of Mrs Wheldon Williams, until the Church Hall was built and enjoyed a strong membership in its earlier days.

The group closed in 1998.

Freemasonry

Upton Weal Stone Lodge was warranted on 6th November 1946 and consecrated on 27th January 1947.

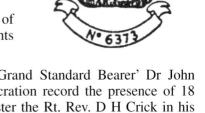

Frederick (Frank) Chidlow was a founding member and became the first Secretary of the Lodge. He suggested that *"This ancient stone being fashioned by men to enable them to fulfil their several obligations one to another and in so doing to promote and enrich the common good and well being of their fellows - it thereby presented a fitting symbolism worthy to be preserved in the name of the Lodge"*

(Frank Chidlow (b.1898) was Headmaster of St. Mary's school for many years. See comments in Reminiscences Chapter 18.)

The first Worshipful Master was 'Past Grand Standard Bearer' Dr John Ambrose Cooke. The minutes of the Consecration record the presence of 18 Founders and 96 others. The Bishop of Chester the Rt. Rev. D H Crick in his capacity as Provincial Grand Chaplain gave the Oration.

Shortly after the consecration, the Vicar of Upton, the Rev. John Wheldon Williams was admitted to membership of the Lodge retaining the parish church's tradition of close association with local freemasonry. The centenary of the church held in 1954 started with a service for Freemasons. The Rev. Wilfred Sparling had been a member of a local Lodge.

The mother lodge for Upton Weal Stone is the Independence Lodge, both of which continue to meet in the local Masonic Hall, Cheshire View in Christleton.

Up to the middle of the 20th century many of the well known figures in Upton would have been Freemasons. One could expect to find members of the established professions, civic dignitaries, clerics & other church officials, landed gentry - all members of one or other of the local lodges - only some of these would have chosen to transfer to the Upton Weal Stone Lodge. Current membership stands at around 30.

Horticultural Society

A Horticultural Society seems to have flourished from c1894 until 1914 as shown by old records of Flower Shows These shows were held in various large houses in the area. The present Society was reformed in 1946, when a *'Flower, Fruit, Vegetable and Farm Produce'* show was held, along with a pony gymkhana on Mr Roberts' field at Upton Cross. The show committee, seeing how successful it was, reformed the following month and founded Upton-by-Chester Horticultural Society. The aim of the society was to promote the cultivation of flowers, fruits and vegetables by means of shows, lectures and meetings.

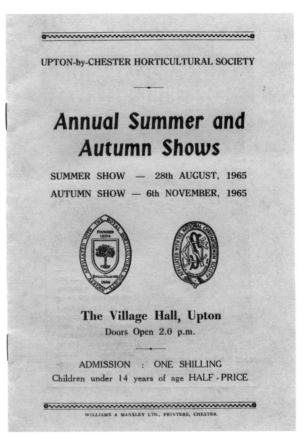

UPTON-by-CHESTER HORTICULTURAL SOCIETY

Annual Summer and Autumn Shows

SUMMER SHOW — 28th AUGUST, 1965

AUTUMN SHOW — 6th NOVEMBER, 1965

The Village Hall, Upton

Doors Open 2.0 p.m.

ADMISSION : ONE SHILLING

Children under 14 years of age HALF - PRICE

WILLIAMS & MANSLEY LTD., PRINTERS, CHESTER.

At the first committee meeting, held in October 1946, Mr C. Watkin was elected chairman, Mr S. French secretary and Mr C. Cassidy treasurer. Shortly afterwards Mr D Miln, of Miln's Seed Merchants, was elected as president. Initially they met in the Scout Hut on Mill Lane, then in 1947 they were able to use the Village Hall, where they have been holding their meetings ever since. The committee who, in the early years paid for the hire of the meeting rooms, were asked to loan the society 10/-, to help with set up costs; they were also asked to enrol 5 new members each. One month later 24 members had been enrolled, each paying 2/6^d for subscription and the loan of 10/- was repaid to the committee members the following February. Membership was restricted to those who lived in the Parish of Upton but associate membership was allowed to those who lived in the neighbouring parishes with ladies not being allowed to join until the following year. All membership applications had to be approved by the committee, and not everyone who applied was granted membership. Two of the earliest lady committee members, Mrs C Norman and Miss E Main (co-owners of Normain College, now The Firs School), expressed an interest in playing a more active role but were politely prevented from doing so and had to continue to be invited, occasionally, to attend committee meetings.

The first annual show was held in on Saturday 22nd November 1947 in the Village Hall. It consisted of 4 sections, totalling 60 classes; the sections were Chrysanthemums (members only); Chrysanthemums (open); Fruit and Preserves. The entry fee for each class was 6d and the 1st prize for most classes was a princely 7/6d.

The following year Summer and Autumn Shows were held and open classes were made available to residents who lived within a 6 mile radius of Upton Cross. A total of 150 metal vases were bought in 1948, to be used for exhibits in the shows - which are still used today.

The New Hut in 1983

The other notable event in 1948 was the opening of the Society's Stores on Long Lane (where Dulas Court now stands). This moved in 1983 to its present location off Caughall Road. This is open on Saturday afternoons from March to October and is staffed by a rota of volunteers. It is here that members can buy garden tools such as canes, plant pots and fertilizers at reduced prices.

Thank you gifts, made to the Show Judges, were a little different in the early days; a gift of 10 cigarettes was common-place and the prizes for the winners of competitions were unusual too; dressed chickens, large balls of string and a load of manure were awarded to some lucky members. Three times the society has played host to BBC's Gardeners Question Time radio programme, in 1951, 1983 and in 2004.

As with most societies, members come and go, in 1951 membership stood at 220, in 1965 it stool at 300 with members paying an annual fee of 3/6d.

By 1984 membership had risen to 629 and today it stands at a respectable 450. A thriving and active group, they meet nine times a year; have a plant sale in May; hold Spring, Summer and Autumn shows; have a bi-annual 'Garden Trail' through Upton as well as organising trips and visits to places of interest.

At the 1986 show, the all male committee lunch………

Frank Whaley, Frank Beckett, John Pritchard, Ken Stamp, 2 visiting judges, and Charlie Clark.

…..…...while the women wait outside

Wyn Beckett, Betty Pritchard, Mrs Cassidy and Rose Snelson.

Badminton Club

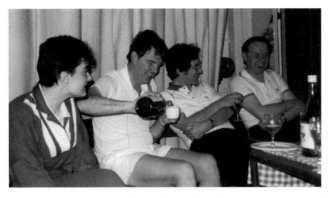

Upton Badminton Club started its life in 1949 when the members used to meet at the Gilwern TA centre in Abbots Park. They transferred to Upton Village Hall in 1957 when they would meet twice weekly, once for a club *'practice'* night and once for match night. In those days they played in division one of the Chester & District league and several players either played or went on to play at County level. They continued to meet weekly on a Tuesday evening from April to September and from the evening club, a group of members branched out to play on a Thursday afternoon, also in the Village Hall.

Hinde's Riding School

Hinde's riding school was set up in 1950 by Jean Hinde (Daughter of Frank) at Northfields on Long Lane. Jean had 12 ponies at the school, either owned or liveried, and taught local children to ride as well as entering local Gymkhanas, fetes and point to point events.

The school closed in 1959 when Jean married and moved out of the area.

Scouts

In the Souvenir Programme for the Official Opening of the Headquarters Upton Drive Mr E R France, Group Council Chairman wrote *'The group was formed in January, 1952, as a result of an appeal from the Vicar of Upton, and initially met in the Village School. The response was so encouraging, it was immediately realised that to operate efficiently a building of their own was essential'*.

Through the generosity of Mr Justice Basil Nield and his family, this object was achieved, and the first Headquarters opened in Church Lane in May, 1953. It was subsequently necessary to move from these premises, and they were fortunate in having the present piece of land donated by Messrs. Capstick & Owen Ltd., and a semi-temporary building was erected in the summer of 1958. During this period the Group Council realised that, with the continued growth of the area, bigger and better accommodation was necessary, and in February, 1963, a general appeal was sent to the residents of Upton, which was to form the basis of a fund for the building. This realised the sum of £310. Further efforts were made and in January 1967 sufficient had been raised to enable definite arrangements for the building to be started.

Leaving for camp with the help of Rev. Wheldon Williams

The Scout hut at Upton Drive was officially opened by His Grace the Duke of Westminster on Saturday 12th October 1968. It is pleasing to note that, since then, no less than 12 Queen's Scout Badges have been awarded to the Group and the boys have had the honour of being selected to attend Jamborees in Canada and in the United States. It has also been possible for expeditions to be arranged for some of the senior members to travel on the Continent and in Scotland. This, in addition to the annual Scout camps in various parts of the British Isles. The Cub Section has also had local camps annually.

The 1ˢᵗ Upton Cub Scouts, at a presentation by the local manager of the TSB. Pictured outside Scout HQ with Akela and Officers in 1980

Young Wives

Upton Young Wives Group was inaugurated in 1956 when Mrs N Ingham was appointed Leader and the annual subscription was set at 2/-. The first meeting, held on the 24th October in the Village Hall, welcomed 58 new members and Mrs Williams, the vicar's wife, presented a gift of £1 to the group on behalf of the Mothers Union. The programme for the first year of the group covered topics such as 'Children Growing up', a Christmas Party, 'Six Essentials for a Happy Home' and a film about the 'Oberammergau Passion Play', plus a mystery outing.

Trying on hats at a fashion show in 1971

At a committee meeting held on 1st September 1959 it was noted that there was £27 in the Young Wives fund; part of this money (up to £20) was to be spent on a clock for the new Church Hall, and members would be asked to make cakes for the opening ceremony. The meeting held on 30th September started with a short service in Church, then moved on to the new hall, which became their regular venue.

In March 1977 the first 'Easter Egg' coffee morning took place, with proceeds going to the Upton Carnival. Easter eggs were made by committee members, personalised and sold, 70 eggs were sold that first year. Of the £29.10 proceeds, £20 was given to the Carnival Fund and the rest reserved for decorating the Young Wives float. By 1981 the committee was making nearly 300 eggs to meet the demand.

An annual Craft Market took place on the first Saturday in November for several years; nearly 30 local craftsmen paid £2.50 for a stall and sold their produce to the hundreds of local residents who turned out to buy early Christmas gifts.

The group closed in 1990.

Flower Club

Doris Pearce

In 1960 Doris Pearce and a group of friends from Upton formed Upton Heath Flower Club. Early committee meetings and club nights were held in the chairman's home, in Upton Park, or in the Village Hall; either in the afternoon or the evening. At one meeting the treasurer was 'delighted' to report that there was £180/12/1^d in the bank.

The entrance fee for the 10th Anniversary celebrations was 3/- although a mistress of St. James Secondary Modern School wrote to ask for reduced terms for a visit by her girls, consequently they were charged 2/-. Raffle tickets were 6^d or 2/6^d per book. A typical allowance for a demonstrator was £10 for the flowers and £25 for their fee.

Full to capacity meetings held in the Village Hall

Membership in 1972 was 39 but by 2003 it had grown to 100. Various competitions and shows have taken place.

In June 1961 one class was named 'Fragrance' and the judges on that occasion were blind. The show that year was held at the Town Hall and the proceeds of £37.10.0 were split between Chester Blind Welfare Society and Guide Dogs for the Blind. Over the years the group has helped members and their families to celebrate special occasions by presenting them with lovely floral arrangements, or supplying and arranging flowers for their anniversaries or weddings.

As well as flower arranging for pleasure, many events have raised funds for local charities including:- Dorincourt; The Hospice of the Good Shepherd and Guide Dogs for the Blind.

Arrangements have been made for special events - including a visit by the Queen to the Cathedral; functions at Peckforton and Bodelwyddan Castles, local churches and stately homes.

Many members have gone on to become professional demonstrators or teachers, while others enjoy entering local and national competitions. Some who have been attending the Flower Club for many years just enjoy sitting and watching a demonstration and arranging flowers at home for their own pleasure.

Olive Minor, Brenda Saunders, Nancy Turton, Ann Harrop,
Sue Dernie, Marie Christian
and other members of the Flower Club

Youth Club

In March 1965 a Youth Club was founded, which met in the Village Hall. It was open to anyone aged between 14 and 20 and enabled the youngsters to take part in a variety of indoor activities. Making an effort to acquire premises of their own they formed a committee, consisting of members and parents, to oversee the project. Among those involved were Irene Hulme, Les and Cath Feather, Maureen Barraclough, Iris & Dick Richards, Bob Clift, Ian Herbert, Tony Trotter and Dorothy Rushton.

Les Feather worked for the education department at the time. He was a great help in co-ordinating events, once planning permission was granted for Mill View School. It made sense to use the same contractor to build the Youth Club as it would be situated next to the new school and could be built directly the school was finished.

Brian Martin plays his shot at bagatelle

The committee needed to raise £2,500 before they could apply for a grant of £10,000 to aid the project so a couple of years serious fund raising took place. Jumble sales, door to door collections and coffee mornings were organised along with anything else that would help them to reach their target.

Once the building was complete, in 1968, the committee was still totally involved in running the club. They manned the canteen on club nights, served refreshments, organised dances. They also helped when the club members invited all the local residents who were aged over 60, for afternoon tea, which became an annual event. Eventually the club became self sufficient and was able to employ an official youth leader.

Upton Playgroup

Joan Quayle, Pam Parkinson, Val Powell, Sally Symes, Joyce Binns
and Jimmy Quayle (Father Christmas) 1983

The playgroup was originally set up in the summer of 1968, in the Upton Youth Club building, by Jean Jonas and Margaret Willey. When Jean left she was replaced by Joan Quayle and when Margaret left she was replaced by Sally Symes. From 1974 to 1988 'Aunty Sally' and 'Aunty Joan' ran a very lively playgroup, with the help of 3 staff, Pam Parkinson, Val Powell and Lorraine Hearse, where 25 children arrived at 9.30 each morning and stayed till 12 noon.

The children started from the term they reached the age of three and stayed until they reached school age. During that time they would learn social skills such as playing fairly with other children, the discipline of sitting at a table and doing organised games and of course there was a story to end the morning. They all had the chance to appear in a Summer Concert or the Nativity Play each Christmas, always well supported by Mums and Dads.

The children also took part in the Upton Carnivals, the first one being in 1977 to celebrate the Queen's Silver Jubilee, when the theme of their float was Nursery Rhymes. One subsequent carnival saw them all dressed up as 101 Dalmatians but the weather was so bad that it was decided not to subject the children to the appalling conditions. However they had their own little party at the playschool on another day.

For a while there were weekly visits to Dorin Park nursery, where the children would all play together. It was good for the two groups to meet each other and make new friends and it made Upton playschool children appreciate how the less able-bodied children coped. Each Christmas a visit would be made to Millview School to watch their Nativity Play. This was a very special event and it enabled the children to familiarise themselves with the 'big school'. Occasionally students from the High School would spend a couple of weeks at the playschool, gaining work experience.

The playschool is currently run by Mrs Pat Miller.

Upton Tennis Club

The idea for a tennis club in Upton originated in 1975. David Hart, an Upton resident, saw in a local newspaper that the Parish Council was asking if anyone was interested in starting up a club to make greater use of the public tennis courts at Wealstone Lane. He was interested, being a tennis player himself, and having noticed much to his surprise that the courts were not at all well used. In fact the attendants went off duty and the courts were locked up every Saturday and Sunday evening.

After having an initial meeting with the Council, he sounded out local interest via posters; press etc. then by having a meeting at his home. Around 50 people turned up with another 50 having contacted him to say they, too, were interested.

The first official committee meeting was held on 13th May 1976. Chairman was David Hart and the other members were Frank Mawdsley, Cliff Evans, Alison Finlay, Beryl Diment and John Todd with Tony Bass, himself (at the time) a junior, representing the juniors. At that meeting one topic discussed was membership numbers, the concern being the possibility of there being too many members for the limited playing times they were allowed by the Council. Membership Fees were set at £3 for adults and £1.50 for juniors. Membership was a magnificent 84.

At these early meetings, the Club philosophy evolved. First and foremost the intention was to be a *'Friendly sociable Club, welcoming members of any standard. There were to be no cliques'*. Positive efforts were made to ensure that players mixed, with anyone prepared to play anyone else regardless of standard. Right from the start, juniors were seen as important members of the Club and early on, junior coaching on Saturday mornings was started by John Ashton. Social events throughout the year were to be important.

On a beautiful sunny October 3rd 1976 the first Club Annual Tournament Finals were held with Mrs Sheila Garston, friend and supporter on the Parish Council, presenting trophies - rather small they may have been, but engraved and kept by the winner. Later, an honours board recording the winners' names was installed in the pavilion

In 2001 the club celebrated its 25th birthday. Events included a fun tournament where members played with old wooden rackets they would have been using in the seventies. Also, wearing those tight shorts, which brought tears to the eyes, as well as bringing back happy memories.

1976
Left to right: Ian Williams; Alison Carter; Tony Bass; Dot Whitehead; Andrew Jessop;
Nicola Shepherd with Councillor Shiela Garston

Upton Bowling Club

Upton by Chester Bowling Club was founded in April 1976, at the instigation of Leo Jackson and Len Vincent, secretary and chairman of Upton British Legion. Meetings were held (and still are) at the crown green in Wealstone Lane since it, too, opened in 1976. For the first nine years they played friendly matches and club competitions. Proving a popular pastime with local residents, membership soon grew to 60.

In 1985 they decided to spread their wings and joined Chester and District League, where they have enjoyed membership ever since. Most of that time they have spent in division C but for a few years enjoyed fame in division B. In 1986 the bowling club joined the Chester Veterans League, progressing over the years to generally 3rd or 4th in the League Table.

In December 1986 the club applied to the parish council to use the crown green on Thursday evenings, to help with league fixtures. The council agreed to this, but only if they gave up one of their other evenings - as they already used the green on Sundays, Mondays and Wednesdays. For the benefit of all who used the green, the team helped with the construction of a shelter. It was soon finished and much appreciated.

In 2002 they severed their connection to the Upton Royal British Legion, in the hope of gaining new members, as membership had fallen to just 20.

League games are played on Monday and Thursday evenings while the veterans play on a Tuesday afternoon. Over the winter, just to keep their bowling arms supple, the group play indoor bowls each Wednesday when they travel to Prestatyn for the pleasure.

Angling Club

Upton Angling Club was formed in 1983 after a small group of four friends became disappointed with the steady decline of the local farm ponds which had been fished from their childhood days. The ponds had been neglected and were silted and weeded up, leaving very few spots left to fish. Around 200 years ago every field in England had a pond but changes in farming have seen them decline rapidly. A 1988 survey estimated 182,000 had been lost since the Second World War! These four friends put £20 each into a fund, stated their objective to improve fishing and conservation locally, placed an advert in the Upton Post Office window for members, and the club was born.

It was agreed that they should approach the Zoo, on whose land so many of the ponds lay, with a view to renting the fishing rights on one or more of the pools. The response from the Zoo was very positive and following a meeting with their estates managers, the newly formed club had the choice of any or all of the ponds on their land. To this day the Zoo has never accepted rent from the club, although when funds allow donations are made to the charity. Approaches to Mr Dutton and Mr Ithell whose farmland also held ponds, were likewise well received and in no time the club had control of almost all the ponds in the area around the Zoo. The advantages for the land owners, of the club using the ponds, were seen in the removal of litter; repair of fences and gates; and some degree of control over who used their land. In return for the work the anglers acquired comfortable, secure fishing and protection of the ponds' future.

Work on the ponds started in earnest and by dragging out weed, dredging silt, trimming overgrown trees and building platforms to fish from. News spread fast and the club grew rapidly as like minded local people, who had also seen the decline, joined to help. HQ remained at a founder member's home where the club was run with a full committee and boasted around 500 members! Even with a membership of that size generating funds, it was impossible to maintain all of the ponds, there were simply too many, so some were left as wild conservation wet areas, where wildlife could thrive. Great Crested Newts, common in yesteryear but endangered now, are living happily just down the road from you.

As the club grew, demand for organising competitions also grew and matches were run on the canal, the River Dee, and some of the ponds. The popularity of the club matches would, at their height, see 80 anglers lining the canal bank on a Sunday morning. The competitions developed talent and attracted other anglers and soon UAC teams were competing in, and winning, local and national competitions. The Club can boast two World Champions amongst its members, with Matthew Dickinson becoming Junior World Champion in 1995 and their most famous member Wendy Locker, Ladies World Champion in 1997.

Community Links

Following a long standing link between the high schools in Upton and Arradon, the parish council in Upton and the commune in Arradon decided to extend the links and in 1992 the Twinning Charter was signed. Following that, 'Upton Community Links' was born, and although it has the full support of the council, it is a financially independent group.

The committee in Upton organised fundraising events, to help support exchange projects and on two occasions have received European Union funding.

Holding the Twinning Charter

Charles Holmes, Upton Royal British Legion; Yves Besnard, French Consul; Monsieur Gall, Mayor of Arradon; Cllr Gerald Grant; Jacque Kercadis, Arradon; Cllr Eric Delaney; Michel Pelissier, Upton High School.

The two twinning committees have worked closely together to organise a rich programme of links, visits and exchanges that have involved a growing number of people from Arradon and Upton. Each year there is a coach visit, to Brittany, by Upton residents and a return visit by people from Arradon. These reciprocal exchange visits have been the highlight of the twinning and have created strong links and great friendships

In May and June 2002 Arradon and Upton celebrated the tenth anniversary of the twinning.

Upton Local History Group

While researching and publishing a book on Upton Park, recently retired Phil Pearn, met several residents who showed an interest in compiling the history of Upton. He called a public meeting in September 2002 to discuss the idea of forming a Group. He had cheekily printed off membership forms which were signed and paid up that night. The Group was soon underway with a membership of approximately 100 and the monthly meetings were typically attended by 50 members.

The first AGM in November 2003 saw the inauguration of their President, Joyce Cook; well known locally, Joyce had taught in Upton for many years. As a commendation to Joyce, and proof of her popularity, many past pupils came along to renew their acquaintance with her and to add their own comments to the evening. Impressively, Joyce could remember something special about each of her ex-pupils and, considering their ages ranged from 30 to 60 that was some feat!

Another highlight for the Group was the Local History Exhibition held in the Village Hall in March 2004. Over 500 visitors attended and were amazed at the amount of material already collected. That volume has increased considerably to far more than this book can contain.

The Exhibition held in March 2004

CHAPTER 15

Churches

Upton is served by four churches, the oldest of which dates back to 1854 and the most recent to arrive was in 1987. As well as being places of worship, churches traditionally have been at the hub of village life. This can been seen by the popular use of the church/community halls. The value parishioners put on their churches is shown by the expansion of the buildings, over the years, to keep in line with the growth of the population.

Church of the Holy Ascension

The Churchyard is entered through the Lych Gate over which is carved a short prayer: '*Grant, O Lord that through the grave and the gate of death we may pass to our joyful resurrection*' The gate was a gift of the Potts family who lived at 'The Oaks', (now the golf clubhouse). From the Lych Gate the path leads to the church with its 93ft spire.

Nearby is the ancient plague stone, which is covered in detail in chapter 3.

Entering the Church through the porch with its side seating there is a plaque recording the grant of £100 towards the building fund from the '*Incorporated Society for Promoting the Enlargement of Churches*' on condition that '*184 seats should be reserved for the poorer inhabitants of this parish for ever*'. Going on into the Nave these seats can be seen. Apart from the '*free*' seats Upton Parishioners would have been able to choose where they sat by paying a seating fee, those paying the highest fee would have first choice. The recommended rate was 7 shillings per seat or 2 guineas per pew; pew rent was paid in advance twice yearly and was used for various church needs such as cleaning, repairs, candles and two shillings for the Bishop.

The focal point of the church is the altar and associated with it, the east window. When the church was built there was an 'Ascension' window in this position but in 1885 it was removed – to where is a mystery. The space left was increased by 3½ feet and the new window, the crucifixion scene, put in.

Built as a Chapel-of-Ease to St. Mary's on the Hill, Chester, Holy Ascension was under the ministry of Rev. William Massie. The first Sunday Service was on 4th June 1854, conducted by curate Rev. Henry Ireland Blackburne. The singing was led by Colonel E Evans-Lloyd of Plas Newton, at first with a pitch pipe until the following August when a harmonium was provided. A tablet on the north wall records his 30 years service as organist. He was also treasurer of the Church School, and churchwarden from 1854 until Upton became a separate parish some 30 years later.

William Massie died in January 1856, aged 50, there is a memorial to him on the floor of the south transept and his picture hangs in the vestry. The churches he built and the Chester Archaeological society which he founded are continuing signs of his life and work. His successor at St. Mary's was Canon Charles Bowen whose grave is in Upton Churchyard near the Lych Gate. For the first fourteen years of its life, Upton Church was a Chapel of Ease to St. Mary's and was served by various clergy from the mother church, but from about 1868 the Reverend H M Towers was curate-in-charge until the appointment of the fist vicar in 1882.

c1930
Unknown, Unknown, H Griffiths, Ms Morris, P Snelson, Mrs Stacey, Mr Stacey, Ms Corfe and Ethel Corfe

Mrs Westbury, Ms Davies, Ms Duff, Mr Westbury, Rev Sparling, Ms Smethurst, Emily Griffiths, Betty Harrison, Frank Hewitt.

The Duke of Westminster appointed his son's tutor, the Reverend Wilfred Sparling MA, to be the first vicar. He was a Cambridge rowing 'blue' who was ordained at St John the Baptist Church in Chester and served as curate-in-charge of St. Barnabas. He died on 10th May 1933 having served Upton for fifty years. His grave is in the old part of the churchyard and a record of his long ministry is carved on the wall near the lectern. Seven years after his appointment it was decided that the new parish should have a vicarage and by the efforts of Colonel Evans-Lloyd a fund was started, supported locally and the balance made up by the Duke. The decision to build was made in March 1889, the foundation stone laid by Mrs Emily Logan on August 15th of the same year and the vicarage finished and occupied eleven months later! Wilfred Sparling's successor was the Rev. F S Gardner Brown who stayed only three years before being replaced by the Rev. T O C East whose ten year tenure included the difficult days of the Second World War. In 1946 he left Upton to become vicar of Neston.

Rev. T O C East with members of the parish, early 1940s

With the end of the war came a building boom and the population of Upton increased rapidly. The man to whom the chance came to deal with this new situation was the Rev. J Wheldon Williams and the impact of his leadership and ability was felt immediately.

A high point was reached on the occasion of the church's centenary in 1954. For this occasion the church was not big enough to accommodate parishioners during the eight days of celebrations. It was necessary, therefore, to hire a marquee together with 500 seats and a stage. At Festal Evensong on the first Sunday the preacher was Canon S J Marriot, Sub Dean of Westminster Abbey, there then followed 8 days of services, dramas, concerts, and parties until the final Festal Evensong when the Lord Bishop of Chester preached. The marquee was on the open field between what was then the British Legion hut and the War Memorial. The hire charge for tent, seats and stage was only £111.

During the months following the celebrations, several possibilities for enlarging the church were considered but the plan finally adopted in September 1955 was to build transepts. The first phase included a south transept and new choir vestry. Completed by the end of 1957, these were consecrated by the Lord Bishop of Chester on 16th February 1958, and none too soon either, Easter Communicants were rising in number, there were 841 in 1956.

Plans for the north transept, were put on hold as there was a more urgent need, the decision to build a new Church Hall was taken within a month of the south transept consecration. Two sites were considered, one roughly where Grangeside now is, and the other at the end of the Vicarage garden. On this latter site the hall was built and opened in September 1959 by Mrs Ellison, wife of the Bishop of Chester. A dance took place that evening at five shillings per head. Money for the hall had actually been partly raised by an unusual method - door to door collections by approved volunteers round Upton houses.

After the addition of the south transept in 1957

The newly opened Church Hall in September 1959

Then the north transept, clergy vestry and organ project went ahead. The organ was not entirely new. Overhead platforms were built at the west end of the church to carry the pipes, and a detached console was placed by the choir-stalls. An opening recital was given by Dr Roland Middleton, the organist and Master of Choristers at Chester Cathedral. All this work was consecrated by Bishop Eric Mercer the Suffragen Bishop of Birkenhead on 7th May 1967. By this time new choir-stalls, communion rails and other furniture had been designed and installed, all in beautiful light oak and all given in memory of various church members whose names are recorded on small bronze plates.

The Rev. Wheldon Williams, died suddenly in July 1969. The Rev. Fred Lapham came to Upton in 1970 then moved to Warrington in 1981. The present incumbent Rev. Glyn Conway has been in office since that time.

The Vicarage Garden Party has been a major annual event for many years. Post-war everyone looked forward to this occasion, good weather was 'ordered' and usually happened. In Wheldon Williams' time it was nicknamed 'Vicars Weather'. For many years Kay and Alix Joseph arranged the Rose Queen ceremony and a beautiful bouquet was given by Peter Snelson from his rose nursery. Entertainment was arranged by Miss Gladys Davies, usually country or maypole dancing; latterly local schools or youth organisations have been important participants. Successive Rose Queens were crowned by well known ladies of the village but in 2004 the mould as broken when Brian Cox officiated.

Some past Rose Queen ceremonies

Some interesting first events, recorded in the parish register:-

The first baptisms were on 4th June 1854, five babies were baptised

The first marriage was solemnized on 1st June 1875, between William Holland and Mary Ellen Stockton.

The first burial was on 1st December 1853, that of E. Smith.

The first confirmation service was on 27th March 1893 when there were 21 candidates.

From Stan Whaley's memoirs, 1920s

For many years, the Upton Sunday School had an excursion in August, going alternately to Rhyl and New Brighton. This was a major event in the village because it was still something of a thrill to ride in a coach and Jimmy Hazelden's good nature allowed everyone in the village to join in, including some who had never once been near the Sunday school. The chance of a free ride was too good to miss and the expenses of the outing were defrayed by the church. But it was on these annual outings that Jimmy showed what a tremendously generous person he was. He bought many of the pupils ice creams, and always insisted on treating the teachers to tea. On the New Brighton outings, he always took us to the fun fair and for a ferry boat sail over the Mersey. Sometimes the old Vicar (Rev. Sparling) joined us as well, but for him it must have been an ordeal and he used to walk slowly up and down the promenade until it was time to return. He was conspicuous because of his saintly white beard, his black shovel hat and his umbrella.

United Reformed Church

Until 1860 the Congregational Church in Upton held their meetings in the Wheelwright's shop, the owner being one of the group's enthusiastic members. It was a comfortless place, lit with naphtha lamps, the oil from which used to drop on the clothes of the villagers who sat on backless wooden benches. In 1860 a Chapel, capable of holding 120 people, was erected at a cost of £250. The opening service was conducted on 27th November by Dr Raffles of Liverpool and it is believed to be the last service he conducted as he died soon afterwards. The sermon was preached by the Reverend Charles Chapman the Minister of Queen Street Chapel. This building still stands and is now Jackson's, a village newspaper shop (see chapter 6).

Towards the end of the nineteenth century, largely due to the vigour and earnestness of Mr and Mrs Clarke, membership increased and better provision for the ministry was deemed necessary. The old Chapel was in a state of disrepair and in view of the ever increasing population, it was decided to build an entirely new Church at a cost of £1,500.

The new Church was designed by Messrs J H Davies and Sons of Newgate Street, Chester and the builders Messrs George Wright and Sons of Kelsall. It was to be built in gothic style in Ruabon Brick and would seat 300 people. An unusual feature was a carved ornamental screen which separated a large schoolroom from the main Church. This could be removed so that the schoolroom could be utilised as part of the Church. The site of the Church was given by Mr Anthony Bradley of Chester who also presented a beautiful stained glass window, representing Christ blessing little children, in memory of his brother William Bradley.

Wednesday 20th June 1900 was a great day, at a special ceremony the foundation stone was laid, appropriately, by Mrs Mary Clarke and Mrs Sidney Clarke. Over one hundred and fifty members and friends also contributed by laying bricks. After the stone laying ceremony an evening meeting was held in a large tent in the field in the centre of the village, with records stating '*over 200 people sat down to a sumptuous tea*'.

The building progressed well and less than six months later on Wednesday 5th December 1900, the opening ceremony took place. The proceedings were conducted by Rev. D Wynne Evans and a hymn sung which was specially composed

Inside the new Church

for the occasion, by Mr. J W Jones of West Lorne Street, Chester. Following which the memorial window to the late William Bradley was unveiled by Mrs. Musker and Mr Anthony Bradley. The commission for the window was given to Messrs William Bros. of the Kaleyards. The Church was still affiliated to Queen Street and was to remain so until early in 1947

The next event of note came in April 1920, when the opportunity arose to buy the land between the Church and the Wheatsheaf, an area of 900 square yards, costing £113. The deaconate and members agreed to purchase the land through a loan from Parr's Bank and by January 1921, the transfer had been completed, the trustees being Messrs Gray, Hinde, Pearson and Young. In 1928 the first extension of the building took place. The Church had been connected to the main drainage system and it was proposed that adequate toilet facilities be built on to the building. This was made possible by a donation of £100 by Mrs Pearson.

1946 was one of the most important year's in the Church's history, time to make a call for their own Minister and become independent for the first time. The Moderator introduced to the Deacons a Mr E F Gurney who had been a missionary in India. Mr Gurney was invited to preach at Upton in December and subsequently invited to be Minister. A house in Heath Road was bought as the Manse and Mr Gurney settled in Upton in March 1947, where he was to reside for two years.

In May 1947 a building fund was set up, with a view to providing a new Hall on the ground adjoining the Church. Also in the summer, a series of open-air services took place outside the Zoo at Upton, conducted alternatively by Rev. E F Gurney and Rev. Wheldon Williams from the Parish Church. It was at this time that the members saw the departure of their first full-time Minister in October 1949. He was succeeded in July 1950 by the Rev. Donald Robertson. During the interim period the existing Manse, 'Greenfields' in Heath Road, due to the heavy cost of repair, was sold to Mr Gould, one of the Church Deacons.

In September 1955, Mr Robertson moved to Accrington and for next three years the ministry was shared by lay preachers and local Ministers. Rev. H T Donaldson, M.A. of Ward Chapel, Dundee was inducted as Minister on Wednesday, 11th May 1960. Prior to then a house in Mill Lane, Upton - 'Rose Cottage' - was purchased as a Manse with the assistance of a mortgage. During the next three years plans were formulated and approved for the erection of a Church Hall adjoining the Church. A great deal of the money raised was due to the efforts of Mr Donaldson including donations from previous Churches at which he had been Minister and £100 from Upton Parish Church.

Due to ill heath, Mr Donaldson had to retire from the ministry just as plans for the Church Hall reached the 'tender' stage in May 1964. The years he had been at Upton had *"Been happier than any of the other years spent in my fifty years ministry"*.

George Eastwood and Son were awarded the building contract and work on the Hall began in June 1964. This was completed in January 1965, the same month the Rev. J W Barraclough was asked to become minister. On 27th March

1965 the new hall was officially opened, fittingly by Rev. H T Donaldson. The ceremony was attended by the Minister elect and many local Church dignitaries including the Rev. C E Wright who presided, and the Vicar of Upton, the Rev Wheldon Williams who gave the address. A wall plaque commemorating the event and Mr Donaldson's Ministry, was later placed in the New Hall.

Rev. Barraclough in his Upton AA kit c1966

Rev. Barraclough was ordained and inducted as Minister on 8th October 1965. In March 1967, Northgate Congregational Church was closed and many of the congregation joined Upton. In May it was decided to proceed with plans to extend the Church and sanctuary. After consultation with the architect, Mr K W Patterson, plans for enlarging Church and hall were approved by the members.

In July 1968, Rev. Winston Barraclough, decided to give up the ministry to train as a teacher. Rev. D M Mr Buckle B.A. was duly inducted on the 29th November. The year ended with the acceptance of Messrs George Eastwood and Sons tender for the extensions and as 1969 began, members at last saw the work begin. During the demolition of the front of the existing sanctuary, the foundation stone of the building laid in 1900 by the Misses Clarke was removed and a tin box, placed underneath the stone at the foundation ceremony, was found. It contained copies of the local newspapers, the Chester Chronicle and the Cheshire Observer, together with the Church and London Mission Society publications of the day, some of which were still in readable condition.

Along with the extension, the enlarged sanctuary and car park were completed in 1969 so that Upton Congregational Church and its members entered the 1970s very well equipped. In 1970 Rev. Buckle left and the Church saw Rev. S M Thornton inducted in 1971. It was during Rev. Thornton's time that the Congregational Church became part of the United Reformed Church. In 1981 Rev. J H Oldershaw took over the ministry and subsequent ministers have been Rev. A F E Wise 1989 - 1993; Rev. G Thompson 1993 - 1994; and the present day Minister Rev. J Kingsley from 1995.

Meanwhile the Church continues to grow. 2002 saw a new front entrance onto the building; the back hall enlarged; the sanctuary refurbished and front pews were replaced by chairs.

Saint Columba's Church

Saint Columba's was the first Roman Catholic Church in the Diocese of Shrewsbury to be dedicated to Saint Columba, the Irish missionary who sailed to Iona in a coracle.

A modern Scandinavian design ahead of its time

In the early 1960s Canon Murphy, with the help of James Tatton, made arrangements to buy a large site fronting on to Plas Newton Lane. The plot had not been built on before, probably because it was susceptible to flooding, due to being criss-crossed by small streams but modern day drainage soon solved the problem. The site had an interesting history as it had once belonged to the Catholic Church. Originally owned by the Earls of Chester, it was donated to the Abbey of St. Werburgh where it remained until the dissolution of the monasteries when ownership passed to the Dean and Chapter of Chester Cathedral. Eventually the land passed into the hands of the Hurleston family and in 1738 Ann Hurleston married John Needham, Viscount Kilmorey, whose country seat was in Ireland.

Having settled on the site, Canon Murphy chose Messrs L A G Pritchard, Son and Partners as the architects and Costain's as builders. Canon Murphy was given a free hand in decision making by Bishop Graser. The modern Scandinavian style of the New Chapel of Ease was considered ahead of its time, yet reminiscent of the rotundas in ancient Rome. The 675 worshippers St Columba's is designed to hold, congregate around the Alter in a semi circle, where everyone is within 50 feet of it.

Contractors started in 1963, the foundation stone being laid by Canon Murphy in September 1964 when 200 people attended the ceremony. The foundation stone, inscribed at a cost of £110, bears the Latin inscription

AD MAJOREM DEI GLORIAM
ET IN HONOREM SANCTI COLUMBAE
LAPIDEM HUNC PRIMARIUM SACRAVIT DEDICAVITQUE
ADM REV. D FRANCISCUS CAN. MURPHY
DIE 6A SEPTEMBRIS 1964

Translated it reads
*To the greater glory of God
in honour of Saint Columba,
this foundation stone was blessed
by the Reverend Canon Francis Murphy
on 6ᵗʰ September 1964*

The estimated cost of the new church was £80,000 and at this ceremony contributions were collected in wheel barrows - and amounted to £62.

In December 1964 the Church Spire (rising to 115 feet) was lowered into position, this was built in one complete section and weighed 6½ tons. The entrance hall situated centrally, together with the old baptistery, supports a timber framed gallery which is occupied by the choir each weekend. The main alter, weighing almost 2 tons, is in Kilkenny and White Perlato Marble. The wooden carving of Saint Columba on the side alter was created in Newry, County Down. One unsatisfactory installation was the underground heating which was totally inadequate. On bitterly cold winter mornings, Father Warnock had been known to mumble *"Too cold for a homily"* and would move on to the Creed to the relief of shivering parishioners. Gas central heating replaced the earlier system at a cost of £13,000.

By the end of 1965 the building was finished and Canon Murphy blessed the new church on Saturday 18ᵗʰ December at a ceremony attended by 200 people and the first mass, which was held the following day, was attended by 600 people. The official opening, in February 1966, was a grand affair. A high Mass took place which was attended by Colonel and Mrs Adrian Howell, Mayor and Mayoress of Chester and M.P. for Chester Mr Temple and Mrs Temple.

The new church was used as a Chapel of Ease for the next two years with masses being said by the priests of St. Werburgh's but marriages, burials and baptisms took place at the Mother Church. As there was no presbytery Canon Murphy bought the house next door, as soon as it became available, number 1 Newhall Road. The site at the side of the church was developed as a car park at a cost of £20,000.

On 8th November 1967 the Bishop appointed Father James Malloy as the first priest of the new parish of Saint Columba in Upton and Plas Newton. In 1971 the duties passed to Father Warnock who looked after the parish until, following illness, he moved to a smaller parish and Saint Columba's passed into the capable hands of Father Lennon in 1983. Father Lennon was ordained in 1959 and celebrated his silver jubilee while at Saint Columba's in 1984.

In the early 1970s there was an obvious need for a church hall, but plans were put on hold until 1978. With the church supplying the materials and the Manpower Services Commission supplying the labour, it became a reality. As no professional builder was involved, a building committee was formed with Charles Houlden as foreman-in-charge. He had nine young workers under his command that became affectionately known as 'Charlie's Angels'. Work was completed on time and the hall was officially opened by Bishop Grasar on 5th July 1978.

Father Lennon

The Church suffered the loss of the stained glass window to the rear of the building. The design, depicting St Columba in the coracle, was set in soft wood which began to rot and the whole structure became loose and dangerous. In 1986 Father Lennon sought estimates to replace the windows but the cost of £100,000 proved too great. For safety reasons the windows were replaced with plain, toughened glass at a cost of £75,000 (almost as much as the building of the Church). However, Father Lennon eventually managed to purchase a new stained glass window for his beloved St. Columba's.

Father Lennon died in September 1997 and at his own request was buried in Ireland. The new priest to be appointed was Father Russell Cooke who moved from St. Saviours, Ellesmere Port in December 1997.

Of the two choirs in the church; the main, adult, choir sings at 9.15 Mass and on special occasions and the junior, folk, choir sings on alternate Sundays at the 11 am Mass and is ably supported by guitars, flutes, recorders and keyboard.

Upton Baptist Church

In the late 1970s the Baptist Church in Grosvenor Park, Chester needed to find a new location due to the extensive road building programme in that area. In September 1979 the Church began a dialogue with Chester Zoo about a plot of land in Flag Lane South in Upton. This plot eventually went for auction later that year and when the Church's bid was put forward, it was accepted.

The Church of about 35 members moved to Upton in September 1980, changing its name to Upton Baptist Church. Meetings were held for some years in Upton Manor (now Upton Heath) Junior School, conveniently adjacent to the building plot, while the old building was sold and the new one designed and built. The building work was carried out in three phases: firstly the base; then the 'A' framework, which was prefabricated in Scandinavia and finally the interior. In the summer of 1987 the work was complete and the first service of worship held in September.

From its roots in 1875 as Chester oldest surviving Baptist Church, they are now in their 3rd building where, in September 2004, they celebrated their 17th anniversary and appointed Jim Waterworth as their new Pastor.

2004 the Church hosted an International Students Weekend

CHAPTER 16

Schools

Upton is served by five Primary Schools, one High School, one special school for children with disabilities and one private school, so the education needs of children are well catered for. The oldest recorded school is St Mary's which was first built in 1843 and the 'newest' school is the High School, built in 1968.

St Mary's School

The original St Mary's school was built in 1843 on a site known as *'Footway Field'*. From the 'Reports on Schools' inspection of 8th August 1853, by Rev. H R P Sandford, the following is known -

'Buildings very fair; mistress' house very small. Desks along the wall but not facing it. Books, tolerable supply. Apparatus not sufficient. Organisation in four classes, under the Mistress and her sister as assistant. Methods fair; pains taken to keep the class attention. Discipline good. Instruction fair, such as to produce correctness in what is taught. Though not a trained mistress, Miss Frith has her village school in very fair order. Some of the girls answered fairly, the boys were behind hand, especially in arithmetic. The plan of taking the farmers' children into the National School at a higher rate than the poor (3^d - 6^d weekly) seems to have succeeded here'. Census records of 1851 show that the schoolmistress, Miss Emma Frith, was 28 and her sister, Ann, 30.

The building of the new St Mary's school began in July 1884 *'For the benefit of the Parish'* and was of a size to hold 170 pupils. The Duke and Duchess of Westminster were invited to the opening ceremony, in April 1885.

After a short period Mr Bullock, the headmaster, received complaints about the playground and the cloakroom. It was felt that the boys' playground should be separate from that used by the girls.

There were 77 pupils in 1894 and records show there was low attendance in school during race week. Even in those days, school inspections were rigorous; it was pointed out that *'Spelling needed more attention, arithmetic of some pupils was weak, desks were of an unsuitable size and slate pencils were too short as they cramped the fingers'.* On the positive side, singing and needlework were good and object lessons were very popular e.g. the rabbit, the cat, the Post Office No comment was made about the fact that sometimes the temperature in the classroom was only 48°F.

When Mr Bullock retired in 1899, there were 13 applications for the vacant post which paid £100 per year; it was filled by Mr John Evans. During this period the playground was re-laid using 23 tons of Spar. The school day started at 9am and the day normally finished at 3.30 but when Queen Victoria visited

Chester the children were allowed to leave at 3.15 pm. The school was used for *'Evening Continuation Classes'* from October 1899. These included two hour sessions on Mondays and Wednesdays, teaching subjects such as Commercial Arithmetic, Correspondence, Geography and Drawing. The fee was 2/- per session, Mr Evans was the teacher and received 3/9d per hour.

After the death of Queen Victoria in 1901 the children were given a holiday to enable them to hear the proclamation given by King Edward VII. In 1914 Mr Evans was replaced as head teacher by Mr E Hacker, who was succeeded by Mr F Hewitt in 1925 and Mr Chidlow in 1930. Mr Chidlow stayed in the post for 22 years and saw many changes. Until 1947 children were educated at St Mary's until the age of 14. After this date, however, they were transferred to the Grange Secondary school in Ellesmere Port at the age of 11. Once Upton Primary School was built, children moved there at the age of 7, making St Mary's an infant's school.

St Mary's in 1908

During the difficult period of the war years, school carried on as near normal as possible. One ex-pupil, Anthony Evans, remembers the windows being blacked out *"With wooden frames covered in thick black paper, some of the lower frames were removable to allow a bit of day-light in but the higher ones were permanent. All the glass, in the windows and the partition between the classrooms, had rug canvas glued to it to make it shatterproof"*. He also remembers going into school an hour earlier than everyone else, to set and light the fire. Known as 'the furnace', this was a large cast iron box with doors on the front and loose lids on the top for the kettle. *"The furnace heated the whole school via 4 inch cast iron pipes and cast iron radiators"*. During this time the children would also help in Mr Chidlow's garden, digging, weeding and watering the growing vegetables under the 'Dig for Victory' campaign. Weekly air raid practices were held when the children would be taken to the underground shelter behind the Village Hall. According to Anthony *"It was often 6 inches deep with water and attracted lots of frogs, thank heavens we never needed it for real"*.

After Mr Chidlow retired through ill health, in 1952, the temporary head complained about the low temperature of the main classroom and the two old stoves were replaced. Interviews were held for the post of head and Mrs G Waterworth was appointed in January of the following year. Later on in the year lessons were held in the Village Hall due to major alterations taking place in the school. The first open day was held on December 16th and a party and concert took place in the Village Hall.

After 20 years of service, Mrs Waterworth retired in 1971 and Mrs Irene Staples was introduced as the new head. At this time there were 178 children on the roll. Mrs Staples introduced the first out-of-school visit when the children travelled to the Liverpool Museum and Walker Art Gallery and the first Parents Evening was held on 9th May.

To celebrate Queen Elizabeth's Silver Jubilee in 1977, parents organised a carnival float for the children to ride on and a party was held on June 24th. Each child received a commemorative mug from the carnival committee and jubilee crown from the school.

During its long history the school has had few breaks in its continuity. In June of 1894 the school had to close for a short while due to bad weather, in 1898 there was an outbreak of diphtheria and *'The closets were disinfected'*. In the early 1940s there was an outbreak of Scarlet Fever which again closed the school and again necessitated fumigation. In 1979, nearly a hundred years after the school was built, it closed for a very different reason. During February there was no oil for the heating, due to a lorry drivers' strike. What would Mr Bullock, the first headteacher, have thought of this?

July 1998 saw the last pupils leave the school and Mrs Staples retire, after 26 years, before its official closure on 31st August. Over one hundred years of education had taken place at St Mary's and to celebrate, the school held a series of Victorian themed events. Pupils and teachers wore period costume, enjoyed the delights of a Victorian lunch which consisted of gruel, found out what it would be like to wear the dunce's hat and used chalk and boards for drawing on. Each child was presented with a leather bookmark as a memento. The following term saw the school merge with Upton Manor to form Upton Heath County Primary School.

The building is now a privately run day nursery.

Upton Heath Primary School

August 27th, 1951. *'The morning on which the school opened was very wet but in spite of the weather all parents who had brought their children to the new school had seen their children's names entered on class lists and left the school premises as requested by 9.20am. The number of children admitted was 222 consisting of 130 boys and 92 girls'.*

With these words entered in the school log book, by head-teacher Mr E L Hughes, Upton County Primary School completed its first day. The account continues with comments on the smoothness of the opening, in spite of continuing work on the playground and main drive. The first meal was very good and various dignitaries called to thank head and staff for all their hard work.

It was soon realised that a rapidly expanding Upton would need more pupil places than the new school could provide and so the original village school, St. Mary's, became a feeder infant school quickly followed by a new infant school, Acresfield, on the Caughall side of Long Lane. Later, Primary changed to Junior in the school name and this title remained until the name Upton Manor was adopted. The final name change occurred in September 1998 when Upton Manor School and St. Mary's Infants amalgamated and the present name, Upton Heath C.E. Controlled Primary School, came into use.

The head, Mr Hughes, universally referred to as Len but invariably addressed as Mr Hughes by everyone from the smallest first year junior to the Director of Education, was utterly dedicated to the well being of the children in his charge.

He formed one of the first PTA's in the county, organised school trips and encouraged social events which had a bonding effect long before the term became known! In fact his name is mentioned in the Plowden Report. He removed grim, formal exams and replaced them with an annual Eisteddfod which encouraged children to write stories and poems, paint pictures, make models and sing, play and recite before a large audience. His Deputy Head, Joyce Cook, sought musical excellence and achieved it most notably with a string of choir successes in the 60s and 70s at the Bromborough Festival, a prestigious event which attracted choirs from all over the North West. Her culminating success was victory in the television programme 'A Good Sing' In turn this led to a choir performance in a concert at the Philharmonic Hall in Liverpool and in *'Christmas at Tatton'* for a few years.

Jock Addison will always be remembered for his gentle manner and unfailing good humour. He joined the school shortly after its inception and served devotedly until his retirement in 1981. Dennis Pugh and Caerwyn Jones both went on to head schools of their own after productive years at The Manor. The former could be seen blowing his whistle in the introduction to 'Match of the Day' in the 70s.

Len retired in 1977 and Mr R Matthews was chosen as his successor. A quiet, gentle person, Ray was sadly dogged by ill health and retired in 1985. In 1986 Glenys Owen, who had been a member of the Manor School's staff, became the new head teacher. The school continued to keep up the tradition of music and drama and sport and many more activities continued to flourish.

1958:   P Lux, C Brown, P Guckenheim, J Addison, P Low, E Tingay, P Butcher
V Lowe, J Cook, L Hughes, M Catchpole, M Warburton

In 1997 the decision was reached to bring Upton Manor and Upton St. Mary's together on the Manor campus and by Spring 1998, a new specialist infant extension at the North end of the school was ready to receive pupils. Mrs. Irene Staples, Head of St Mary's, decided at this point on a well earned retirement and Mrs. Owen became head of the new school. With the help of Deputy Head Lorraine Brookman and her team of teachers from St. Mary's, Upton Heath C.E. Controlled School came into being.

Although now a very large Primary School with some 420 pupils on roll, the school has never lost the ethos of a caring village school. Wednesday morning assembly is held for the whole school, during which a class or year contribution is usually the central point and the Rev. Conway is often present. The school has forged links with schools in Soweto and one teacher, Sylvia Williams, has exchanged with a Township teacher.

Perhaps the growth, change and creative energy so evident at Upton Heath are symbolised by the Mini Wood. In 1992 an army of children, staff and local dignitaries including Gyles Brandreth, the then MP for Chester, marched to the far end of the school field, each one clutching a tiny sapling. These were planted with much muddy fun and today there stands, at the corner of Demage Lane and Long Lane a beautiful, mature copse.

An early photograph with headteacher Mr Len Hughes

Upton Manor in the mid 1950s

Extensive photographic records of the early years of Upton Heath Primary School were made by Joyce Cook and are currently kept at the school.

Worthy of a book in their own right?

Acresfield Primary School

Acresfield School is situated in Upton Heath and was opened in 1959 in extensive grounds. Originally built as an infant annex for Upton Manor Junior School, they shared the same headmaster Mr Len Hughes. In 1975 the school was extended and the designation changed to primary, with that change came Mr Selwyn Matthews as the new head. During this time there were 60/70 pupils on roll.

1993 saw headteacher Selwyn Matthews leave to be replaced by Mrs Sue Smith who is still in post today.

The school building is light and airy with 1 open plan classroom and 5 traditional classrooms. It also has a reference library housed in the junior corridor. There is a speech and language centre on site which can take up to 10 children aged 7 - 11. A mobile classroom, installed in October 1995, provides accommodation for older infants.

A school grounds development programme was started in 1994 with the planting of over 300 shrubs and trees. This was followed with further plantings on subsequent years until 700 trees and shrubs had been introduced to the land.

A building programme, begun in 2000 has provided a small computer suite, cloakroom, PE store and caretaker's room. The following year saw the completion of a library/study area and meetings room. The large hall, well equipped with PE apparatus, also doubles as a dining hall.

Starting in November 1995, parents of the children transformed the grounds by constructing a soft play area, digging out a pond and building a fence around it. The process of ground development has continued in subsequent years with a range of seating and play facilities. A woodland trail has been laid through the now maturing woodland area. In 2002 the school won first prize in the Chester City in Bloom Schools Section.

In 2002 the reception children were filmed as part of the 'Great Britons' television series and appeared in the Charles Darwin episode. The following year older children were filmed for a BBC Education 'Watch' programme at Chester Zoo.

Before the last building programme could commence an archæological survey was carried out as Roman practice camps have been discovered in the locality (see chapter 2). Although no Roman remains were found, the remains of a prehistoric votive (fire) were uncovered. This was identified as a trench with charcoal fragments and small rounded pebbles.

In March 2004 children in year 4 and 5 took part in a project 'Pastimes' for the National Singing Strategy. This culminated in singing at the National School Proms, at The Albert Hall, in November along with 600 other children.

The 181 children on roll are organised into 7 teaching groups.

*Images of year 6
taken from the school's website*

Westlea Primary School

Westlea Primary School, built to accommodate the growing population of children in Upton, opened on 30th April 1962 admitting 158 pupils. The catchment area ranged from Weston Grove to the Chester City boundary and from Long Lane to Wealstone Lane. Designed as a one-form entry primary school, it comprised four junior and three infant classrooms, however there was no intake of year 7 pupils at this time. 91 pupils and all the teaching staff, including Mr F Skitt the headteacher, stayed for the first school dinner.

An open evening was held on 23rd May for inspection by parents and other interested parties. The official opening, attended by Mr John Temple, M.P. for Chester, took place on 20th July.

The number of pupils on the roll after the summer holidays rose to 171, which included the new intake of year 7. The number of pupils rose steadily over the following years. Within twelve months of inception the Parent Teacher Association was active and when the football team was formed the PTA were able to provide their first strip. Those participating in the lunchtime clubs of country dancing, recorder playing and choir singing all enjoyed a trip to the Llangollen International Eisteddfod.

From Easter 1964 the school agreed to accept children from Vicars Cross and Boughton, pending the provision of schools in those areas with two new demountable classrooms being provided. These, together with an extra infant class working in the dining room, meant the school now had 10 classes in total.

By February 1966 pupil numbers had reached 386. A special meeting was called of the managers of the school to discuss overcrowding. The following month saw the headteachers of Westlea Primary, Upton County Primary and St Mary's Infant schools meet with Deputy Director of Education and Divisional Education Officer to discuss accommodation problems. This led, eventually, to more de-mountable classrooms being used. Pupil numbers reached 411 in September 1967.

In March of the following year a group of 29 children and 3 adults left for a week long holiday at a Wildlife Youth Camp, the first holiday visit ever made from the school. Pupils also took part in the Chester Mystery Plays depicting 32 animals in the Noah's Ark scene. Animal heads and costumes were made, by staff and parents, for classes 6 and 7 who took part. An inscribed book of Bible stories was presented to the school in recognition of their efforts. In December 1967 the school closed for Christmas holidays and said farewell to 77 children who would be starting, the following term, at the newly opened Mill View School. The following summer would see the older children moving on to the also newly opened Upton High School.

Although by 1969 the school had a television, for the Investiture of the Prince of Wales, the infants were sent home early to watch the proceedings while the junior children watched together at school. This enabled as many children as possible to see the event.

The first school outing, to the International Eisteddfod, at Llangollen 1963

The animal heads and costumes created for the Chester Mystery Plays were utilised again in November 1973 when a party of pupils visited London along with a team from the World Wildlife Fund. The event this time was the Lord Mayor's Parade when they walked the six miles in their costumes as part of the largest Lord Mayor's Parade ever, attended by 750,000 people.

A major event in 1976 was the decision to open a Speech Therapy Unit which would accommodate up to 10 children. The unit opened the following May under the supervision of one teacher, one senior speech therapist and a class room assistant. The first intake consisted of seven full time children and one part time, aged between 4 and 8 years. The unit gives children the chance to spend time improving their language skills before returning to their local school.

In September 1979 Mrs D Nall took over as head teacher after Mr Skitt's retirement. Mr Skitt would not lose touch with the school however, as he returned some years later as 'Father Christmas' at the infants and playgroup parties.

Due to the extra junior school in Upton and the falling child population, numbers at Westlea gradually fell over the years (although the language unit was constantly at capacity). The decline continued until the late 1980s when the roll was less than 100. In the early 1990s the population began to rise again and numbers at the start of 2005 stand at 142.

Mrs Nall retired at the end of 1995 to be replaced by Mrs Christine Jackson under whose leadership the school continues to develop.

The school now has a nursery class and the language centre. The playground has been developed and there are several adventure play areas for the children to use. There is a technology room where ICT and Design and Technology take place, something that would not have been on the curriculum in 1962.

Mill View School

Mill View School opened in 1968 when existing catchment boundaries were re-drawn and very clearly defined. Boundaries were very important at that time, not only between the local schools but between City and County schools. Children on the south side of Rosewood Avenue, for example, went to Newton school; those on the north side went to Upton Manor. The style of the building was very simple and typical of all County schools being built at that time. There were four junior classrooms built at right angles to the three infant classrooms with an open patio area adjoining the hall. The school cost approximately £68,000 when it opened, fully equipped, but the new roof in the late eighties and the new windows and cladding in the nineties cost three times that figure.

Bryan Lambert was appointed head teacher of this new school, built, according to many mystified parents, on the 'wrong' side of Wealstone Lane. They had a point. At that time every child in the catchment area had to cross that busy road and a crossing patrol was speedily established. A bend was removed from the lane that caused headlines in the local paper *"A long lane has no turnig"*. This spelling mistake inspired the staff to create a strange red felt creature, which lived in the staff room and became the school mascot known as Turnig.

1968: A Jones, D Williams, J Church, J Drew, J Roberts, J Tovey.
M Westgarth, M Higgs, B Lambert, D Nall, E Grinter.

Mr Lambert remained headmaster until 1978. The infant department, unusually, had two parallel classes of middle infants and reception children who started school in the term in which they had their fifth birthday. The oldest children from both classes moved up to become the top infants in September.

Horizons were broadened when pupils were taken on school trips, not only to the Outdoor Pursuits Centres but also abroad. Mr Lambert organised visits to

Belgium, which included a trip into Holland, and later, during the Headship of Mr Bob Springett, exchange trips were made to Angouleme in France in the Cognac area. The school also received visitors from Finland and Mr Springett took a group of the older juniors on a return visit, the first English teacher ever to make such a journey.

Mr Lambert left and in 1979 Mr C Royston Evans was appointed head. He stayed two and a half years before moving to Neston.

Mr Bob Springett was appointed Head in 1982, arriving at School in the early days in black leathers, astride his powerful motor bike. In deference to the feelings of Upton parents, he changed his mode of transport to a small Fiat Uno which, he complained, had only half the power of his bike!

During the 1980s the school developed links with Chester College when students were received on teaching practice. Mutually beneficial exchanges took place when Mill View children were bussed to the College for swimming lessons and the College sent science students to work with the younger children, in school and on field trips. When the College's new Primary Education Centre was opened by Princess Margaret in 1989 the Infants were invited to demonstrate their scientific activities during her visit.

Maypole Dancing with Mrs M Higgs

In the 1980s, the junior cloakroom became a designated Library area for the juniors and the Infant corridor was used similarly for the younger children. The central patio area was roofed over to provide extra accommodation and the whole of the entrance hall was incorporated into a new Library area in the late nineties.

Mr Springett took early retirement in 1996 to be replaced as headmaster by Mr Richard MacRae. Major improvements have since been made to the building, which now boasts a computer suite, resource area, new staff-room and science area.

Upton High School

The high school in Upton opened in September 1968 as Upton Secondary Modern School, although the official opening was in July 1969. For the first five or six years it was under Ellesmere Port Education Authority until boundary changes moved responsibility to Chester. Previous to its opening, children living to the south side of Plas Newton Lane went to Chester City Secondary School and children living to the north of Plas Newton Lane went to one of three schools in Ellesmere Port; John Street, The Grange or Stanney.

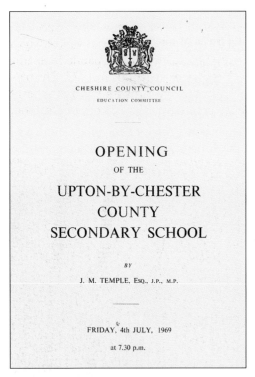

CHESHIRE COUNTY COUNCIL
EDUCATION COMMITTEE

OPENING
OF THE

UPTON-BY-CHESTER
COUNTY
SECONDARY SCHOOL

BY

J. M. TEMPLE, Esq., J.P., M.P.

FRIDAY, 4th JULY, 1969

at 7.30 p.m.

It was in 1972 that it became a comprehensive and changed its name to Upton-by-Chester High School. Included as part of the uniform for the new school was a badge which related to an ancient Upton family (the Brock family), and a Cheshire wheatsheaf. The total cost of the buildings, furniture and equipment amounted to £266,000. The first head teacher was Mr Gordon Rigby, who, with the help of deputy head Mr John Farey and 20 staff, oversaw the intake of 200 pupils.

As with many building projects the school was not completed on time and for several months the builders were still on site. The new furniture did not materialise on time either, so suitable furniture had to be begged and borrowed to furnish the premises. For the first two years, pupils had to be bussed back to John Street School, Ellesmere Port, to use their sports field until Upton's was created next to the school. This was on a site that was formerly a pond. Consequently in early summer of the following years, there were lots of frogs on the cricket pitch looking for their old spawning ground.

In the early days it was a 3 form entry (3 forms for each year), the original intention was to take just first and second year pupils but this was over-ruled by the Educational Authority who insisted that the new intake should include all four years. This upset some pupils as they had, perhaps, only a term or two of education left before being eligible to leave. Over the years the intake increased to a 10 form organisation with 1650 students, fed by all the junior schools in Upton plus many of the outlying villages such as Mickle Trafford, Guilden Sutton and Mollington, as well as pupils from the city junior schools (parental choice). The school has developed a large and thriving 6th form with most 6th form students progressing to university, including Oxford and Cambridge.

Originally the school consisted of one main block of seven classrooms plus a library, dining room, gym, and a technical block. More accommodation had to be created before becoming a comprehensive school in 1972, so the first of several extensions was built. Over the years four more blocks have been added making it the large complex it is today.

When Mr Rigby left in 1972 he was replaced by Mr Norman Butterworth and he, in 1985, was replaced by Miss Jennifer Jackson who remains Headteacher to this day. The board of governors, chaired originally by Mr Richard Tucker, has always been an integral part of school life.

Pupils have always been encouraged to take part in community issues and charitable causes. The older students have been involved in such diverse assignments as helping at local residential nursing homes, preserving public footpaths such as the one at Picton and aiding the Carnival preparations in 1977. The parents of one ex-pupil set up a fund to reward the student with the best A level results (in the form of a book token) which they did this in memory of their son, who died tragically from diabetes.

Upton High School Staff in 1972

For many years the school housed a De Haviland Vampire jet plane in the grounds, this came about through a contact in the R.A.F. who knew it was about to be scrapped. It was transported to the school on a pantechnicon and hoisted into the quadrant where it fascinated students and visitors alike. Eventually the plane was removed for restoration and the staff and students established a garden where it had been located.

Dorin Park Special Needs School

After thorough consultation and a well-attended public meeting where local people were invited to express their opinion, the planning and building of Dorin Park School went ahead. It was designed to be non-intrusive in style and to merge well into its setting. It is situated on the site of the former Government House and where the playground now is, was a paddock surrounded by trees with a small stable in the corner. Dorin Court Residential Home was built more or less at the same time at the other end of the site. The original brick boundary wall is still there, facing on to Wealstone Lane.

Lee, Rose and Kyle playing in the sand, helped by nursery assistant Enid

The school opened in June 1977 under the headship of Mr David Lloyd Jones, with Mrs Sheila Garston as chairman of governors. For the first two months, the head had an office in Dorin Court.

The school was originally designed for 120 pupils, but the highest number to attend has been 95 due to the space required for wheelchairs to move freely. The children have to cope with physical disabilities such as spina bifida, hydrocephalus and cerebral palsy; one of the great strengths of the school has been its close contact with paediatricians from the hospital which means that parents received support from the earliest days. Clinics are held in school and parental involvement in activities and on the governing body has resulted in some memorable and very heart-warming contacts, not to mention phenomenal fund-raising activities, which have enabled the school to help the children in so many ways.

Because of the nature of the school population, the catchment area began with Chester and surrounding areas, soon extending to Malpas and Kelsall, Ellesmere Port and later, Clwyd. Eventually more came from Wales and there were even, at one time, one or two pupils from as far afield as Llangollen. All these enriched the school population which ranges in age from two to nineteen years.

The ethos of the school has always been to try in every way to *'equip pupils to become as independent as possible'*, hence the recognition of the place of the therapists – physiotherapists, occupational therapists and speech therapists in the development of the children. The school has its own nurse. The swimming pool is not only used therapeutically for the school but also for some groups from the Hospital – not to mention toddlers and children and for evening classes.

The welfare of pupils and staff has been at the centre of school life and respect and dignity are two features of the care of children, who sometimes are not able to do a great deal for themselves physically. Lifting and moving place a strain on helpers (there is a special band of assistants as well as teachers in the school) so pioneering care for staff by the provision of hoists was introduced. In a different way, computers were introduced to enhance communication and early work on computerised speech was undertaken through contact with Wythenshawe Hospital. This opened a whole new field of learning – even the publication of a book of poems by one pupil.

The school developed strong community links both with donors and volunteers. Because of this and the dedication of the staff, the children visit special school camps and enjoy many activities. Horse-riding is supervised under the auspices of Riding for the Disabled. The advent of the Multi-Sensory room a few years ago, added a new dimension for the severely disabled, who responded to the gentle light and sound features.

Mr Philip Kidman became Head teacher in 1997. His expertise has been much valued and he has been in great demand to share knowledge and experience. He has built on the sound foundations of the past - developing and expanding the success of the school.

To those who know it well, it is a very special Special School.

Lauren, Ashlee and Abby with Pooh Bear

The Firs School

The beginning of the Firs School goes back to the Second World War when Mrs Florence Longman was teaching at Westminster Road School in Hoole. As a result of the 1944 Education Act the 11+ examination provided free places in Grammar Schools and alongside this were the entrance exams for the King's and Queen's Schools. In order to supplement her income Mrs Longman decided to coach children for these exams after school. This was such a success that it was suggested that she should start her own school. Subsequently, Mrs Longman started her first school in a small room in Abbey Street, opposite the Cathedral. In 1949 Mrs Longman was renting rooms in Mill Lane Upton when she heard that Western Command had some vacant married quarters in the grounds of a large house (since demolished) called The Firs. As she already met the educational needs of several army children, their parents were keen to support her in her request to rent several wooden huts for use as a school. In 1950 the school moved in and thrived. The number of pupils soon grew to about 80 and gained a reputation for sound academic methods.

The main building in these grounds, Heywood Lodge, housed a private secondary school known as Normain College, which saw its numbers dwindling rapidly by 1961. The logical conclusion of the owner was to offer to sell the building to Mrs Longman, which she readily accepted. In 1962 Mrs Longman and her pupils moved into the new building, lock stock and barrel; just in time, as it happened, as the wooden huts burnt down only two weeks later.

Outside the 'New' School Building in the early years

At last settled in permanent accommodation 'The Firs School' prospered and by 1971 was able to buy land adjacent to the school to site a Reception unit, as pupil numbers had grown to 230. For a long time one long wooden hut remained, which supposedly came from Chester Racecourse It deteriorated to such a degree that pencils would be lost between floorboards and an ancient piano descended to a mythical floor below.

Mrs Longman headed the school until 1987 when she handed over the reins to her son Rev. Ted Longman, while she enjoyed her retirement in a bungalow built for her in the grounds of the school. In 1990 Mr Michael Ellis took over as head teacher and the school continues to develop and improve.

The school grounds have been planted with a wide variety of trees and shrubs to provide interest for the children and resources for staff use.

In 1995 the school celebrated its Golden Jubilee.

CHAPTER 17

People

This section of the book is dedicated to some of the people whose lives have had a significant impact on the life of the village. This could have been because they held a valuable role in the village or something important happened to them or that they were an integral part of village life. We particularly chose people who are no longer in the public limelight and there is no order of preference in the listing.

Rev. Canon John (Wheldon) Williams,

Following WW2, a period of rapid expansion occurred in Upton and the population increased enormously. The opportunity for the Church to be at the centre of the new community presented itself, and with it came the ideal leader – indeed, as quoted in The Story of the Church of the Holy Ascension, Upton-by-Chester by Jim Wheldon 1987, *'cometh the hour, cometh the man'*. He arrived with his wife Mary, a much loved member of the parish for so many years, and two little daughters, Ann and Shan. They were soon established happily at the centre of things.

Born in Tregarth, Wales in 1909 Wheldon was 1 of 10 children. He left school at 14 and went to work in the slate quarry at Penrhyn before going on to study Theology at St David's college, Lampeter. Following ordination at Bangor Cathedral in 1937 he served as curate in Blaenau Ffestiniog, Llandudno and Nantwich before becoming Vicar of the Parish of Upton in 1946.

As Vicar he took part with zest in all parish activities. He gave the impression of thoroughly enjoying what he was involved in and in this way drew his parishioners together into a thriving church family. He could be seen driving in Chester, catching sight of a member of his flock and waving happily regardless of other traffic! Nothing seemed to disconcert him, even the swallow that attended Evensong and swooped perilously over the pulpit during the sermon, or the time New Year was rung in by a member of the choir whose surplice became entangled with the bell rope so the bell gave a resounding 'ping' rather than its cracked but fuller note.

The spiritual life of the church thrived throughout Wheldon's ministry. He visited each of his parishioners regularly and if anyone was not in when he called he would leave a note and call back. He had his own way of personalising services such as weddings, by speaking to one or two of the wedding guests and complementing them on their hat or outfit which made them feel particularly special. When he noticed a newcomer in his Sunday congregations he would take the time to speak to them making them feel welcome. All these personal touches made him a very popular minister as can be judged by the memorial windows to him in the south transept of the church.

Wheldon established a men's group which met, among other places, at the Men's Institute, now Guide Headquarters, and indeed he was instrumental in helping the Guides to achieve their goal of having their own meeting place after years of meeting at St Mary's School. He revived the traditional involvement of the Vicar with the Upton Dramatic Society and he and Mary would be made very welcome at the annual dinner. He encouraged young people and supported their activities. He was central in organising the events to celebrate the Church's centenary (see chapter 13).

In 1948, the Vicar became a Territorial Army Chaplain and was appointed Officiating Chaplain to the Forces for duty at The Dale Camp in 1949, thus cementing the Parish connection with The Dale. In 1961 he was made Rural Dean of Chester.

He was always ready to help out in other areas and other churches and denominations and 'volunteered' his Readers from time to time as well. He was instrumental in forming the Chester Council of Churches. On December 18th 1965 he was installed as a Canon of Chester Cathedral.

He had a phenomenal knowledge of the newly developing areas in the parish and was able, at times, to help the postman or others seeking out a new resident. During those post war years he kept pigs, as his family had during his childhood. One pair of pigs was called Dot and Dash and another pair were David and Jonathan although it is said that he never ate bacon.

His love of his native Wales led him to relax in remote places. He especially enjoyed fishing and it was while doing this favourite pastime on Conway Lake that his life ended unexpectedly on the 24th July 1969 aged just 59. So many people attended his funeral at Upton Parish Church that some had to stand outside in the pouring rain.

Despite the fact that he must often have been in great pain from progressively developing arthritis, as Jim Wheldon said *"He never allowed it to interfere with his single-minded devotion to his Lord, his Church and his parish"*.

The curates who were under him during his ministry found him a strict, no-nonsense man who set them up in good stead for when they gained their own parish, as Perris Williams would confirm. He worked with Wheldon as curate in the 1960s, *"We would hold staff meetings on a Monday morning and Wheldon would give me a list of households to be visited during the week. If there were any left unvisited by the next staff meeting Wheldon would want to know why, as he considered pastoral contact with parishioners most important"*.

"Anything that is good in my ministry of 40 years can be attributed to Wheldon Williams".

Wheldon and his wife Mary

John Ross O.B.E.

John was born in Hoole, in 1923 and educated, firstly at All Saints School, then in Chester. When he left education he was fortunate enough to find employment with British Rail in Chester. During his time with British Rail he was moved from Chester to Stoke-on-Trent and then to Liverpool, where he spent most of his career.

After learning to play the piano as a child John had organ lessons at Chester Cathedral under the tuition of Rowland Middleton. This led him to become organist at the Welsh Presbyterian Church in St Johns Street, Chester and then organist and Choirmaster at Upton's Holy Ascension Church.

When he was called up for his National Service, John joined the Air Force and while he was stationed in Sudan, he was able to play the organ in Khartoum Cathedral for the services that were held there.

In the early 1950s he had cause to be admitted into Chester Royal Infirmary, where he met his future wife, Hazel, who was nursing there at the time. Hazel always knew that if John wasn't in his sick bed, when he ought to have been, she would be able to find him 'chatting' to the nurses over a cup of tea in the kitchen area. During the time that they were courting, Hazel went to Edinburgh, for 18 months to train as a Midwife. On her return she told John she was thinking of going to Hong Kong to do her Queen Alexandra Nursing, John was a bit dismayed and said *"It's either Hong Kong or me"*, so *"me"* won and they were married in 1954.

John had been choirmaster at the Parish Church since 1951 so the then incumbent Rev. Wheldon Williams was only too happy to perform the marriage ceremony for them. Following their marriage Hazel moved into John's house in Hoole but shortly after they moved to Upton, temporarily initially, but liked it so much they stayed and raised their family.

During his 40 years as choirmaster at Upton (1951 - 1991) he worked with three different incumbents, Rev Wheldon Williams, Rev Fred Lapham and Rev Glyn Conway.

In the early days the choir was men and women only, who met weekly for choir practice and for services on a Sunday. John would say affectionately *"I have a cock and hen choir"*, due to the lack of youngsters. Boys were admitted to the choir for the first time in 1967, John and Hazel's elder son (Jeremy, born in 1960) was one of the first to enrol and his brother (Anthony, born 1965) joined as soon as he was old enough. All the boys were good at attending choir-practice with the adults on a Wednesday evening; at one time there were 16 boys in the group. Saturday morning was recreational time for the boys and a football team was formed and many a good game was played on the Westlea School playing field.

Anthems were sung on most Sundays and at Easter, special music - Stainer Olivet to Calvary or The Crucifixion was rendered; at Christmas, Bethlehem was appreciated by the congregation. Residents of Upton were also able to benefit from the talents of the choir with musical evenings, especially in the autumn, when a 'Harvest Home' was presented. It started in the Village Hall, production manager Mr H Ingham, but after the church hall was built in 1959 Jim Wheldon produced the plays for four years followed by 3 years by Gordon Jones, with John as musical director. These were light hearted and amusing evenings and were happy occasions. His church involvement also extended to the Mother Church of our diocese, the Cathedral, where he was chairman of the events committee, as part of the Cathedral appeal.

The field of education was important to John and he was on the governing body of the Upton schools. He was Chairman of Governors of Upton Manor School (now Upton Heath) and Upton High School, as well as being a governor of Chester College for a period of 10 years.

He served the local community as a Parish Councillor for Upton and was elected to Chester City Council for a period of 13 years (1973 - 86) during which time he became Sheriff of Chester (1978 - 9).

John retired from his career with British Rail in 1985, but continued with his many activities. These included being Magistrate for 29 years, Chairman for 5 of those years (1987 - 82); also serving with the Police Authority and Chester Police Forum. A member of the Health Authority for seven years – serving as Chairman for five of those. He was on the board of the Chester Mystery Plays, which are produced every five years in the city, as chairman from its formation in 1985 until his death. John enjoyed people and his connections and friendship of the members of the Chester Pitt Club, City Club, Merchants and Wealstone Lodge, and Rotary Club - President 1996 - 7 for which he received the Paul Harris Fellowship, the highest honour Rotary can bestow.

Although Hazel never managed to get John into the kitchen, cooking up exotic meals, he would gladly help her in the garden and they thoroughly enjoyed their 2 or 3 holidays each year. John was a keen Chester football supporter, and attended matches in his earlier days with Wheldon Williams. After being picked up, the two would travel to the Deva Stadium together, stopping on the way for a bracing Scotch from Wheldon Williams' hip flask - to keep the cold out. Latterly John took his sons to watch Chester play.

In the 1995 New Years Honours List, John was awarded the O.B.E. for services to the community.

Sheila Garston

Although Sheila Margaret Nesta Garston was born in South Wales in 1924, Chester became her home when her family re-located here in the 1930s and she was educated at Chester City High School from 1935 - 1940. On leaving school Sheila found employment as a civil servant with the War Department, Command Secretariat, where she had an administrative roll. In 1946 she transferred to the Ministry of Labour where she stayed until she was married.

It was during this time that she met her husband, John. John had been invalided home from war duties in the Far East and spent time at Moston Hospital. He joined the local drama group in Upton and it was there that he first met Sheila, who was a particularly active member of the group either acting or producing as well as being Vice President of the Society. John and Sheila were married at Upton Parish Church (where Sheila was a choir member) in April 1952. The first house they moved into was The Lodge, at Backford Hall but they moved back to Upton where they settled and brought up their son Richard.

Sheila always had a keen interest in local government and joined Upton Parish Council in 1966, serving as chairman for part of that time. Running alongside that, she served on the Chester Rural District Council and the City Council where she was elected Mayor in May 1977.

The list of Sheila's involvement in local organisations is as long as it is varied; her sense of public duty is quite outstanding. She has been chairman of the board of governors, of most of the local schools; trustee and member of the Village Hall Management Committee; President of the women's section of Upton Royal British Legion; Vice President of the Chester District Scouts and Cheshire Forest Girl Guides Association; Member of the Upton-by-Chester Golf Club, where she also enjoyed being Lady Captain.

As well as these, Upton, commitments Sheila has also served as Director of Chester Race Company; as board member of MANWEB and the Local Electricity Consultative Council, the list is endless. On top of all this she managed to help with several fund raising projects locally, whether house-to-house collections or jumble sales Sheila did it with enthusiasm and dedication.

In her spare time (?) she enjoyed visiting the theatre, reading, amateur dramatics and golf.

Bob Clift

When he married in 1961 Bob Clift and his wife, Dorothy, made their home in Upton. He came from an army background his father serving in the Coldstream Guards for 34 years. Several of those years were as R.S.M. at Chester Castle, so it was natural for Bob and two of his three brothers to join the same regiment. He was able to draw on this background in the various activities he became involved in later in life.

Bob helped with the Marine Cadet Corps in Chester as well as the fund raising and opening of the Youth Club in Wealstone Lane. He also organised the local Scout Jumble Sales for some time, this was hard work but with dedicated helpers, it was always a good money raiser for the Scouts.

The Clift family were well known in the area for their cycling activities and many young people were introduced to cycle touring and hostelling through Bob's enthusiasm. He was called upon to appear on the North West Tonight television programme for an item on the dangers of cycling in certain parts of Chester. As Bob had cycled back and forth to work at Ellesmere Port for thirty two years, only being prevented by weather on one occasion, he was interviewed by Radio Merseyside, who gave him the title of 'Cyclist Extraordinaire'. Bob thought this was amusing, but did feel he must hold the title for having cycled the most times up Moston Hill.

In 1983 Cheshire County Council asked if he would devise a 'Cheshire Cycleway' route. In due course, after covering many miles by bicycle, he marked out the route. This started just outside Chester and continued for 100 miles through quiet lanes (crossing a number of main roads) to Macclesfield. Cheshire County Council, with a few minor changes, adopted the route and signposted it. Bob also devised a 'reliability ride' based on this route which attracted over 200 entries each year.

Bob died at the age of 56 following a short illness, but his legacy lives on. The reliability ride is named after him (the Bob Clift Memorial Ride, held annually) and still attracts many entries.

In 1990 Cheshire County Council extended the route with an option through Ellesmere Port and Neston. At a re-launch event at Tatton Park a presentation was made to Bob's wife Dorothy. It was inscribed Cheshire Cycleway in memory of Bob Clift and was a fitting tribute. A year before he died Bob planted daffodils at various sites around Upton, each spring they appear giving pleasure to local residents.

The Hinde Family

The Hinde Family lived in Upton for many years. In 1901 Thomas Hinde and his wife Elinor lived in Flag Lane, from there they moved into a new house, 'The Mount' built by Thomas, on Long Lane. Some time after that Thomas built another house for the family, 'Northfield', on land adjacent to The Mount. It was from here that he ran his abattoir and the butchers' shops in Chester. The abattoir was situated just behind Northfield, also in this area was a large pond that Thomas frequently fished. The former children's home on Long Lane was built on land donated by Thomas.

Thomas & Elinor

Thomas' family consisted of three daughters and five sons. The first daughter, Dolly, married butcher Sid Horswell from Ellesmere Port; Ethel married Will Grey; the third daughter Evelyn never married.

The sons, William (Arthur), Tom, Stanley, Fred, and Frank all worked closely together. Tom and Stanley were butchers looking after the two shops in Newtown and Boughton while Frank, Fred and Arthur were cattle dealers. This would mean them travelling over a good part of the country buying cattle to bring back to Chester by train. From Chester station they would herd them back to Upton, to a field they rented from Sir Philip Grey Egerton, on the site that is now Kingsmead. To help with this mammoth task they enlisted the help of local boys by paying them 6^d each.

Arthur married Rose; Tom married Dorothy; Stanley married Miss Kershaw; Fred married Lou Morris whose father was the landlord of the Frog pub; Frank married Nellie. Arthur bought Upton Hall from Mr Ithell but left there in 1932 due to the repairs to the building becoming too great a burden (it was demolished in 1933). He had a house built opposite the Dale Camp called Bankfield and Arthur took the horse drinking troughs, that were at Upton Hall, with him to his new house. Arthur's nephew Jim remembers playing at Upton Hall as a child and investigating the underground passageways that would emerge near Bache Hall.

Tom lived over the butcher's shop in Newtown with his wife Dorothy, who was in service to the Duke of Westminster. When the family came along they moved to a house on the corner of Upton Lane and then to Church Lane where Tom bought a plot of land from Fred Owen. This was adjoining the 1st hole of the newly formed golf course (he also became a founder member). Later the Duke set Arthur & Dorothy up as steward & stewardess of the Palatine Club in Chester.

Mr William Dutton

Mr Dutton was educated at Sussex College Cambridge where he went up in 1920 with an open classical scholarship. To have obtained a first class classical degree and also to have ridden the winner of the Grand National is surely a unique achievement for a young man of twenty six. Mr Dutton could run as well as ride, for in his last year at University he was a prominent member of an extremely successful college cross country team and was awarded his athletic colours and ran more than once in the university hare and hounds team. He was also a successful amateur cross country rider.

Son of farmer Mr J D Dutton, William (Billie) was a fully qualified solicitor articled to his uncle's firm of Messrs Mason and Moore Dutton in Chester. In 1925 Billie won the foxhunters race, over the famous Aintree course, riding Upton Lad, a horse bred at Upton Grange by his father (from a mare originally owned by Mr Tyrer of Plas Newton). Upton Lad was also ridden by Billie in the 1927 Grand National.

The horse he rode to victory, Tipperary Tim (owned by Mr H S Kenyon) had won not more than half a dozen steeplechases at small Tipperary meetings. He went on to win The Grand National, at a starting price of 100 - 1, on Saturday 31ˢᵗ March 1928. Forty two horses started the race but only two made it to the finishing line.

Following the success of that race Mr Dutton was granted a licence to train and took over the tenancy of Hazel Slade, Hednesford.

Tipperary Tim with Rider William (Billie) Dutton, owner Mr Kenyon and others

Fred Owen

Creator and founder member of the Upton by Chester Golf Club, Fred Owen worked for Chester Council as Borough Surveyor, as did his father before him. He was married to Mary and had three children, Susan, Mary and Robert (Bob); following in his father's footsteps, Bob also became a surveyor.

Although he never golfed before creating the golf club, Fred was keen to learn and was a charismatic Upton resident throughout the 30s and 40s.

When Fred retired he moved to Bournemouth, but still had contact with Upton through his family, particularly his son Bob.

The Joseph Sisters

Mr & Mrs James Joseph and their family of five daughters, Doreen, Kathleen, Marjorie, Muriel and Alix, moved from Liverpool to Chester the 1920s when Alix, the youngest, was a baby. Sir Francis Joseph, Mr Joseph's elder brother was living at Alsager at that time.

The Josephs made their home at Bron-y-Garth, a large house set well back from Liverpool Road in spacious grounds covering the area where Garth Drive is now. Alix remembered the times when cattle would be driven up Liverpool Road to the market and the frantic rush to see that the big gate was closed. In their early years, life was much centred on the church and at various times all the girls were members of the choir, Alix for 50 years. Mrs Joseph and Kathleen (Kay) were both members of the PCC and at one time or another, the girls were members of Upton Dramatic Society.

Doreen, the eldest, trained as a nurse when war came, at the Southern Hospital, eventually becoming a District Nurse at Delamere until her retirement. Muriel, the only daughter to marry, did so soon after leaving school and went to live in Scotland, she had three sons. Marjorie trained as an almoner and worked in London. Kay remained at home and assisted Miss Sparling with Brownies; she celebrated 40 years as Brownie Guider in November 1969 and was 'in harness' till her death

ness' till her death in 1973. The garden at Guide HQ was dedicated to her memory in 1974. She was a firm, no nonsense, much loved Brown Owl. Alix and Kay were the mainstay of Guiding in Upton for many years.

Alix trained as a Fröebel teacher and taught at Miss Giles' school and the Queens School Preparatory Department before opening her own school, Wakefield Grange, on Liverpool Road. She devoted much of her life to Guiding, as Brownie; Guide; Guide leader of the 1st Upton Company; District, then Divisional Commissioner for 10 years; County, Commonwealth and International Advisor; County Vice President and Chairman of the divisional Trefoil Guild. As guide leader Alix brought much fun to camping and as a friend put it *'Alix and her mallet were a formidable combination'*.

After Mr Joseph died the family left Bron-y-Garth, moving first to Eversley Park and finally to Upton Rise where the three remaining sisters retired and lived until the last, Alix, died in 2000.

Reverend Wilfred Sparling and Monica Sparling

Reverend Sparling became the first Vicar of the new Parish of Upton in 1882, preceding this he had been tutor to the Duke of Westminster's son.

He was a much loved minister and popular with his parishioners as he became more and more involved with village life. He introduced annual Sunday School Outings and in 1889 the distribution of Ascension Day buns to the children.

At the age of 65 he was reputed to have climbed the church steeple to fix the lightning conductor as there were no other volunteers.

Reverend Sparling's daughter Monica was also deeply involved with village life. It was she who started the first Brownie Pack and subsequently the Guide Troup in Upton in 1919.

The garden in front of the Village Hall is dedicated to her memory.

Ray Griffiths

Ray Griffiths, the elder of two brothers, was born in 1933 and spent his entire life in Upton. His Grandfather, Henry, lived in Flag Lane South and ran his wheelwright business on Long Lane in the late 1800s (see page 158). Henry's son Harry took over the business and carried on until he retired in 1950. Harry and his family lived on Long Lane, where son Ray and his friends would play football and cricket on the field behind the family home. This love of cricket continued when he later played for Crosville, Christleton and the Labour Party.

Ray's education started at the village school of St. Mary's, then continued, from the age of 11, at Ellesmere Port. On leaving school he served his apprenticeship with The Crosville Bus Company, as an electrician, before completing National Service with peace keeping forces in Korea. In 1954 Ray met his wife-to-be, Kathleen, through a mutual friend; they were married in 1960 at Hoole and settled in Long Lane next door to Ray's parents. It was there that they raised their two sons Peter and Jeffrey. As an enthusiastic gardener, he won competitions for his displays of vegetables with the Horticultural Society

Ray's belief that *'It's people that matter most'* led him to join the Parish Council. He went on to join the Chester City Council, in 1980, as Upton Heath's first ever Labour Councillor. He was also an active Trade Unionist who was treasurer for many years and a Union delegate to the Constituency Party. He was re-elected in 1984 and 1988. A keen environmentalist, Ray served on the committee of Chester's Environmental Services, as chairman, as well as many others such as the Highways Sub-Committee, Housing and Personnel. Along with his many other campaigns he fought vigorously for the abolition of burial charges for stillborn babies and was successful in his quest.

In 1992 Ray decided not to seek City Council re-election, but stayed extremely active as a member of Upton Parish Council, serving as chairman from 1996-99. He had particular interest in play areas and amenities

Remembered for his sense of humour, colleagues appreciated the 'one liners' which would lighten meetings. Frequently his 'dead pan' deliverance would leave others wondering whether or not he was joking, he usually was. Ray holidayed in Britain but claimed he had travelled widely – which meant he had moved next door when he married.

Arthur Godwin - milkman

Arthur Godwin was a colourful character known by most of the village as their milkman. He delivered the milk from the old post office / grocers shop opposite the Egerton Arms at the Bache, using a horse drawn cart until he retired in the 1950s.

Polly his horse was the love of his life; in frosty weather he would gently walk it up the hill to start his daily milk round. With the help of the newspaper boys he would push and pull the float up the hill so as not to put any undue strain on Polly. After Arthur's retirement Polly was taken on the usual round, just for the exercise.

Many tales are told of old Mr. Godwin - he was the delight of the local children but they also made fun of him - teasing him with practical jokes.

Although he is reputed to have never taken a day off during his full working life, it is said that each Sunday afternoon he would take the bus to Woodside, Birkenhead; cross the River Mersey by ferry and walk round Liverpool's Pier Head before re-crossing on the ferry and catching the bus back to Chester.

When Mr Godwin, and his horse Polly, gave up the local milk round in the early 1960s, the residents of Upton Park made a collection to buy him a wrist watch. This was presented to him at Hawthorns, the home of Bill and Joan Wilson.

Mr Godwin died in c1972.

CHAPTER 18
Reminiscences

This chapter contains a selection of memories of a rather different Upton than it is today. Memories are just that; we each remember things in our own way and there is no claim here about the accuracy of the facts mentioned but it does make enjoyable reading.

Eddy Edison remembers...

My first recollection of Upton, as an evacuee, was arriving at the now defunct Upton Halt station. Climbing the big oak steps some 30 to 40 of us were met by Ladies & Gentlemen who ushered us into cars to St. Mary's School. We waited in the school before being allocated to our respective foster homes. I was allocated to Mr & Mrs Hughes and my two younger brothers to Mr & Mrs Griffiths next door. The two cottages, Nos: 1 & 2 Lawn Cottages were in Smoke Street, now known as Upton Lane. Coming from Liverpool, Upton seemed a thousand miles away.

Exploring our surroundings, we found that we had a big garden at the front of the house and the back door opened onto the main road – Upton Lane. There was a huge house next door which I believe was initially occupied by Sir Charles Cayzer and later by Sir Basil Nield and his sister Beryl. I often saw them strolling around the grounds both in uniforms.

Opposite to the cottage where I lived was Mr Powell who bred and slaughtered pigs. Next door to him was the Council Yard and behind this an allotment, Mr Collins, Headmaster of Chester's Blue Coat School, would bring boys to work on this allotment.

Sir John Frost of Frost Flour Mills lived at Upton Lawn which was a huge house, also on Upton Lane. During the war the house was let as flats. At the entrance to the grounds of the house, was the Lodge which is still in use. In my younger days this was occupied by the Misses Rivers. They were small in stature and were dubbed the seven dwarfs, though I am not sure how many of them there were. To the left of the big house were woods which stretched as far as the Wheatsheaf Inn. My friend, Frank Peris, and I built a den in the trees and also one made of bricks in which we would while the night away.

Around the corner in Demage Lane was the Vicarage and opposite this the local cobbler. The building is still there – now used as a garage. I got to know the old cobbler and would take him hot water to make his tea. Moving on past the cobblers was the refuse tip where Frank and I would spend hours at night shooting at rats. Further on into Demage Lane there was a gate into a field where the soldiers from the RAMC would come to play football and cricket. If we children ever dared venture into the field the farmer, Mr Arthur Hinde, would chase us away; it was different in the summer when he needed help with his haymaking. Further on at the top of Demage Lane was a farm owned by Mr Davies, the farm is now part of the zoo.

The Zoo was the brainchild of Mr G Motteshead. When as a boy I met him, he was a huge man in stature with a walrus moustache. Often we would go down the 'Butterhill', top end of Flag Lane, past the Judges House and climb into the Zoo. We passed the 'cows', which we were told later were buffalo and bison. The elephant keeper was an Indian man Khanadas Karunadasa (known as Kay). He would take people for rides on his elephant.

Two hours around the zoo in those days and you had seen everything.

Turning right at the top of Demage Lane and on into Flag Lane you came to Dick Jones and his Blacksmith's shop on the corner. Whilst at St Mary's school we would be taken to the blacksmith's to see him shoeing the horses. Coming along Flag Lane back into Heath Road, Brookfield Stores was opposite, on the corner of a small lane that led you to the playing fields and also to the back of the row of houses on Heath Road. I think the field was donated by Sir John Frost. Just beyond Brookfield Stores was the Wheatsheaf Inn.

The Scout hut was next to the Wheatsheaf. The Scoutmaster was a Scotsman called Mr Boyd who lived next to the Chemist Shop on Long Lane. At the age of ten I joined the 1ˢᵗ Upton Cubs then later, the 1ˢᵗ Upton Scout Troup.

The air raid shelter was located opposite the Wheatsheaf and during school we would have air raid drill when we would walk up to the shelter. One night the raid was particularly bad and my foster parents and I were on our way to the shelter when we heard a whirring noise followed by a loud bang. Next day we discovered there was a huge crater on the Golf course. It seems that the pilot had seen a spark from a train going along the line in the Bache area.

From the Wheatsheaf, it was a short walk down Heath Road to St Mary's School, opposite which was another wood that stretched nearly as far as Church Lane. A Miss Nickson had her riding school to the left of the school and the village hall was to the right. There were only two houses separated by a path next to the Village Hall. The path took you into Newton in the vicinity of St. Columba's Church. Before St Columba's was built, mass was held in the Village Hall. Then there were fields as far as the end of Upton (now Wealstone) Lane. The fields were owned by a Mr Jim Ithell whose farm was in Wervin. He had a team of Land Army girls to plough and sow crops for the war effort.

Half way along Wealstone Lane a gate led you through Upton Park to the Mill. I had a Saturday morning job at Dean's bakery putting the slit in the top of the bread and helping with deliveries.

On the other side of Heath Road is Church Lane and just past the Church on the left-hand side were four Army huts. These bordered the home of Sir Basil Nield. After the war one of the huts was purchased by the Secretary of the Upton British Legion, a Mr F Morris who lived in Demage Lane. It was taken down and erected where now stands the British Legion. My foster parents and I helped Mr Morris to scrub and clean it out to make it presentable. Two snooker tables were put in and an office sectioned off. This new building caused a lot of members to leave the Upton Men's Institute, still there on the corner of Caughall Road but now the Guide Headquarters. During the war this was a First Aid Station.

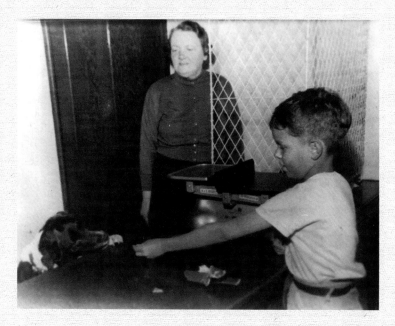

Inside the Post Office

I remember going into the Post Office in Mill Lane, run by Miss Nixon. It was a dark dismal little shop even though there was an open fire during the winter months. Whenever you went into the shop it smelled of the dog which seemed to live under the counter, it was usually chewing on a bone and when you went in, it would bark once, then go back to its bone.

Other things I remember are, the pond at the top of Marina Drive where we would see crested newts and frogs and beyond that a sand tip, giving us two in the village. Upton seemed to have two of everything at that time - sand tips refuse tips, blacksmiths (apart from the one in Flag Lane there was Mr Darlington, situated in the dip before the dale camp). After the war the ponds, sand and refuse tips were filled in with waste from a power station, before houses were built on them.

Joyce Cook remembers...

My earliest connection with Upton dates back to 1946 when I obtained a teaching post at St. Mary's School. After working as a Probationary Teacher in the heart of Liverpool, I was thankful to find myself in such a peaceful and pleasant little village. The whole of my career was to be spent in Upton and so it became my 'second home'.

Upton County Primary School (later know as Upton Manor, then Upton Heath) opened in 1951 and I worked there until I retired in 1980. This brand new school, filled with all the latest equipment, had a big Opening Ceremony. Afterwards the Director of Education escorted some of the important visitors around the new classrooms. He spotted my home-made xylophone (made from medicine bottles) played a tune and suggested that I should fill them with whiskey instead of coloured water, perhaps this was the beginning of my interest in the teaching of music!

In those days, I had no idea that my ancestors had been musical; I taught music because no-one else wanted to. When a visiting Inspector suggested that I should form a choir, I had to borrow library books in order to make a start. However, it was by entering Music Festivals and listening to adjudications that I became really interested. Each year, auditions were held (for members of the top classes) and I felt very sorry for those who could not sing in tune. So I made sure that there were other musical activities, playing instruments, composing, dancing and for the football-mad boys who could not be persuaded to learn the recorder, the Manor Morris Men.

During the 1950s, the 'News Chronicle', a popular daily national newspaper of the time, announced a special competition for schools. Each day, a picture of something of historical interest would be printed and children were encouraged to find something similar in their own town or village. Since one of the first items was a new school we became interested. The competition, to make a book of findings, had been arranged by 'Big Chief I-Spy' whose little booklets such as 'I Spy Castles' and 'I Spy Seashells' had kept generations of children amused and occupied during long car journeys and holiday outings. We decided that our book should be called 'I Spy Chester' though we realised that some of the clues might be found in Upton. It was hard work but fun. Little groups of children would meet in the evenings and on Saturdays, making sketches and notes. Eventually our book was posted off to London and there was much rejoicing when a telephone call announced that we were in the top three entries for England and Wales. I was invited to Fleet Street to see the exhibition and to meet Big Chief I Spy. He was then invited to Upton to present gift books to the 'leavers'. The top class put on a performance of 'Hiawatha' and he enjoyed this so much that he fancied a repeat!

Big Chief I Spy came to visit

Later in the year he returned and we found a boy and a girl to guide him around the City Walls so that he could write an article for his newspaper. This led to a huge competition known as 'I Spy Chester' to be held on the Roodee. Sadly, on the appointed day it poured with rain and hundreds of competitors had to cram into the Drill Hall. Students from Chester College helped to mark the entry forms and the wonderful prizes, which had been stored at school, were presented by Bernard Breslaw, a TV personality of the 1950s.

Perhaps the most exciting event for any Manor Choir was in 1978 when the BBC sent a producer and Director to see if we might be suitable contestants for a forthcoming programme entitled 'A Good Sing'.

We were! A coach took us to Manchester and the boys were very excited when they spotted a famous footballer in the foyer! Eventually we found ourselves in the recording studio and when the word 'transmission' appeared in red lights I raised my arm and we sang 'Mairi's Wedding' and 'Mango Walk'. It was with great relief that we returned to our seats and held our breath as the international adjudicator reported '"Here was something quite remarkable – these little people singing totally in tune.....they sang with rhythm, attack and life.....everything they did was so vital....".

We were awarded 86 marks and had won the Children's contest, even though the opposition had been so formidable.

Joyce with her class watching 'A Good Sing'

More than all the excitements and successes, I remember the wonderful children, parents and staff at Upton Manor. As one ex-pupil noted on 'www.friendsreunited', 'they were halcyon days'.

Stan Whaley remembers …

I was allowed to start school before my fifth birthday in 1918 and thought it wonderful. This was easily arranged in that our two girl neighbours. Mabel Fletcher, aged 8, and Phyllis aged 6 were already walking there twice a day and they rather proudly took possession of me. They gave me much juvenile advice on what to do and what not to do - and for girls were surprisingly knowledgeable in such matters as the best sections of hedgerows to find birds nests and how to test the speed of approaching horses by putting your ear to the ground. The delightfully winding Upton Lane was bordered by tall trees all the way and as yet was almost completely undisturbed by cars.

Upton St Mary's C of E School was in the charge of the tall thin austere headmaster, Mr Hacker, although I don't think he ever spoke a single word to me. I was the concern of Miss Jones, teacher of the infants. I remember her as a small, mousy, fussy teacher who made me sit on the front row and must have regarded me with some suspicion.

I can recall only one incident during my stay under her jurisdiction. It was a handwork lesson and each pupil had been given a square piece of coloured paper and a pair of blunt scissors to cut it with. We were instructed to draw a circle inside the square and then to cut a fringe half an inch deep around the circumference of the circle. This must have taken approximately two minutes. But Miss Jones had disappeared and as we waited with increasing impatience for her return, and further instructions, we quickly became bored. Then as a diversion, the small bright boy who shared my desk suggested cutting off the fringe and throwing the bits at the boys in the next desk. This we did, and it was easy to cut another fringe so that teacher would not notice. So, to obtain more ammunition, we had to repeat the operation, and with all the class joining in, our pieces of paper were soon reduced to miserable scraps the size of a sixpence and there was a fair amount of litter on the floor. When Miss Jones finally did reappear she was furious and all the culprits were called out to the front to be caned. Because of my strategic position I was dealt with first and had to hold out my hand while she slapped it with a ruler. I am afraid that I laughed. There must be few children today who can claim that they were caned before their fifth birthday, at school!

Mum and Dad thought it highly desirable that we should attend church services regularly and from about 1924 onwards sister Norah and I went to Upton Parish Church every Sunday morning and Sunday school in the afternoons. The church was built in 1854 - the same year as our home, Mona Villa. The congregation was small but we came to know some of the regular worshippers quite well - Sir John and Lady Frost, Mr J H Haseldon and old Kenny Tyrer from Plas Newton.

The benign and venerable Reverend Wilfred Sparling was popular and respected and he took an interest in village people and affairs. After 1928 we came to know him well - and his tall, spindly, beaky-faced wife. On one cold chilly morning, when the interior of the sandstone church was even colder than usual, Norah puzzled me by fainting during the singing of the canticles. Mrs Sparling came out to sit with us in the porch as Norah recovered and then walked all the way home with us and I was surprised to find how human and sympathetic she was.

The well-intentioned, earnest, hard working superintendent of the Sunday school, Jimmy Haselden, simply could not cope with the gang of rude, mischievous and impudent village boys who came along week by week during the winter months simply to keep out of the cold and to seek as much fun as possible. They ragged poor Jimmy persistently and outrageously, and the more he pleaded with them to be sensible and well-behaved the more obstreperously they swore and fought between themselves.

I often wish that we had come to know Jimmy better, as he took a genuine interest in us. He also lived in the Park and seemed to enjoy our company as we walked home together. It must have been comforting to meet some fairly civilised children after the rough and tumble of the afternoon's wrestling. He told us tales about his civic duties, he was City Councillor for the St Oswald Ward and sheriff of Chester, about his ironmongers business in Delamere Street and about his business interests in Liverpool. It became his custom to invite us into his home for a few minutes to play in the parlour. This was after I had begun to help him out as Sunday school teacher and player of hymns.

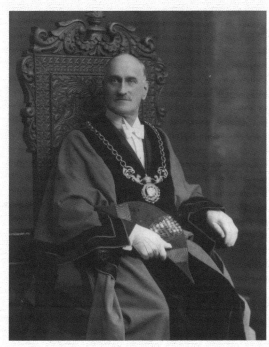

Jimmy Haselden, Sheriff of Chester

For those involved, the Confirmation Service was impressive. A packed congregation saw the Bishop of Chester in all his regalia perform the rites and I felt suitably angelic as Wilf presented me, along with a number of other Upton urchins, all unusually clean and silent.

During my last 3 years in Upton I came to know Sparling well and to appreciate his qualities. He was grateful for my help with the Sunday school and encouraged me to practice on the Church organ. He prevailed upon Mr Westbury to let Madame Foden give me organ lessons and these I enjoyed immensely. Brother Don generously came along to 'blow' for me and on Good Friday 1930 and 1931 I accompanied the especially plaintive Good Friday Service. Rev. Wilf occasionally invited me into the huge library of his big vicarage and I was deeply impressed by the extensive shelves around the walls all filled with books. Proudly displayed over the door was the oar with which he had successfully rowed for Oxford in the Boat Race of 1876. Wilf presented me with an inscribed Prayer Book when we left in 1932.

Derek Barnett remembers…

Naturally we had to go to school. This was a small, red brick Victorian building on the edge of the village. I remember the smell of chalk dust, of newly opened exercise books in which we wrote with 'Waverley' and 'Relief' nibs, and the fresh woody aroma of plain brown utility pencils. The headmaster, Mr Chidlow, was a strict but kind man in grey flannels

St Mary's School

and brown tweedy jacket with leather patches at the elbows. He took us for more advanced lessons as we got older and also for 'games' such as handball in the small rear playground. We wore coloured bands of red, green, blue or yellow across the shoulders like bandoliers to distinguish opposing teams.

The teachers were mostly elderly maiden ladies with their hair done up in buns. Miss Baker, whose fingers always seemed to be stained with red ink she used for marking our work, taught us reading, writing and arithmetic, and sometimes took us into the woods to learn nature study first hand by opening up horse chestnuts or dissecting wild flowers and showing us how they were pollinated by the bees. Then there was Mrs Houlbrook, who did her best to teach us a love of music. She would strike chords as she stood at the piano (we always wondered why on earth she didn't sit at the instrument) and then point to a boy or girl and fire the question "What key was that in?" We were sometimes allowed to sing as she played and the room would resound to the out-of-tune but lusty strains of 'Rose of England' 'Hearts of Oak' or 'Killarney'. Miss Williams was courting an army officer who would sometimes meet her at the school gate at four o'clock when they would stroll off arm in arm. We always giggled and thought it "soppy".

A popular game was 'Pie Crust' I have never heard of it being played in any other part of the country. A group of boys would make a human chain by bending forward from the waist and locking arms around the hips of the boy in front. The opposing side would run from behind and leap one after another on to the bent backs in much the same way as cowboys in the Westerns would jump on to their steeds from behind for a quick getaway. The idea of the game was to make the chain of backs give way by sheer weight.

280

Mum (Emily)
Reg (with Peggy), myself & Ken

A more hazardous game was called 'duckstone' and involved hurling fairly heavy stones at another on the ground as boys took turns trying to retrieve their own stones from around it. Hands were frequently bruised or chipped in this reckless pastime. Sometimes, in the middle of a game a fight would break out between a couple of boys. If Mr Chidlow happened to see the 'scrap' from his window he would rush out, drag the pugilists apart and hustle them inside for a caning.

Mr Chidlow did not object to our having a little fun but came down hard on anyone guilty of infractions of school rules, particularly when they concerned safely. One of these rules was never to interfere with the stirrup pumps and fire buckets placed in the cloakrooms in readiness for air raids. Well, one hot summer day, I and a fellow ruffian, now a respected builder in the Chester area, decided that the other pupils standing in line waiting for a singing lesson, needed cooling down, and while I was at the pump and buckets he manned the hose. The cloakroom was filled with hissing water and the cries of boys and girls running hither and thither to escape the inevitable wetting.

Suddenly there was a silence. There stood Mr Chidlow, eyes blazing with anger and head dripping from the spray which had caught him as he opened the door to investigate the din. He cuffed both of us soundly around the ears and administered a vigorous and, on reflection, deserving caning for that particular outrage.

We rejoiced at anything which took us out of the classroom, especially when we were taken in a crocodile to see geography or other documentary films in the village hall. Surprising though it might sound to today's more sophisticated children, we were taken several times to the village's one and only telephone box to learn how to use the phone! Even more popular were the times when we descended into the damp-gloom of the school shelters to learn the drill for air raids or gas attacks, carrying our gas masks in square cardboard boxes with string shoulder straps. Sometimes the departure from the schoolroom was purely imaginary. This was when, about twice a week, we listened to the BBC's 'History for Schools' programme on the school's radio.

American military convoys frequently passed along Long Lane, the main road which we had to cross on our way back to school after lunch. They seemed never-ending and regretfully, made us late for lessons. The GI's would invariably throw lots of good things to us as they went by – chocolate, chewing gum, cigars and cigarettes in particular. They probably thought we would give the latter to our mums or big sisters! However, when we finally got back to school Mr Chidlow always asked us to turn out our pockets "Just to be sure you haven't got anything that boys shouldn't have. I know what these Americans are". We were allowed to keep all the chocolate and gum. "But I'll have to confiscate the cigarettes and cigars," he'd say with mock solemnity. We all knew what that meant.

The Americans had a 'clean rubbish' tip at one end of the village. Well, it might have been rubbish to them but to us it was a source of pleasure...and much needed income. "I've found a fountain pen!" "Just look at this cigarette case"..."Who wants a super flashlight".

We also did newspaper rounds, which yielded a few shillings a week from Mason's newsagent's shop, the one from which we obtained our illicit 'smokes'. Mr Mason was a kind, hearty man who always doled out a few sweets to his boys before they left the shop on their rounds at 6.30 each morning. Plum 'rounds' were those which included one of the three or four army camps where it became traditional for the lucky paper boy to be given porridge and bacon and egg alongside the soldiers at breakfast in the mess hall. These rounds were the preserve of older boys who benefited particularly at Christmas time when they experienced the delight of being served Christmas dinner.

At home during air raids our family slept in bunks which my father built under the stairs while on leave once. Later we were given an indoor Morrison Shelter. This had a sheet steel top and corner posts and steel mesh sides. At first we got out of bed to use the shelter only when the sirens wailed to herald an attack. But we began so to enjoy the novelty of sleeping downstairs in it that we never bothered to go upstairs at all. Upton must have been on the flight path of German planes heading for Liverpool to bomb the docks, and only about half a mile across the fields at the back of our house was a Royal Artillery ack-ack battery. At night we watched the searchlights stabbing the sky. When they picked out a German plane they would open up, rocking houses and rattling windowpanes. Next morning there might be the wreckage of a plane in the surrounding fields, once we children were allowed by the services to view one of these. It must have been considered as a boost to the morale!

Our association with the local army camp lasted right through VE Day (Victory in Europe) and VJ Day (Victory in Japan) when celebration parties were held there. By that time the camp was much different. In place of tents were wooden huts with hot and cold water laid on. I think it was towards the end of hostilities that German and Italian prisoners of war in the area were allowed out to work on the farms and spend afternoons and evenings at weekends walking around the village and lanes. They wore British soldiers' uniforms dyed dark brown and with a large pale blue circular patch on the back for identification. Curiosity got the better of us children and we were soon on friendly terms with them. We spent hours talking about their own countries and learning words and phrases of their languages. The Italians used to make rings for us from sixpenny and shilling pieces.

How fast the days of boyhood fly! But the memories linger on to warm and cheer the heart as the years go by.

Hilda Shenton remembers…

Walter and his son Frank (my husband) took over Moston Nurseries in 1952. The nurseries had been owned by Mr Charles Dandy, who lived in a big house on the nursery but which is now separated from it by the A41. He gave up the nurseries when he reached 91 years old and couldn't manage them any longer.

The stall on Chester Market

Walter's father had been a farmer at Stamford Bridge and Walter was chauffeur/gardener. Walter could see the potential in opening a café beside the farm to serve passing trade, such as truck drivers and day trippers, with refreshments. He then started growing tomatoes and some vegetables and buying fruit, such as oranges and bananas from Liverpool, to sell in the café. The café was sold after the war when they bought Moston Nurseries. In taking on the business Walter also inherited the stall on Chester market that went with it and the two employees were more then happy to stay on and work for Walter. The gardener, Mac, tended the seeds and seedlings, working a lot of the time in the greenhouses In his youth he had played water polo for Chester and in later years he still cycled from his home in Handbridge to Moston each day. The other employee, Albert Futcher, prepared things for the market stall. Along with the land came the very old truck, nicknamed 'Charlie' it was a 1936 Morris Commercial with a Cheshire number plate CFM 1

When they moved into the premises at Moston, the land was covered in fruit trees, it seems that any trees that Mr Dandy did not sell at market, he brought home and planted. The trees were very old and not at all productive so had to be removed and the land converted back to market garden standard.

Walter's son, Frank, had served his time as a carpenter and joiner before joining the army in 1939, where he stayed for the duration of the war. After the death of his father in the early 1960's Frank took over the nursery.

They grew flowers and vegetables for the market in Chester and did a good trade in cuttings and seedlings which customers bought to cultivate at home. It wasn't too long before they acquired a stall on Ellesmere Port Market and added two more greenhouses to the six they already owned. In the springtime, which was the busiest time of the year for them, they employed up to six women from Upton to prick out the seedling bedding plants, I would also help as did Frank's two sisters Tiny and Audrey, either on the stall or in the nurseries. When our son Ian left school he worked full time in the business, driving a van, and when there were any problems with the vans, or with any of the machinery, our younger son Christopher repaired them as he was a mechanic in Chester at that time. It was truly a family business.

Frank died in 1982 and following this Ian came to live in the nursery bungalow. Our sons Ian, Chris, David and Peter look after things now growing and selling Christmas trees.

Bill Morgan Remembers…

Our family moved to Plas Newton Lodge around 1925/6 when I was approximately 2 years old. My father, William Morgan, was promoted to head gardener, his employers at the time were Mr Alfred and Mrs Ida Tyrer of Plas Newton. Mr Tyrer was a solicitor in Liverpool and a very keen Polo player. Other staff employed at Plas Newton included 5 indoor household servants, three gardeners, a gardener/farmhand and a chauffeur/groom.

Plas Newton and the grounds were made up of 8 acres of arable land and grazing, lawned areas to the west and south of approximately ½ acre, a putting green to the west in front of the house; a Japanese garden with its own miniature bridges with streams and waterfall and arches and figurines – all of which were shipped directly from Japan. To the north and west stood their pride and joy, the walled kitchen garden with almost half an acre of heated greenhouses (coke fired) and also the stable yard and horse boxes. A large orchard was also the home for a variety of poultry and indeed a fox on numerous occasions. The saddle room in the stables held the most fantastic aroma of polish and the apple storage room had its own exotic perfume. A cemetery for the numerous dogs that lived a life of luxury on the estate was for their demise together with suitably inscribed wooden crosses. Our dog (Peg), a red setter which lived to the good age of fifteen, was buried there.

Alfred & Ida Tyrer with head gardener William Morgan

Garden parties were held on the front lawns and on occasions the General Railway Station brass band provided entertainment. A marquee was the focal point from which to obtain free drinks and cigarettes.

The whole of the Plas Newton Estate was owned by Mr A E C Lloyd-Jones who lived lower down the road at Newton Cottage. He also owned a large proportion of the style (or stile) fields which ran from Plas Newton Lane right across to Upton Village Hall and St Mary's School. Beef cattle were shipped in from Ireland and unloaded at the General Railway Station. From the cattle pens they were driven up Hoole Road and along Newton Lane to eventually arrive in the style fields, having wreaked havoc on many private gardens and lawns on the way.

The six years spent at Upton school leave me with lots of happy memories. Our headmaster Mr Chidlow and my teacher Mrs Baker were so very clever and understanding and worked very hard to cope with classes of 40 pupils and upwards. Getting across the style fields with books and egg butties for lunch was a challenge and an art, not only of dodging the bulls which might be grazing but also to cut down on the time by avoiding the styles and leaping over the adjoining hedges. The gaps in the hedges got lower and lower as time went by and my Mother used to say she knew when to put the tea on because she could hear my shouting long before I arrived.

At the age of twelve I passed the necessary entrance examinations for Love Street Secondary Modern School as it was known in those days. For that achievement I acquired a second hand bicycle. The road from our house down to Newton Corner was routed through the walls, at the entrance to Newton Hall, and down quite a sharp hill to Wealstone Lane. I very often used to meet Mr Kenny Tyrer, who lived at Newton Hall, taking his five dogs to Picton for their morning exercise. On these occasions I was expected to touch my cap, dismount, stroke the dogs and hand over my homework for scrutiny, He was a very keen cyclist and on one particular morning he informed me that I was to call at the Hall on my way home from school in order to inspect his new bicycle that was being delivered from France that very day. The maid who answered the front door told me that I was expected and I was ushered into the courtyard where a spanking new bicycle was standing upside down. At the point of me giving it my well rehearsed praises he informed that it had to go back to the factory. "Surely not" "Why"? He spun the front wheel and eventually it stopped with the valve appearing at the top of the wheel. "You see, my boy, it should have stopped at the bottom, and so it proves that the wheels are not properly balanced". And indeed, back it went!

The Firs was an Army establishment during the war and sentries were posted at the entrance. It was not unusual to be challenged "Halt! who goes there" and having to 'advance' and produce your identity card. In the early days of the raids our family scrambled into the shelter, together with blankets and flasks but my youngest brother developed whooping cough during the night and thereafter my mother decided that under the kitchen table would be as safe as the shelter and so it remained that way.

When my eldest brother & I joined the forces in 1941-2 my parents moved down the road from The Lodge to Plas Newton Cottage (the house next door). On arriving home in 1946 I was greeted by flags and bunting hanging from all the windows. Whilst serving in the Royal Navy I was drafted to a new ship which was lying in Liverpool; this entitled me to a 24 hour pass. I arrived at Chester Railway Station in the early hours of the morning and rather than wait until it got light I decided to walk home together with kitbag and hammock. The blackout made the walls at

Newton Hall even darker than usual and halfway through I was hit by something that must have laid me cold for a short while. Feeling around and finally recovering my luggage I discovered that I had hit or had been hit by one of three carthorses which had got out of Miss Darcy's field close by and it was in a greater panic than I was.

At the end of the war German prisoners were employed on the farm at Newton Cottage and Polish families were housed in wooden huts on the style fields.

David Hooper remembers….

I came from Hoole with my family when I was not yet seven years old. Our house in Hamilton Street had only tiny gardens and there was only the park for play under the strict eyes of the park keeper. Coming to Upton meant larger gardens and fields everywhere for recreation. Fortunately my parents seemed to agree with the advice "Better drowned than duffers. If not duffers won't drown" from 'Swallows and Amazons'.

My interest in pond life meant that I fell into many local ponds which contained caddis and dragonfly larvae and other exciting creatures. We went on walks and knew footpaths for miles around. Careful to avoid growing crops we roamed almost anywhere we chose.

My friends and I often played in the sand quarry off Sandpit Lane (Upton Lane). There were cliffs of say 3 feet of soil and clay on top of about 15 feet of hard sand. We discovered that narrow ledges could be dug out of the sand and it was great fun to extend them at different levels. However we decided to try constructing caves and the inevitable happened, I was about a yard inside when it collapsed, at the same time I jumped safely to the bottom of the cliff where plenty of loose sand broke my fall.

When war broke out in 1939, we lads in the Demage Lane area formed a 'Royal Upton Regiment' as a kind of Home Guard. No uniforms but a light blue flag made form an old cloth flour bag; no weapons but sticks and clods of clay. We had the 'Aeroplane Spotter' to identify enemy air-craft and collected shrapnel after air raids.

When evacuees arrived, to our respective regret, they provided a sub-stitute for Nazis and there were a few battles before a kind of unofficial truce was called. Eventually we played football together, usually on the field now covered by Daleside using goal posts put there by the RAMC from Moston. We watched the RAMC team at weekends. The field was also used by cows with mucky results when we played.

What else did we do? Most winters were cold so we went sledging on Butter Hill. At home we played board games like 'Invasion', 'Buccaneer', 'L'Attaque' and 'Monopoly'. School pressures were minimal and we had a wonderful time in spite of rationing and the war!

Dolores Pickstock remembers…

I came to live in Upton in 1935/6 and attended St. Mary's School. Mrs Baker was a good teacher and I learned a love of nature study and botany from her lessons as well as neat needlework. Her daughter Shirley was my best friend.

Mrs Baker's class was the smaller room, divided from the big class-room by a heavy moveable wooden screen, always referred to as 'The Partition'. The big classroom was where Miss Williams and Mr Chidlow taught. Mr Chidlow was a very knowledgeable Roman scholar and could be side-tracked from a lesson with a well chosen question about what the Romans did in Chester. We had some artefacts, probably loaned by the museum, on the window sills. One was a terracotta brick stamped with XX Legion. Mr Chidlow was always keen for us to go to the cinema if there was a film from which he thought we would learn something. One was 'Elephant Boy' and another was 'Fire Over England' but he used to go crackers if we called the Gaumont 'Gormont' "It's Go-mont, Go-mont" he would shout. He was very keen on correct pronunciation.

In the summer we did PE in the little playground at the back and learned country dancing to a scratchy gramophone but the boys did a very nifty 'sword dance' whereby they interwove flat laths and ended up with a six-pointed star, a bit like a Star of David. Some of the boys in the class were Ian Scrambler, Fred Roden, Alan Davies and Frank Halliwell (son of the construction family).

The winters always seemed very cold with frost and snow lasting a long time. One year we built a snow house on the front playground by rolling a big ball of snow, some of us scooped out the inside, while others piled snow on the outside. After a couple of days it was big enough for several chil-dren to stand up in. Each classroom had a big iron stove and in the winter the crates of school milk were placed around it to take the chill off.

Every Christmas someone came into school present a Cinematograph show. One film was called 'North of the Fifty Five' about monkeys dressed as Canadian Mounties riding Alsatians and on the last day of term before Christmas we were given an apple and an orange to take home.

Shirley and I had a desk at the back, between the door into the infant's room and the door to the cloakroom. There was a single row of desks heading for the blackboard apart from the main class, creating an aisle. There were a few of us older girls Sheila Morris, Pam Rowlands, Florence Prior, Joyce Roberts, Margaret Ashcroft, Marion Teague and Ada Woodwood. We girls at the back must have looked some-times as if we weren't paying attention because the call would come across the room "Wake up there, down in Sleepy Hollow".

Mrs Baker with daughter Shirley

The woods across from the school we called 'The Plantation', which must have been the perimeter of the grounds of the Frost's mansion. The daughter of the family organised a Rose Queen procession one year and issued us with pastel shades of silky fabric to get our dresses made. Another time there was a Pageant in Chester with all the schools involved. We made our own costumes for that, which were yellow, I think we were part of a rainbow in the background.

Every November 11th we went to Upton Cross and laid a wreath. As a WW1 veteran Mr Chidlow was very strict about how we behaved and we had to show great respect. Once when we had been there he told us about a sandstone block that was situated behind the cross. It had a hollow in it about the size of a sugar basin and he called it the Plague Stone. He said that during the plague, the townspeople used to come out to the village to buy farm produce and would put their money in the hollow which was filled with vinegar (for sterilising).

We seemed to have a lot more respect for grown-ups in those days and I remember Rev. T O C East's Friday RE lesson very well. Another notable resident in Upton at the time was Sidney Gustard the organist, who used to play on the wireless a lot as well as playing at the cinema in Chester.

In Newton Lane in the fields, where the houses are now, was a lovely old Victorian cottage where a jolly farmer named Parry lived. Across the road from there, on the edge of Dicksons nursery was a smallholding, the man's name was Frank Morris. The gentleman was usually the MC for the whist drives and dances and during the war gave rabbits as prizes but you had to skin them yourself.

Faichney's were the coach people. They bussed scholars in from Wervin, Stoke and Stanney and took us once a week to Hoole and Newton school for cookery and the boys to woodwork. I also remember Mrs Houlbrook supervising craft lessons and the boys making stools with woven seats. When the war came Mr Chidlow's front garden was turned over to vegetables and the boys worked hard there and the girls did the weeding.

For a few weeks, during the bombing of Merseyside, the siren blew at dinnertime every day, when a solitary German reconnaissance plane came over to see how much damage they had caused at Liverpool docks or to see if there were any convoys in. On the way to the school air raid shelter, if you looked up, you could see the plane like a dot in the sky, with little puffs of smoke following it because the guns were firing at it. In the shelter was a tea chest full of balls of wool and knitting needles and we had to pick one up as we went in. We were supposed to be knitting blanket squares but I always seemed to get someone else's bad piece of knitting and spent my time putting dropped stitches right. It was not long before the all clear went and we had to go back into school and continue with our lessons.

Mr Chidlow warned us never to play near a pit that was fenced off (near where Alpraham Crescent is now) as it was a quicksand pit. Supposedly there was a moving river of sand that started at Parkgate and continued under the sandstone shelf that our part of the county sits on, then surfaced again in a field at Backford where the commercial sandpit was situated. It ran under what is now the A41 on the village side of Hoole roundabout and when they worked on the road the contractors had to sink concrete 'mattresses' (this was the way Mr Chidlow described it) reinforced with metal rods. One day many years later, the roads were being dug up and I could see these concrete slabs. Mr Chidlow came to mind and I remembered the interesting thing he told us. He was a lovely learned gentleman and I'm sure many of his ex-pupils remember him with great affection.

CHAPTER 19
Tale Ends

Tales, told and retold, odd sightings and things that go bump in the night.

Animal Tales

Nobby, father of Jubilee, the first elephant to be born at the Zoo, escaped and on his way down Flag Lane, turned into No. 46. Jim Wheldon's mother rang him at school, where he was headmaster, to tell him there was an elephant in the garden! *"Oh yes Mum, really?"*. After this had been confirmed by his wife, he arrived home to find to his indignation that Nobby had tiptoed round his old garden shed, which he wouldn't have minded in the least being replaced.

Nobby then set off for the main road and sadly had to be destroyed. He was buried on the opposite side of the bridge from the Elephant enclosure and for many years there was a large burial mound there.

....

Les Hills former Elephant Keeper at the Zoo, was at a Holiday Camp with his wife when at breakfast time an announcement came over the loud speaker to say that Mr & Mrs Hills had a new addition to the family - a boy weighing ...... lbs! That was Jubilee!

....

Jubilee was very mischievous and took an almost human delight in playing tricks. Les Hills used to cycle to and from work, as he lived just a little way from the Zoo. One morning Mrs Hills saw him approaching at a furious pace, dripping wet from head to toe and not smelling very salubrious. Jubilee had watched Mr Hills cleaning round the edge of the pool in the Elephant House, sidled up to him and with a nudge, had pushed him into the water. One can almost imagine Jubilee relishing the occasion.

....

The small lake, from the former brickworks, behind The Mount on Long Lane, was stocked with fish by Thomas Hinde. On several occasions when Sammy the seal escaped from the Zoo, this is where he would be found.

....

Nancy Turton recalls coming home from shopping one day to discover a crowd, including policemen, around her house and garden. She immediately thought she had been burgled but on closer inspection a deer had escaped from the zoo and had become trapped in the ditch beside her house. The zoo vet had to be called out, the deer tranquillised and led back home.

....

Nancy also tells of the time her grandparents lived in Caughall. As a child she would cycle to visit them and on more than one occasion she had to made detours to avoid the Bison on the lanes.

....

Ghostly Ends

A Tale of Upton Hall

According to one resident's grandmother: An old lady was left alone in Upton Hall while the rest of the family were away for the evening. As she sat quietly sewing in the kitchen she heard a sound like the towel on the door being moved behind her. She turned and saw nothing. A second time she heard the sound and asked *"What do you want?"* thinking someone must be at the door. A voice replied *"Follow me"*. She got up and found no one at the door. Again she heard *"Follow me"* so she went in the direction of the voice and was led to a flagstone and there told to take it up and she would be rich. She obeyed the instructions and found a lot of money. The voice disappeared and was never heard again.

....

At Upton farm, a ghost is supposed to have walked through the walls and disappeared again, on the occasion of a wedding in 1928.

....

At Upton Lawn there have been reports of a carriage and pair which used to drive up to the door on windy nights.

....

Clarence is the resident ghost at Bridge Farm Cottage in Linksway. He is a benign presence dating to sometime at the beginning of the 1900s. A country man, perhaps a farmer, dressed in rough brown tweeds, with trousers tied with string just under the knees. He first appeared just as the present owners were moving in; a figure in the doorway, who disappeared when looked at directly.

He is not fond of change, and when alterations began he has been responsible for lights flashing; kitchen flooding; setting off alarms; pictures falling and scaring visitors half to death. One visitor woke one night to find Clarence standing over them, this would not have been so bad, but on closer inspection they realised the figure was actually standing IN the wall. The story was corroborated by a barman at the golf club, who used to stay in the house as a boy, and woke one night to see a man walking through the wall towards him. When questioned as to which room he was sleeping in, it was the same room and same wall where Clarence had been spotted by the new residents.

When the kitchen was being re-fitted he first of all scared off the electrician, and then appeared on a photograph as a strange spiral of smoke. The negative was examined and found to be genuine, not a fault on the film, or someone blowing smoke in front of the camera. However, at this time a wall was opened up and evidence was found of an old door, Clarence seems to have been more at peace since then. Perhaps it was the door he used in this world, and did not like his path blocked – hence his habit of using the walls instead of the doors.

'Clarence'
and Carolyn

These pictures were taken just 30 seconds apart and definitely no one was smoking. The negatives were checked by an expert, who claims they had not been tampered with

INDEX

GAZETTEER

(Grid ref. relates to map page x)

Ready Reckoner, to help put historical costs into perspective.

Based on the Retail Price Index approximate values would be:-

Related to the average wage, indicting what people could afford:-

£1 in 1905 = £67 in 2005
£1 in 1925 = £35 in 2005
£1 in 1945 = £27 in 2005
£1 in 1965 = £12 in 2005
£1 in 1985 = £2   in 2005

£1 in 1905 = £350 in 2005
£1 in 1925 = £150 in 2005
£1 in 1945 = £82   in 2005
£1 in 1965 = £25   in 2005
£1 in 1985 = £2.50 in 2005

Hence the 1928 Chrysanthemum Show, held in the Village Hall, which raised £338/19/- for the building fund, should be seen today as over £11,000. But seen as what the average wage earner could afford, related to average earnings, we should relate this to around £45,000 (see page 170).

About the Publisher

www.historyofuptonbychester.org.uk

The Upton-by-Chester Local History Group was founded in September 2002. With a membership in excess of 100, the Group meets monthly with a typical attendance of fifty. We also welcome 'out of area' members who share our interests.

The Group continues to compile a local archive of facts and artefacts with the website its main means of publicity. We were awarded a Lottery Heritage Grant to purchase a computer projector – this enables us to display web-based information to those without internet access. The website will feature any book corrections as they become apparent. Similarly, it is hoped that publication will trigger considerably more historical information. Where appropriate, this will be web-published. We welcome constructive comment in the 'Guestbook'.

Further publications will be based on book, booklet, leaflet, CD or web as appropriate. These are expected to be on specific topics within the history of the Upton area. This will necessitate significant research and archaeology – which we are planning.

The Group wishes to have wide appeal. To this end, the programme will continue to be varied and membership costs kept at a minimum. We intend to increase our status by presentation of papers and by further partnership with the academic world and other local history groups.

We would welcome any Upton based items of historical interest.

Via the 'Guestbook' on our website
or direct email via uptonhistory@hotmail.com
or postal to either – 80 Upton Park   CHESTER CH2 1DQ
        or – 8 Thornton Drive CHESTER CH2 2HZ

Joyce Cook   Margaret Nash   Kate Roberts   Barbara Smith

Phil Pearn   Paul Wilbraham   Eddy Edison